Injuries

Injuries

Causes, Control Strategies, and Public Policy

Leon S. Robertson
Yale University

LexingtonBooks
D.C. Heath and Company
Lexington, Massachusetts
Toronto

Library of Congress Cataloging in Publication Data

Robertson, Leon S.
  Injuries—causes, control strategies, and public policy.

  Includes index.
  1. Wounds and injuries—United States. 2. Wounds and injuries—Prevention. 3. Wounds and injuries—Government policy—United States. 4. Accidents—United States—Prevention. I. Title. [DNLM: 1. Wounds and injuries—Prevention and control. 2. Public policy—United States. WA 250 B651i]
RD93.8.R63   1983   363.1   81-47553
ISBN 0-669-04664-7

Copyright © 1983 by D.C. Heath and Company

All rights reserved. No part of this publication may be reproduced or transmitted in any form or by any means, electronic or mechanical, including photocopy, recording, or any information storage or retrieval system, without permission in writing from the publisher.

Published simultaneously in Canada

Second printing, November 1983

Printed in the United States of America

International Standard Book Number: 0-669-04664-7

Library of Congress Catalog Card Number: 81-47553

*To the memory of
Louis E. Dotson,
mentor and friend*

Contents

	Figures and Tables	xi
	Preface	xiii
Chapter 1	**The Scope of Injuries as Public-Health and Research Problems**	1
	Incidence and Severity	2
	Fatal Injury	8
	Economic Costs	10
	Researching Injuries	11
Chapter 2	**Characteristics of Agents and Vehicles of Injury**	23
	Mechanical Energy	24
	Major Vehicles of Injurious Mechanical Energy	28
	Asphyxiation	33
	Heat Energy	35
	Chemical Energy	36
	Electrical Energy	38
	Ionizing Radiation	40
Chapter 3	**Human Vectors and Hosts**	45
	Human Limitations	45
	Temporary States and Permanent Traits	49
	Developmental Stages	54
	Screening Traits	58
	Sociocultural Environment	63
	Conclusion	65
Chapter 4	**Injury-Control Options Analysis**	71
	Factors and Phases of the Injury Process	71
	The Ten Strategies for Injury Control	73
	Public-Health Principles	80
Chapter 5	**Control Strategies: Educating and Persuading Individuals**	91
	Education	91
	Clinical Settings	97

	Health-Department Inspections	100
	Mass Media	100
	Behavior Modification	103
	Altering Perception	108
	Conclusion	111
Chapter 6	**Control Strategies: Laws and Regulations Directed at Individuals**	**117**
	Alcohol	118
	Speeding Laws	125
	Other Studies of Deterrence	127
	Laws Requiring Protective Behavior	129
	Generalizations	133
Chapter 7	**Control Strategies: Policies Directed at Agents and Vehicles of Injury**	**139**
	Motor Vehicles	140
	Rail Transport	145
	Air Travel	146
	Boats	148
	Occupational Injuries	148
	Mining as a Special Case	151
	Consumer Products	152
	Standard Development for Industry and Government Use	154
	Private Professional and Industrial Standards: Development and Application	155
	Studies of Local Regulations	156
	Conclusion	157
Chapter 8	**The Economics of Injury Control**	**163**
	The Estimation of Costs	164
	Benefits	170
	Cost-Benefit Analysis and Public Policy	174
	Conclusion	179
Chapter 9	**Values, Politics, and the Future of Injury Control**	**185**
	Values and Beliefs	186
	Freedom	188
	The Politics of Injury Control	191

Contents

Regulatory Agencies	192
Theories of Regulatory Life Cycles	196
Decision in Organizations	198
Policies for Injury Control	202
Index	209
About the Author	221

Figures and Tables

Figures

2-1	Stopping Distance, Velocity Change, and Injury for Seated, Properly Packaged Normal Adults Decelerating Forward	30
3-1	Conviction Records and Fatal Crashes	61
4-1	Factors and Phases in Injuries	72
7-1	Average Annual Fatal Crashes Per 100 Million Miles, United States, 1975-1978	144

Tables

1-1	Injuries Reported Per 100 People and Average Days of Bed Disability Per Person Injured	4
1-2	Annual Incidence of Motor Vehicle Road Nonfatalities, by Maximum Abbreviated Injury Scale Level, Age, and Sex, United States, 1975	6
1-3	Deaths, Preretirement Years of Life Lost, and Median Age at Death by Major Causes of Death, United States, 1978	9
1-4	Hypothetical Data Illustrating Potential Systematic Errors in Estimating Belt Effectiveness	14
1-5	Age of Workers in Relation to Injuries Per Person-Year Worked and Total Injuries Minus Injuries Expected from Exposure	18
3-1	Stopping Distance of Motor Vehicles Braked at -15 Feet Per Second^2	46
3-2	Drivers in Fatal Crashes Per 10,000 Licensed and Per 100 Million Miles Driven, United States, 1978	57
6-1	Some Suggested Factors That Contribute Differentially to Individual Compliance with Laws and Administrative Rules	133
8-1	Motor Vehicle Price Index and Sales, 1964-1973	168

Preface

Writing a book is easy at the start, painful by the middle, and exhilarating after the finish. In this case, the euphoria is tempered by the realization that we have a long way to go to reach our goal of controlling injuries. This book is an attempt to lay out possible paths to that goal within the limits of our present knowledge. The road to that end result can be boring in spots, challenging in others, or can lead to dead ends for those who have failed to prepare themselves. Although it is possible for persons who have no scientific training to make a major contribution to injury control, efforts based on mythology, good intentions, or traditional approaches that have repeatedly failed or led in wrong directions only hinder achievement.

The knowledge needed to solve the many aspects of the problem is drawn from various scientific disciplines. Persons knowledgeable in one or another discipline jump in occasionally, some to make a contribution and others to create difficulties. One of the problems in the field is that some applications commonly thought evident turn out to be useless. Many such pitfalls and failures are discussed throughout the text.

The nonscientist should not be intimidated by unfamiliar words such as epidemiology, or by concern that the technical points are incomprehensible without a scientific background. A little more concentration is required than that usually devoted to bedtime reading, but esoteric points have been kept to a minimum, and the few simple equations in chapter 2 are explained in English.

At the beginning, in chapter 1, the issues are presented in bits and pieces. For some severe injuries, such as those related to motor vehicles, we can clearly delineate the various factors involved and when and where they occur. Those injuries that occur in the home and other settings in relation to many consumer products are becoming better known through emergency-room surveillance. The data on injuries in the work place are being collected, but in insufficient detail and seldom with proper analysis. A discussion of the use and abuse of data, one of our most important tools, is an important early task.

Chapters 2 and 3 discuss essential evidence from the physical and behavioral sciences, respectively. Chapter 4 provides a variety of methods to achieve injury control through the use of logical and systematic analysis. Some possible shortcuts to our goal are outlined; through them we can achieve far greater benefits than we might have imagined.

Chapter 5 tracks a course through behavioral theories of injury control. A number of these have resulted in an increase rather than a reduction in killing and disabling. Others pertain only under special conditions. A separate tack is reviewed in chapter 6, which defines how and what we can achieve in injury control through rules and sanctions for changing individual behavior. This method has been more successful than strictly persuasive efforts, but rules have different effects on specified groups of people and in various environments. Chapter 7 notes some of the advantages for injury control of built-in and controlled elements in the environment; these have become increasingly important as our understanding of individual human limits has increased.

The estimation of costs of injury control and the problems of balancing costs against risks are the subject of chapter 8. The illusion that cost/benefit analysis supplies an objective formula for such decisions is explained.

The old American problem of the extent to which government can set rules for individual behavior and protective facilities, and how many of the latter will be well-constructed with such rules, is the subject of the final chapter. It is not clear whether attempts to reverse governmental regulations will be supported by the courts or changes in the body politic. It is clear that premature death from injury cannot be reduced at a scientifically feasible and practical pace without government intervention. Opposition to use of state-of-the-art technology in certain industries has placed them in economic jeopardy because of the threat of strict liability suits.

Preparation for this writing effort and help along the way was provided by many mentors, colleagues, family members, and friends who gave unselfishly and will understand if they are not individually mentioned here. Special thanks go to Elaine Zajkowski, who typed several drafts, to Margery Mills for finishing touches, and to colleagues for their insights. Julie Greenberg, William Haddon, Jr., Ben Kelley, Nancy Robertson, Sylvia Tesh, and Phil Shepherd each offered useful suggestions. None of these people agrees with everything that is written here and are, therefore, not to be held responsible for the views expressed.

This project was supported by a grant from the Insurance Institute for Highway Safety to Yale University. The views expressed are those of the author and, in the tradition of academic freedom, do not necessarily reflect the views of the institute or the university.

1 The Scope of Injuries as Public-Health and Research Problems

The narrow epidemiological view of a public-health problem such as injuries focuses on incidence (how many injuries occur), their severity (death or length and type of disability) and factors that place one at greater or lesser risk of these outcomes. In this book that narrow view is confined mainly to the first three chapters. The basic theme of the book is that, technically, we know enough about injuries to prevent many and reduce the severity of the vast majority of them. There remains some basic epidemiological and other research work to be done and the problems associated with it will be addressed. But the major focus is on the conceptual, behavioral, social, economic, and legal barriers to injury control.

The term *injury* is used interchangeably with trauma throughout to refer to damage to the body caused by exchanges with environmental energy that are beyond the body's resilience.[1] Mechanical-energy exchanges in motor vehicle crashes, shootings, and falls are the most common causes of severe and fatal trauma. The result of acute exposure to large concentrations of energy is usually called injury, while the result of long-term, less concentrated exposures, such as to low-level ionizing radiation, is usually classified as disease.

The definition of injury in terms of its necessary and specific cause, energy exchange, avoids the issue of fault that has so pervaded scientific investigation as well as injury-control efforts. The attribution of fault or human error is of prime concern to many persons in cases where the injury was unintended, while the intent of the injured is usually the major focus of attention in the case of suspected suicide or that of the one or more assailants in the case of homicide. This obsession with blame is at least partly the result of a legal system that focuses on allocation of compensation and punishment according to the intent or fault of the persons immediately involved.

Prior intent in the attribution of fault is not measured directly nor often scientifically inferred; it is concluded from statements of the persons involved and any physical evidence of the injury having been planned. While the assessment of intent may be relevant to compensation of the injured party or punishment of the party blamed for the injury, there is substantial doubt that this process has much effect on the prevention of injuries. In contrast, the application of public-health principles has shown great promise in the limited instances in which they have been used. This book discusses those principles and their applicability to specific energy sources and the injuries they cause.

It is interesting that notions of fault and negligence of individuals immediately involved in damaging transfers of mechanical, thermal, chemical, and radiation energy have seldom been applied to interpersonal transfers of harmful biologic organisms. In medieval times, persons thought to be carriers of the plague, but who actually were not, were persecuted and in some instances murdered.[2] But in modern times people seldom if ever think of suing someone who conveys bacteria or viruses that result in disease. Surely the person who knowingly has a disease that is transmitted by sneezing in crowds, kissing, sexual intercourse, or whatever and who then infects others by engaging in those activities is no less negligent than the alcoholic who drives while intoxicated and injures someone. Why do we believe that the latter is somehow more subject to control by legalistic faultfinding and punishment than the former? Infectious-disease epidemiologists seldom if ever concern themselves with blame assignment, although carriers of the more serious diseases may be pursued by public-health physicians for the purpose of treating the disease and stopping the chain of transmission. Yet the primary purpose of police and often of expert investigation of car crashes is to assign fault in reports or to testify in lawsuits for damages.

Traditionally, and in much current popular parlance, people refer to "accidents" when they mean unintentional injuries. The emphasis on intent reinforces the blaming approach, and the broader rubric, accident, includes a large set of phenomena in which no damage occurs. Most people daily experience unintended events that are called accidents (a tie in one's soup, mistakes in typing, locking keys in one's car) but that are not physically injurious. It is only those events that result in human damage that concern us here. If for no other reason than the magnitude of the problem, it makes more sense to think about injury control than accident prevention.

The significance in terms of public health of an injury is not whether it was intended but the extent and ultimate outcome of the damage. Concepts of blame, including blame attributed to chance, acts of God, and the like in the unintentional case, are barriers to injury control. The fact that injuries are not often considered as a public-health problem is one of the reasons that they are a public-health problem.

Incidence and Severity

Because many injuries are minor cuts and bruises that are not medically treated and are soon forgotten, estimates of the total incidence of injuries are questionable. The National Health Survey reports that in 1979 about 74 million injuries occurred to 69 million persons—more than a third of the U.S. population. This estimate is based on recall in interviews of a random sample of the population.[3] Obviously, only a percentage of the minor cuts and bruises were probably included.

Injuries in the survey report are classified by where they happened, age and sex of the injured, and numbers of days in bed as well as days of restricted activities associated with the injuries. Per population in each group, injuries were reported more frequently among males (38.6 percent) than females (25.9 percent) and more often among children and adults up to age forty-four (35 to 39 percent) than among adults aged forty-five to sixty-four (23.3 percent) and older (18.2 percent). The responses indicate that 12.5 percent of the population was injured in the home in 1979, compared to 8.9 percent at work and 2.7 percent by motor vehicles. An additional 14 percent were in the "other" category.

The cliche that "accidents occur most often in the home" may be true, but such statements are misleading with respect to severity. If the reported bed disability days are divided by the numbers of persons injured, a quite different perspective emerges. The bed disabilty days per person injured is highest among those injured in or by motor vehicles, more than twice that in either the work place or home (table 1-1). This statement is qualified somewhat by the fact that for some people the motor vehicle is the work place. Also, injuries are much more likely to result in bed disability the older the person injured, particularly so among the elderly.

At least three factors could account for these patterns. First, persons being interviewed in their homes may selectively recall injuries that happened there more often and/or selectively remember those that happened to the children or other members in the household. Second, the level of violence in motor vehicle crashes is more often severe compared to that in home and work incidents. And, third, resilience declines with age.

Assessment of injury severity based on clinical evidence is usually more accurate than recall of incidents such as bed disability. Substantial progress has been made toward objectively classifying injury severity and relating it to predictability of outcome. For research purposes, though seldom used clinically, the Abbreviated Injury Scale (AIS) is used to rank injuries in five categories, exclusive of death: (1) minor (for example, ache or stiffness); (2) moderate (such as simple rib fracture); (3) severe, not life-threatening (such as multiple rib fracture affecting respiration); (4) severe, life-threatening, survival probable (for example, flail chest); and (5) critical, survival uncertain (such as aortic laceration).[4] In multiple injury cases, each injury is scored but the most severe (MAIS) is often the only one reported.

Follow-up study of 2,128 persons who suffered motor vehicle injuries and who were hospitalized or who died during a two-year period in Baltimore led to an important refinement of the AIS. The researchers noted that survival declined exponentially as the MAIS increased. Also, people who had two injuries scored as 3 and 4 respectively had about the same survival rate as those with one injury scored 5. Further work with the data led to the Injury Severity Score (ISS), "the sum of the squares of the highest AIS grade

Table 1-1
Injuries Reported Per 100 People and Average Days of Bed Disability Per Person Injured

Age in Years	Total		Motor Vehicle		Work		Home		Other	
	IR	BD	IR	BD	IR	BD	IR	BD	IR	BD
All ages	32.0	2.9	2.3	7.0	5.6	3.4	11.5	2.5	14.0	2.5
Under 6	38.1	0.5	0.8	*	*	*	22.4	0.3	15.2	0.8
6-16	34.9	0.8	2.1	4.5	*	*	12.8	0.4	20.5	0.7
17-44	37.3	2.4	3.4	5.2	10.4	2.4	10.2	1.8	15.3	2.2
45-64	23.3	4.8	1.8	13.9	5.4	6.5	9.4	3.7	7.9	4.2
65 and over	18.2	12.5	0.6	27.8	0.8	12.8	9.1	12.0	7.9	11.6

Source: National Center for Health Statistics, *Current Estimates from the National Health Survey: United States, 1979* (Hyattsville, MD: U.S. Department of Health and Human Services, 1981).

Note: IR = injuries reported per 100 people; BD = average days of bed disability per person injured.

*Insufficient data or not applicable.

in each of the three most severely injured areas."[5] The proportion of persons who died was a linear function of injury severity scores above 25. Also, an elderly person with the same ISS as a younger person was more likely to die.

The injury-severity-scoring procedure has been simplified into a standardized instrument that can be used in case abstraction from medical records and subsequently translated into AIS, MAIS, or ISS from a computerized dictionary.[6] The researchers who developed this procedure are applying it to all injuries seen in acute care facilities in five northeast Ohio counties—up to now a unique opportunity to compare injuries from a variety of sources on the same severity scales.

Most studies of injury incidence and severity are limited to a specific source of injury, site of injury, or disability outcome. The AIS was originally developed to score motor-vehicle injuries and it has been most widely used in classifying such injuries. Although a nationally representative sample of all injuries of any kind has never been scored by the AIS or other clinical criteria, national estimates of motor vehicle injury distributions have been derived from samples of crashes in which a vehicle was towed away in a wide variety of areas around the country. The total incidence is estimated to be about 2 percent of the population per year. This means that about 1 in 50 Americans (some 4.2 million) is injured annually in motor vehicles; and more injuries of a similar or greater severity may occur to pedestrians in situations where the vehicle is not sufficiently damaged to be towed.

Since the case findings for these estimates are from official police reports, the actual incidence is probably higher. The Northeastern Ohio Trauma Study of emergency-room trauma cases found almost 46,000 cases related to motor vehicles compared to 32,000 in police records for 1977. The discrepancy for aggravated assault and rape was even larger, the rate in emergency-room cases being four times that in official police statistics.[7] Higher injury rates based on hospital data compared to official police records also have been reported in Britain[8] and California.[9]

The distribution of the nonfatal injuries in the vehicle towaway study by MAIS, age, sex, and age-sex specific population rates is presented in table 1-2. Although most of the injuries are in the less severe categories, more than 1 per 500 population is categorized as severe (MAIS 3) or worse and more than 1 per 2,000 population is classified as life-treating (MAIS 4 and 5). The rates are much higher in the teenage and young-adult groups, particularly among males. About 1 of every 21 males aged 15 to 24 in the population is injured annually in or by motor vehicles in a towaway crash and 1 of every 565 males of that age sustains a life-threatening motor vehicle injury annually, excluding those who die.

Studies of potentially life-threatening and permanently disabling injuries such as spinal cord and head trauma find similar distributions. Almost 56

**Table 1-2
Annual Incidence of Motor Vehicle Road Nonfatalities, by Maximum Abbreviated Injury Scale (MAIS) Level, Age, and Sex, United States, 1975**

Sex/Age	MAIS 1		MAIS 2		MAIS 3		MAIS 4		MAIS 5		Total Nonfatalities	
	Incidence	Rate[a]	Incidence	Rate[a]	Incidence	Rate[a]	Incidence	Rate[a]	Incidence	Rate[a]	Incidence	Rate[a]
Males												
0-14	213,442	78.0	33,670	12.3	20,338	7.4	2,590	0.9	2,590	0.9	272,630	99.6
15-24	695,244	341.5	171,422	84.2	82,460	40.5	25,812	12.7	10,246	5.0	985,184	484.0
25-34	348,562	227.0	80,789	52.6	40,054	26.1	15,039	9.8	2,190	1.4	486,634	316.9
35-44	158,365	142.0	34,435	30.9	25,107	22.5	6,067	5.4	2,422	2.2	226,397	203.0
45-54	126,081	109.7	32,758	28.5	18,390	16.0	4,223	3.7	1,334	1.2	182,786	159.1
55-64	84,237	90.1	22,024	23.6	14,503	15.5	3,121	3.3	1,467	1.6	125,352	134.1
65-74	46,104	76.5	14,915	24.7	8,259	13.7	1,601	2.7	615	1.0	71,494	118.6
75+	21,055	66.9	6,811	21.7	3,771	12.0	731	2.3	281	0.9	32,649	103.8
Subtotal	1,693,091	162.4	396,824	38.1	212,882	20.4	59,184	5.7	21,145	2.0	2,383,126	228.6
Females												
0-14	187,003	71.1	27,148	10.3	8,212	3.1	3,190	1.2	679	0.3	226,231	86.1
15-24	488,508	245.3	114,832	57.7	39,520	19.8	8,440	4.2	3,076	1.5	654,376	328.6
25-34	262,234	168.3	51,321	32.9	20,801	13.4	5,217	3.3	1,432	0.9	341,005	218.9
35-44	139,748	119.7	33,147	28.4	18,242	15.6	2,848	2.4	1,112	1.0	195,097	167.2
45-54	123,585	100.6	35,238	28.7	15,354	12.5	3,620	2.9	535	0.4	178,332	145.2
55-64	89,664	85.9	21,922	21.0	16,939	16.2	1,818	1.7	458	0.4	130,801	125.3
65-74	44,784	57.1	14,555	18.6	13,991	17.8	1,906	2.4	113	0.1	75,349	96.0
75+	24,418	45.4	7,936	14.7	7,628	14.2	1,039	1.9	62	0.1	41,083	76.3
Subtotal	1,359,944	124.3	306,099	28.0	140,687	12.9	28,078	2.6	7,466	1.0	1,842,274	168.4
Total	3,053,035	142.9	702,923	32.9	353,569	16.6	87,262	4.1	28,611	1.3	4,225,400	197.8

Source: Reprinted by permission of the publisher, from *The Incidence and Economic Costs of Major Health Impairments* by Nelson S. Hartunian, Charles N. Smart, and Mark J. Thompson (Lexington, Mass.: Lexington Books, D.C. Heath and Company). Copyright 1981, D.C. Heath and Company.
[a]Incidence rate per 10,000.

percent of traumatic spinal cord injuries and consequent deaths or paraplegia and quadraplegia occur in or by motor vehicles. These, along with those associated with firearms (12 percent), diving (5 percent), and other recreation peak in teenaged and young adult males.[10] The exception is spinal trauma associated with falls (19 percent), which is higher in the elderly population. Approximately 2,500 to 3,000 new cases of permanent disability from spinal cord injury are added annually.[11]

In addition to paralysis, trauma to the head can result in seizures, amnesia, personality changes, psychiatric disorders,[12] and disfigurement[13] if the person survives. Using minimum criteria of loss of consciousness, post-traumatic amnesia, or skull fracture for case finding, one study found an annual incidence of 270 per 100,000 population in males and 116 per 100,000 population in females.[14] Forty-six percent of these injuries were associated with motor vehicles or bicycles, the latter often to people struck by motor vehicles. Falls accounted for 29 percent, and recreational incidents (led by falls from horses and football injuries) contributed to 9 percent, of the head trauma. As in the case of spinal-cord injury, head-injury rates peaked among males in their mid- to late teens and early twenties in the motor-vehicle and recreational cases. Falling from horses was the only case of higher rates for women among the various activities of the young. Head injuries from nonrecreational falls were highest among the elderly. These data come from a northern state where the severity of the winters reduces the extent of activities that contribute to head injuries, such as driving, motorcycling, diving, and horseback riding. In areas where these activities are more frequent, the incidence of injuries is probably worse.

Persons with severe head trauma (brain contusion, intracerebral or intracranial hematoma, or twenty-four hours of unconsciousness or amnesia) suffered subsequent epilepsy many times more frequently than the general population. Epilepsy occurs in less than 0.1 percent of the population; but, excluding those with pretrauma seizures, 7.1 percent of persons who survived severe head trauma had seizures within one year and 11.5 percent had them within five years.[15]

Persons with less severe head trauma nevertheless have substantial problems, including headache and memory problems three months after the injury in the vast majority of moderate injury cases.[16] Among those classified as suffering minor head injury (loss of consciousness for twenty minutes or less), 34 percent who had been employed before the injury had not returned to work, 79 percent had frequent headaches, and 59 percent were experiencing memory losses at a three-month postinjury examination.[17]

The author is unaware of research that systematically separates out by cause the loss of sight, hearing, and various lengths of limbs and other appendages from injuries. Surveys of disability suggest substantial increases in the number of these conditions from 1966 to 1976 in persons less than forty-five years of age; specific causes, however, are not adequately specified.[18] A full accounting of the consequences of trauma would have to include these as well as internal organs,[19] the removal or alteration of which often disables survivors to some degree. Documentation of the extent of mental retardation,[20] pain, suffering, phobias, and impaired human relations involving the injured, disabled, and those around them—including the survivors of those who die prematurely—is less possible in any quantitative sense.

Occasionally persons bereaved by the loss of a parent, spouse, or child are motivated to constructive action. One man whose son was murdered with a handgun in San Francisco quit his job with a major corporation and founded Handgun Control, Inc., an organization that is growing in effectiveness as a lobby for gun-control legislation. But for every one such person, there are tens of thousands annually whose grief, guilt, fear, revenge, or other emotion may lead only to long-term psychological and social problems.

Little is known about the types and extent of such sequelae of trauma. There is evidence that surviving children are treated differently (to their detriment) when a child in the family dies. Children who lose one or more parents are more often divorced and have criminal records when they grow up. Inference of causation is difficult because of the delay in time between the loss and the subsequent behavior, as well as the possibility of commonly shared inheritance and environments that might contribute both to the death and the child's subsequent problems.[21] Nevertheless, the anecdotal accounts of permanently altered emotions and behavior[22] suggest that scientists who develop ways of separating out nontraumatic contributing factors will find that trauma is an important component in the etiology of psychological and social problems.

These data characterize periods during which the nation is not at war. The nature of battle injuries changes from one war to the next, as weapons are invented and others are abandoned or banned from use by international agreements. Because of such changes as well as differences in classification systems, comparisons of injuries among wars and among services in a particular war are difficult.[23] Such comparisons will not be attempted here. The major focus is on severe and fatal injury in peace time.

Fatal Injury

We have greater knowledge about the circumstances of fatal injury in cases where the death occurs soon after the injury than about the causes of nonfatal injuries. More than 152,000 people in the United States died from injuries each year in recent years, about 1 death for every 2,000 people in the population per year. In numbers, injuries are the third leading cause of death after cardiovascular diseases (960,000) and malignant neoplasms (397,000). Numbers of deaths, however, are not the complete story.

Table 1-3 presents, in addition to total numbers of deaths in the six major categories, the median age at death and the approximate number of years lost prior to the age sixty-five, the most frequent age of retirement in 1978. Deaths from cardiovascular diseases and malignancies are concentrated in the elderly: half of the deaths from the former occur to people older than seventy-six years of age and half of the fatal malignancies involve people older than sixty-eight. In contrast, injury is the predominant cause of death for the young. Half of motor vehicle-related deaths occur among persons twenty-seven years old or younger. Because of deaths from falls among the elderly, the median age at death from other unintentional injuries is higher (fifty) but, nevertheless, substantially lower than the median age of the leading causes of death in numbers alone. The median age at death of persons who die from trauma associated with homicide or suicide is thirty-one and forty-two, respectively. The conclusion to be drawn from these figures is that the leading cause of loss of preretirement years of life is injury. More than 2.8 million preretirement years are lost annually from unintentional injury and an additional 1.3 million years are lost from intentional injuries. In total, these injury deaths take more preretirement years than cardiovascular diseases and malignant neoplasms combined.

Such a conclusion, it should be pointed out, does not imply that the retirement years of life are any less desirable or valuable than the preretirement years. Nor does it imply that reductions in cardiovascular diseases and malignancies are less desirable than injury control. It does emphasize the enormity of the cost in economically productive years of life lost—indeed a loss that potentially reduces the quality of life for the elderly because of reduced contributions to Social Security and other programs by the income-earning younger population. In individual cases among the elderly, the loss

Table 1-3
Deaths, Preretirement Years of Life Lost, and Median Age at Death by Major Causes of Death, United States, 1978

	Cardio-vascular Diseases	Malignant Neoplasms	Motor-Vehicle Injuries	Other Unintentional Injuries	Homicide	Suicide
Total deaths	966,120	396,992	52,411	53,150	20,432	27,294
Median age at death	76	68	27	50	31	42
Preretirement	2,142,885	1,740,000	1,678,700	1,150,800	660,492	612,584

Source: Derived from age-at-death distributions in National Center for Health Statistics, *Vital Statistics of the United States, 1978, Volume II-Mortality* (Hyattsville, MD: U.S. Department of Health and Human Services, 1981).

of support by a child or the added responsibility of a disabled one would multiply these burdens.

Without corrective action, the situation is likely to worsen in the 1980s. Current trends in correlates of motor-vehicle fatalities led analysts at the National Highway Traffic Safety Administration to project 70,000 motor vehicle-related deaths per year by 1990, mainly because of reductions in vehicle size, the effects of which more than offset the decline in the youthful population.[24] A projected increase in the elderly population is likely to result in more fatal and disabling falls.

As might be expected from the distributions of injury severity, fatalities are concentrated in particular age and sex groupings. In recent years, about 37 percent of motor-vehicle fatalities occur among fifteen to twenty-four year olds and more than three-fourths of these are males.[25] About 1 in every 120 adolescent males who reaches his fifteenth birthday will die of motor-vehicle injuries before his twenty-fifth birthday. About 27 percent of homicides occur in that age group; 78 percent of those are males.[26] One in every 410 males who reach age 15 dies by homicide, mainly gunshot wounds, before age twenty-five. In summary, injuries from motor vehicles, other unintentional injuries, homicide, and suicide, cause approximately 1 of every 60 males to die of injuries in the decade after his fifteenth birthday.

The only decade of life in which the percent of women who die from injury is comparable to that of males is the seventy-five to eight-four-year-old age group. About 13 percent of the deaths from unintentional injuries unrelated to motor vehicles occur in that age group; and women are involved in a larger proportion than men—52 percent—but their greater numbers of the population at that age keeps the rate per population lower than that for men. Most of these deaths occur from injuries in falls or medical complications, such as pneumonia, that sometimes accompany post-fall immobility.

Economic Costs

In the absence of knowledge of the incidence and severity of trauma of all types, it is not possible to estimate with any exactness the economic losses in even relatively easily calculable direct costs such as medical care, court costs, and funerals. Recent comparison of direct and indirect costs (unrealized wages and so forth) due to coronary heart disease, cancers, and motor vehicle injuries suggests that, if all trauma had been included, injuries would have been found to be the most costly health problem in the United States. These cost estimates do not include amounts for pain and suffering or secondary consequences of trauma or the diseases in damage to psyches and interpersonal relationships.

The costs in medical care are greater for cancers and about the same for coronary heart diseases as for motor vehicle injuries; but because of the large differences in age distributions of those involved, the foregone productivity of those disabled or killed in or by motor vehicles results in motor vehicle injuries being second only to cancers in calculable costs. In 1975 dollars, the economic cost of cancers was $23.1 billion. Using the same accounting methods, motor-vehicle injuries cost $14.4 billion and coronary heart disease cost $13.7 billion.[27] Because motor vehicles are involved in only half of the deaths from unintentional injury, and only half of severe disabilities from spinal cord injury, it is not stretching the matter to attribute the highest total societal costs to injuries. If homicide and suicide were included, the total cost would be even more staggering. Those who would argue that apples and oranges are being compared should remind themselves that cancer is not a homogeneous category: there are several hundred known carcinogens.

Researching Injuries

At numerous points in the following chapters, it is necessary to qualify conclusions because of issues in research methodology. Too much of what passes for research on injuries and injury control is of questionable value. This is partly due to the fact that this field of investigation has only emerged in recent years as a discipline perceived by competent researchers as worthy of full-time endeavors. Almost twenty years ago, Haddon et al. warned researchers that use of concepts and methods from any single one of the traditional academic disciplines often resulted in too narrow an application to this emerging field.[28] Nevertheless, some researchers based in traditional academic disciplines venture occasionally into the field because they believe that some theory or method in their disciplines can be applied easily to an injury problem. In some cases the belief is correct but, like all research, the field is mined with boobytraps for the unwitting who are unwilling to spend the time and energy necessary to find them.

Based on more than a decade of reviewing research proposals and research reports in the injury field, the author finds that most such research endeavors can be classified in one of three groupings:

1. the researcher's main interest is focused on a phenomenon that may have an effect on injuries;
2. the researcher has a research method or ameliorative approach that she/he thinks applies to almost any issue, including injuries; or
3. the researcher is interested in a particular set of injuries and is trying to explain their incidence and severity, and/or how they can be reduced.

Researchers with the first or second of these orientations are the more likely to get into trouble.

Emphasis on a favorite hypothesized cause often leads to neglect of alternative explanations and naivete regarding the appropriate categorizations as well as reliability and validity of data on injuries. For example, the researcher primarily interested in alcohol as a cause of various problems may develop an interest in injuries because of alcohol's potential effect on behavior that increases the probability of injury. Repeatedly one sees studies by such researchers that use police reports of alcohol use in "accidents." Yet, police reports are notoriously unreliable indicators of alcohol use.[29] Furthermore, when care is taken to measure alcohol in breath, blood, or other body fluids, the extent of its presence is highly related to the degree of violence that produced the injury. Illegal blood alcohol concentrations are found in about 15 percent of drivers in all motor vehicle crashes reported to police,[30] in about one-half of fatally injured drivers, and in two-thirds of fatally injured drivers in single-vehicle crashes.[31] Also, the drinking individual whose behavior contributed to the injury, but who is not injured, such as a driver who strikes a pedestrian, often is not tested for blood alcohol concentration. Thus, the extent of estimated "causation" is dependent on the injured population investigated.

Reliance on a favored method often results in neglect of methods that would produce more reliable and definitive results. Recently, the analysis of trends in fatality rates from illness and injuries during long periods of years in relation to other changes in society during that time, has been favored by some epidemiologists and economists. Such analyses are often oriented to debunking the efficacy of deliberate intervention to reduce harm. One epidemiologist has claimed that because many death rates attributable to certain infectious diseases were in substantial downtrends before the use of antibiotics, their importance is insignificant.[32] Aside from the questionable reliability of diagnosis in earlier years and the experimental evidence that antibiotics kill several important microorganisms, the analysis ignores some obvious points. The factors that affect a trend during one period are not necessarily those that affect it during a subsequent period. Improvements in sanitation or housing can reduce exposure to an organism during a period to the point where there is no longer exposure from that source; however, other exposures can continue to occur or increase that, when penicillin or other therapy is used, reduces severity as the therapy is more widely applied. It is even more illogical to infer that, had the therapy been available years earlier, it would have had no effect on the trend because it was already sloping downward. Historical data on relevant variables in the population is usually inadequate to make a strong inference regarding the relative effects of the factors involved.

Public-Health and Research Problems

A few economists and others have attempted to infer a lack of effect of motor vehicle safety standards, introduced in the 1960s, in a similar fashion.[33] But trends in motor vehicle fatalities and their correlates did not behave in the same way in the 1940s and 1950s as they did in the 1960s.[34] The urbanization and suburbanization of large segments of the population had important effects on the vehicles used, the kinds of uses of vehicles, and the age and sex groups using them that are not reflected in correlations of gross death rates to aggregated statistics of miles driven on freeways, percent of population aged fifteen to twenty-four, economic trends, and the like. Much more refined data are necessary to make reasonable causal inferences regarding ameliorative actions (see chapter 7).

A research method that has been too frequently used by psychologists, sociologists, and epidemiologists is the questionnaire or interview. Despite the well-established fact that people do not always do what they claim to do—such as use seat belts—much less think what they claim to think, the use of questionnaires and interviews is a common source of data supposedly indicative of behavior and thought. This problem is illustrated by data showing that 23 percent of the drivers who claimed to always use belts on local trips were not using them when observed near their homes and that 54 percent who claimed to always use them on long trips were not doing so when observed at a long distance from home.[35]

The estimates of the effectiveness of seat belts in reduction of injury severity in crashes has ranged from 7 percent to 85 percent because of the biasing effect of claimed use and the extent of severity of the injuries considered. The hypothetical data in table 1-4 illustrate how these factors could affect estimates of effectiveness. In more severe crashes, use of belts could be verified by belt marks on the persons involved or possibly by studies of damage to belt fibers; but in the less severe cases, the only indication of belt use would be in response to interview. Notice in the table what happens to the belt effectiveness estimate if 500 (5 percent) of those interviewed falsely claimed to use belts. The belt-effectiveness estimate increases from 40 to 53 percent. If one were to try to correct that error by using only injury cases, however, the bias is in the opposite direction—belt effectiveness would be grossly underestimated, 22 to 23 percent rather than 40 percent. The latter bias has long been known[36] and both have recently been illustrated in studies of belt effectiveness.[37]

Researchers who are not pushing a single cause or a single methodological or ameliorative approach also may overlook issues of reliability and validity of data and methods. Focus on the end results in human damage, however, seems to lead to a more systematic review of the range of possible contributing factors as well as of ameliorative strategies and better, if not always the best, means to research their consequences.

Table 1-4
Hypothetical Data Illustrating Potential Systematic Errors in Estimating Belt Effectiveness

	Belt Use		
	Belted	Unbelted	Total
All vehicle occupants in crashes	2,500	7,500	10,000
No injuries	2,040	5,700	7,740
Minor injuries	400	1,500	1,900
Severe injuries	60	300	360
Percent severe of all occupants	2.4	4.0	
Percent severe and minor of all occupants	18.4	24.0	
Estimated belt effectiveness in reducing severe injuries (all occupants considered)	= $\frac{4.0 - 2.4}{4.0}$ =	40.0%	

If 500 Noninjured Occupants Claimed to Use Belts When They Did Not

	Claimed Belt Use	
	Belted	Unbelted
All vehicle occupants in crashes	3,000	7,000
Percent severe of all occupants	2.0	4.3

Estimated belt effectiveness in reducing severe injuries = $\frac{4.3 - 2.0}{4.3}$ = 53.5%

If Only Injury Cases Are Used to Estimate Effectiveness

Estimated belt effectiveness in reducing severe injuries = $\frac{16.7 - 13.0}{16.7}$ = 22.1%

If All Injuries Are Used to Estimate Effectiveness

Estimated belt effectiveness in reducing all injuries = $\frac{24.0 - 18.4}{24.0}$ = 23.3%

Data Sources

When considering the collection of data, use of existent data, or the logic of a research report, one must keep in mind the factors that contribute to potentially invalid or biased results. One way to view the reporting of injuries is to think of the filters or contingencies that increase or decrease the probability that that type of injury will be reported and where.

Public-Health and Research Problems   15

Responses to questionnaires and interviews that solicit the recall of injuries are filtered by the memory and attitudes of the interviewees. An injury that is forgotten or thought too trivial to mention by one respondent may be considered important by another. The extent of bleeding, pain, time lost from work or school, and the like may contribute to the degree to which an injury is remembered or thought important enough to mention in response to a question. To the extent that propensity to report particular types of injuries is correlated to other personal characteristics, a false inference of a causal role for such personal attributes may be drawn.

Injuries that are embarrassing or suggestive of culpability may not be reported or, if severe enough to require treatment, may not be presented as they happened. This selectivity is especially true of spouse and child abuse, assaults, and altercations. Some people will go to an emergency room or physician and/or call the police for injuries that are relatively trivial compared to those that others treat themselves. Reports to police may be predicated on relationship to others involved, social characteristics and demeanor of the injured and other involved persons, and responsiveness of the police. Concern for economic consequences, such as liability suits or insurance surcharges, can influence how and to whom an injury is reported.

Another limitation of data sources is the filtering of information on injuries by the interviewers, police, physicians, and insurance adjustors who gather it. Preconceptions regarding the physical and social characteristics and the behavior of the injured as well as interest or disinterest in particular injuries and/or their circumstances may result in unreliable or invalid recording of information. Standards for reporting, legal requirements, and reporting forms that neglect relevant variables are important factors in the usefulness of official records. Until recently, for example, police report forms used the nonsensical category "noncollision" for motor vehicle crashes in which the vehicle left the road and hit a fixed object.

Police reports that concern factors on which they are not expert or that must depend on the memory and veracity of the injured or witnesses have often been found unreliable. For example, few police are medically qualified to judge the severity of injuries even though they are required to do so. Occasionally a person who is reported by police to have a trivial injury subsequently dies. Even some physicians inexperienced in treating injuries may misdiagnose severe internal injuries.[38] Likewise police reports of factors such as precrash speeds of vehicles and, alcohol, drug, and seat belt use are subject to serious biases.

Records of emergency-room visits and hospitalizations may contain reliable data on clinical aspects or nonfatal injuries, but little or no good data on the agents of circumstances of injuries. Some fatal cases do not reach the hospital and criteria for selection of hospitals by emergency medical systems may vary from one area to another. Whether the injured person is admitted to the hospital or treated in the emergency room depends on variable hospital and physician criteria.

Furthermore, most violent deaths are investigated by medical examiners or coroners, but the quality of the data varies among jurisdictions. In areas where well-trained forensic pathologists conduct the investigations, the available data are often extensive and reliable. Where there is lack of expertise or selectivity in choice of cases for autopsy and alcohol and drug testing, the potential for unreliable or biased data exists. In some cases, cause of death (such as suicide) may be altered or left off death certificates to avoid embarrassment to families.

The extent of standardized, systematic reporting systems has been expanded as federal and state agencies have been given the authority to investigate injuries and develop countermeasures. Inclusion of types and severity, as well as relevant variables on sources of injury and persons involved, varies according to the mission of the agencies, the feasibility of obtaining the data, and the orientations of the persons who developed the systems. Files of injury data related to motor vehicles,[39] consumer products (excluding important ones, such as motor vehicles and guns),[40] occupations,[41] and boats,[42] among others, are maintained by federal agencies. The agencies involved also conduct or support special investigations that may contain more information than in their surveillance-type files. The data are public information and are available to researchers, often at a fee for computer processing of tables or cases that are not ordinarily published.

In some agencies the data are extensive in terms of both persons and products involved. Although one must be cautious about the biases in police reporting of alcohol use, belt use, and the like, the data on fatal motor vehicle crashes are relatively rich in information. In contrast, the Consumer Product Safety Commission reports nothing about the people involved in the injuries in its summary data on products and the Bureau of Labor Statistics does not collect data on the machinery or vehicles involved in worker injuries in its general data-gathering effort. Some good research has been done with these and other extant files; but there is often no substitute for designing research to fit the questions to be answered and gathering fresh data for that specific purpose.

Research Strategies and Designs

Much of the injury-control research that is done in private and government laboratories by physicists, chemists, and engineers to establish human tolerances and to test materials and products is not discussed in technical detail in this book; but its importance will be evident as the effects of standards for materials and products are discussed. In many cases, changes in materials and designs that result in improvements in areas such as energy absorption and reduced flammability have been and can be adopted for use without field testing after they have undergone extensive laboratory tests. It would have been foolish, for example, to fail to use energy-absorbing steering assemblies in motor vehicles until field studies of their effects are completed. Only a nihilist could argue that an energy-absorbing steering assembly of whatever design is less preferable than a steel shaft that spears drivers in the chests in frontal crashes. Field studies can be implemented after a product is generally introduced in order to refine it for maximum benefit.

Most of the physical science necessary for application to injury control (briefly outlined in chapter 2) is well understood by those trained in disciplines such as physics, chemistry, biomechanics, and engineering. However, that does not mean that those so trained always pay appropriate attention to the injurious consequences of the materials and products that they research or design for use in the human environment. One of the reasons that injuries remain such a large public-health problem is that those who are in a position to understand the injury problems their work produces usually are not alerted to such considerations in any systematic way during their training. Moreover, they often work in organizations where management is either unfamiliar or unconcerned with such matters.

The behavioral sciences are relatively underdeveloped and their usefulness in injury control is therefore limited. Some of what is known about behavior that contributes to injury is discussed in chapter 3. Most quantitatively trained behavioral scientists do have the skills to analyze experimental and nonexperimental data when they understand enough of the substance of a problem to ask the right questions and obtain the appropriate data. The evaluation of attempted behavior changes to reduce injuries or the possibility of inadvertent responses to changes in materials or products make the involvement of behavioral scientists or epidemiologists cognizant of behavioral issues in field studies useful.

It is important to recognize that field studies do not preclude the use of tightly controlled experimental designs. For the nonscientist reader, the controlled experiment, in which a change is introduced in one group but not in an otherwise comparable control group, is the least questionable method for inferring a possible cause or consequences of the change. If possible, the experiment's subjects should be randomly assigned in order to decrease the chances that some unrecognized difference between them will make the conclusion about the introduced change invalid.[43] Several controlled experiments in driver education, television advertising, and use of incentive systems to change behavior related to injuries are described in chapter 5.

When the scientist cannot control introduced changes or the groups into which they are introduced (such as the introduction of laws discussed in chapter 6), reliance on statistical methods to "control" for these changes that can simultaneously affect injury incidence or severity is necessary in order to infer the relative effects of various factors.[44] Where the consequences of a law should be abrupt and major in scope, the before-after comparison of trends using appropriate statistical analysis may be adequate to observe and infer the presence or absence of a major effect.[45] The further examination of reasonably comparable groups of jurisdictions in which changes in law or other introduced factors did not occur increases confidence in these conclusions.[46] This process may seem relatively simple but repeated examples are noted in chapters 5 through 7 in which public officials, other interested parties, and more than a few scientists inferred that some program or law had an effect that closer examination indicated could be reasonably attributed to expected fluctuation in other trends or factors.

It should be evident from the discussion of age and sex differences in injuries per population that comparison of groups that differ on these and other factors must include a statistical correction for the differences or comparison of specific age-sex or other comparable subgroups. Also the choice of denominator when calculating rates or the consideration of alternatives to calculation of rates can make a remarkable difference in the inferences that are made.

In illustration, the author and a colleague examined differences in injuries among workers in metal-working plants and found that the rate per person-years worked did not peak in the youngest workers as might be expected (a person-year is one person working a year, two working six months each, and so on). Instead, as shown in the top section of table 1-5, average injuries per person-year were highest among workers in their thirties and forties.

Table 1-5
Age of Workers in Relation to Injuries Per Person-Year Worked and Total Injuries Minus Injuries Expected from Exposure

	Age					
	Teens	20s	30s	40s	50s	60s
Injury Rate Per Person-Year Worked						
Average	0.07	0.16	0.29	0.27	0.15	0.21
Standard deviation	0.16	2.19	1.65	1.14	0.67	2.53
($F = 0.825$, df $= 5$, $p > 0.50$)						
Total Injuries Minus Expected Injuries						
Average	0.48	0.14	−0.03	−0.32	−0.65	−0.24
Standard deviation	1.23	1.19	1.56	1.50	1.25	0.68
($F = 33.940$, df $= 5$, $p < 0.001$)						

Source: L.S. Robertson and J.P. Keeve, "Worker Injuries: The Effects of Worker's Compensation and OSHA Inspections," *Journal of Health Politics, Policy and Law*, in press.

Suspicious because of the incongruity with other injury studies and aware that hazards varied greatly among the departments in the plants, we used the average injuries per person-year in each department to calculate an expected number of injuries for each individual based on the number of years or fraction of years he or she worked in a given department. When this expected number of injuries was subtracted from the actual number of injuries, the average difference was highest among teenagers, declined with age through the fifties, but increased somewhat among the oldest workers—a pattern similar to that for other types of injuries (see the bottom half of table 1-5). The variations around the averages, indicated by the standard deviations, were much more uniform than in the case of rates per person-year. We concluded that management perceived differences among hazards and placed younger, less experienced workers in departments where hazards were fewer. When that differential exposure was accounted for, however, the effects of inexperience and other correlates of age, such as impulsiveness, appeared.[47]

The researcher or the consumer of research should by now be aware that the choice of a denominator for an injury rate, such as miles driven or flown or years worked, involves assumptions about the denominator's lack of correlation to an unplanned or programmatic change that is thought to affect only the injuries in question. If the factor also has an effect on the miles driven or flown, years worked, and/or when and where that activity occurs—in other words, the quantity and quality of exposure to the hazards involved—an appropriate means of indicating that fact must be found for the research to accurately reveal the causal process.

References

1. W. Haddon, Jr., "Advances in the Epidemiology of Injuries as a Basis for Public Policy," *Public Health Reports* 95(1980):411-21.

2. L.F. Hirst, *The Conquest of Plague: A Study of the Evolution of Epidemiology* (Oxford: Clarendon Press, 1953).

3. National Center for Health Statistics, *Current Estimates from the National Health Interview Survey: United States, 1979* (Hyattsville, MD: U.S. Department of Health and Human Services, 1981).

4. Committee on Medical Aspects of Automotive Safety, "Rating the Severity of Tissue Damage I. The Abbreviated Scale," *Journal of the American Medical Association* 215(1971):277. Committee on Medical Aspects of Automotive Safety, "Rating the Severity of Tissue Damage II. The Comprehensive Scale," *Journal of the American Medical Association* 220(1972):717. E. Petrucelli, J.D. States, and L.N. Hames, "The Abbreviated Injury Scale: Evolution, Usage and Future Adaptability," *Accident Analysis and Prevention* 13(1981):29.

5. S.P. Baker, et al., "The Injury Severity Score: A Method for Describing Patients With Multiple Injuries and Evaluating Emergency Care," *The Journal of Trauma* 14(1974):187.

6. J.I. Barancik and B.F. Chatterjee, "Methodological Considerations in the Use of the Abbreviated Injury Scale in Trauma Epidemiology," *Journal of Trauma* 21(1981):627.

7. J.I. Barancik, et al., "Northeastern Ohio Trauma Study I. The Magnitude of the Problem," *American Journal of Public Health*, in press.

8. J.P. Bull and B.J. Roberts, "Road Accident Statistics: A Comparison of Police and Hospital Information," *Accident Analysis and Prevention* 5(1973):45-53.

9. J.F. Kraus, et al., "Some Epidemiologic Features of Motorcycle Collision Injuries: I. Introduction, Methods and Factors Associated With Incidence," *American Journal of Epidemiology* 102(1975):74-98.

10. J.F. Kraus, et al., "Incidence of Traumatic Spinal Cord Lesions," *Journal of Chronic Diseases* 28(1975):471.

11. C.N. Smart and C.R. Sanders, *The Costs of Motor Vehicle Related Spinal Cord Injuries* (Washington, DC: Insurance Institute for Highway Safety, 1976).

12. H.S. Levin and R.G. Grossman, "Behavioral Sequelae of Closed Head Injury. A Quantitative Study," *Archives of Neurology* 35(1978):720.

13. T. Karlson, "The Incidence of Hospital-Treated Facial Injuries From Vehicles," *The Journal of Trauma* 22(1982):303.

14. J.F. Annegers, et al., "The Incidence, Causes and Secular Trends of Head Trauma in Olmstead County, Minnesota, 1935-1974," *Neurology* 30(1980):912.

15. J.F. Annegers, et al., "Seizures After Head Trauma: A Population Study," *Neurology* 30(1980):683.

16. R.W. Rimel, et al., "Moderate Head Injury: Completing the Clinical Spectrum of Brain Trauma," *Neurosurgery* 11(1982):344.

17. R.W. Rimel, et al., "Disability Caused by Minor Head Injury," *Neurosurgery* 9(1981):221.

18. A. Colvez and M. Blanchet, "Disability Trends in the United States Population 1966-76: Analysis of Causes," *American Journal of Public Health* 71(1981):464.

19. W.F. Northrup and R.I. Simmons, "Pancreatic Trauma: A Review," *Surgery* 71(1972):27.

20. J. Caffey, "The Whiplash Shaken Infant Syndrome: Manual Shaking By the Extremities With Whiplash-Induced Intracranial and Intraocular Bleedings, Linked With Residual Permanent Brain Damage and Mental Retardation," *Pediatrics* 54(1974):396-403.

21. R. Schulz, *The Psychology of Death, Dying and Bereavement* (Reading, MA: Addison-Wesley, 1978).

22. R.J. Lifton, *The Broken Connection: On Death and the Continuity of Life* (New York: Simon and Schuster, 1979).

23. J.V. Henderson, "The Importance of Operational Definitions in Design of a Combat Casualty Information System," *Journal of Medical Systems*, in press.

24. National Highway Traffic Safety Administration, *Traffic Safety Trends and Forecasts* (Washington, DC: U.S. Department of Transportation, 1981).

25. National Highway Traffic Safety Administration, *Fatal Accident Reporting System, 1979* (Washington, DC: U.S. Department of Transportation, 1980).

26. National Center for Health Statistics, *Vital Statistics of the United States—1978, Volume II, Mortality* (Hyattsville, MD: U.S. Department of Health and Human Services, 1981).

27. N.S. Hartunian, C.N. Smart, and M.S. Thompson, *The Incidence and Economic Costs of Major Health Impairments* (Lexington, MA: Lexington Books, 1981), p. 370.

28. W. Haddon, Jr., E.A. Suchman, and D. Klein, (eds.), *Accident Research: Methods and Approaches* (New York: Harper and Row, 1964), pp. 14-15.

29. Haddon, et al., (eds.), *Accident Research*, p. 208.

30. R.F. Borkenstein, et al., *The Role of the Drinking Driver in Traffic Accidents* (Bloomington, IN: Indiana University Department of Police Administration, 1964).

31. W. Haddon, Jr., et al. (anonymously), *1968 Alcohol and Highway Safety Report* (Washington, DC: Committee Print, Committee on Public Works, U.S. House of Representatives, 1968).

32. T. McKeown, "Determinants of Health," *Human Nature* 1(1978):60.

33. S. Peltzman, "The Effects of Automobile Safety Regulation," *Journal of Political Economy* 83(1975):677.

34. L.S. Robertson, "A Critical Analysis of Peltzman's 'The Effects of Automobile Safety Regulation,' " *Journal of Economic Issues* 11(1977): 587.

35. P.F. Waller and P.Z. Barry, *Seat Belts: A Comparison of Observed and Reported Use* (Chapel Hill: University of North Carolina Highway Safety Research Center, 1969).

36. Haddon, et al., (eds.), *Accident Research*, pp. 705-6.

37. L.S. Robertson, "Estimates of Motor Vehicle Seat Belt Effectiveness and Use: Implications for Occupant Crash Protection," *American Journal of Public Health* 66(1976):859.

38. H.R. Gertner, et al., "Evaluation of Management of Vehicular Fatalities Secondary to Abdominal Trauma," *The Journal of Trauma* 12(1972):425.

39. National Highway Traffic Safety Administration, *Fatal Accident Reporting System, 1979.*

40. *1979 Annual Report* (Washington, DC: U.S. Consumer Product Safety Commission, 1979).

41. Bureau of Labor Statistics, *Occupational Injuries and Illnesses in the United States by Industry, 1978* (Washington, DC: U.S. Department of Labor, 1980).

42. U.S. Coast Guard, *Boating Statistics 1979* (Washington, DC: U.S. Department of Transportation, 1980).

43. D.T. Campbell and J.C. Stanley, *Experimental and Quasi-experimental Designs for Research* (Chicago: Rand-McNally, 1963).

44. D.G. Kleinbaum, L.L. Kupper, and H. Morgenstern, *Epidemiologic Research: Principles and Quantitative Methods* (Belmont, CA: Lifetime Learning Publications, 1982).

45. H.L. Ross, "Law, Science and Accidents: The British Road Safety Act of 1967," *The Journal of Legal Studies* 2(1973):1.

46. L.S. Robertson, "An Instance of Effective Legal Regulation: Motorcyclist Helmet and Daytime Headlamp Laws," *Law and Society Review* 10(1976):467.

47. L.S. Robertson and J.P. Keeve, "Worker Injuries: The Effects of Worker's Compensation and OSHA Citations," *Journal of Health Politics, Policy and Law*, in press.

2 Characteristics of Agents and Vehicles of Injury

The epidemiological model of human damage includes the interaction of hosts, agents, and vehicles (or vectors). The host is the person injured. The agents of injury are the various forms of energy.[1] Mechanical energy is the usual agent for injuries that result from transportation crashes, falls, and gunshots. Heat energy is the injurious agent of burns, including those that occur in transportation crashes. The lack of oxidation, an energy transfer necessary for life, is the agent for drowning, chokings, and other types of asphyxiation, including those initiated by mechanical energy and combustion. Other forms of energy—chemical, electrical, ionizing radiation—also account for some injuries.

In epidemiological usage, the term *vehicle* refers to any element in the environment that conveys damaging agents. The term *vector* has traditionally been used to refer to animate carriers, while vehicle refers to inanimate carriers. Most of the carriers of potentially injurious energy are vehicles: cars, guns, gravitational fields, flammable materials, water. A few are vectors, including human beings. This chapter focuses on some of the characteristics of agents and vehicles and the environmental factors that affect their interaction in the injury process. Human vectors are discussed in chapter 3.

From the viewpoint of injury control, the characteristics of agents, vehicles, and hosts that, if changed, would eliminate all or most injuries, or reduce their severity, are of paramount interest. In most causal processes there are conditions that must be present for particular outcomes to occur— called, appropriately, "necessary conditions." In illustration, injuries in motor vehicle crashes or to persons struck by them are dependent on at least four necessary conditions: 1) motor vehicles must be manufactured; 2) motor vehicles must be placed in motion; 3) motor vehicles must intersect other objects, animate or inanimate, at the same times and places; and 4) the energy transferred to the potential host in collisions must exceed the threshold of tolerance to such energy exchange of the host's tissues. In the absence of any one of these conditions, the injury would not occur.

While the necessary and specific agent of injury is energy transfer,[2] it is clear from the motor vehicle case that necessary conditions can be characteristics of the agent, vehicle, host, or the environment in which these elements interact. The fact that a number of necessary conditions for damage can often be identified means that choices regarding amelioration can be made on the basis of the extent to which those conditions can be manipulated and to what advantage in the economic, political, and social environments. This chapter's treatment of these factors is selective, but the selectivity is not arbitrary. The concentration here is on characteristics of agents and vehicles that can be changed to reduce the incidence or severity of injuries.

Mechanical Energy

The agent common to the majority of deaths from injury in the United States is mechanical energy. Deaths associated with transportation vehicles, falls, bullets, and other moving objects account for one-half to two-thirds of these deaths. This estimate of proportion would be more precise if deaths were classified by their necessary and specific agents, as well as by vehicle and host characteristics. For example, published statistics[3] do not allow determination of the exact extent to which deaths in cars, trucks, planes, buses, and trains were the result of mechanical or heat energy.

Modern physics has specified many of the processes of the interchangeability of energy and matter. Not only is one form of energy convertible into another, material can be converted to energy and vice versa. Fortunately, it is not necessary to understand all of these processes to comprehend the major sources of energy damage to people. The important characteristics of mechanical energy relevant to injuries have been known since Sir Isaac Newton published the *Principia* in 1686.

The reader with no formal training in physics probably has at least some intuitive grasp of references to mass, velocity, acceleration, and deceleration. These phenomena are related to one another in ways that can be characterized by mathematical equations. The weight (w) of an object in a field of gravity is a function of its mass (m) and the acceleration of gravity (g):

$$m = \frac{w}{g} \qquad (2.1)$$

Mass is thus proportional to weight.

The velocity (v) of an object is the distance (d) it moves in some unit of time (t). In the United States, a car "doing 55" is theoretically moving at a constant speed of fifty-five miles per hour. In countries where the metric system is used, the distance covered at "55" would be different because 55 would refer to kilometers (55 kph would be 34.2 mph and 55 mph would be 88.4 kph). A constant speed is difficult to maintain, however, because the environment includes friction of the road surface and air in front of the vehicle that decelerate it without other force, mainly that generated by the burning of gasoline, to accelerate it. One of Newton's greatest contributions was his mathematical treatment of acceleration-deceleraton. He derived a means

Agents and Vehicles of Injury

of calculating acceleration, called the calculus, that can be used to study the rate of change of any measurable phenomenon relative to other phenomena.

Most of us have an intuitive grasp of the concept without deriving it from calculus. In the case of velocity of an object such as a car, any change in speed per unit of time is acceleration or deceleration depending on whether the rate of speed is increasing or decreasing. The change may be expressed in miles per hour per hour, or in other units such as feet per second per second. The repetition of units is not an error: it expresses the actual units of change. If the speed of a car is decreased steadily over two hours from fifty-five miles per hour to forty-five miles per hour, it is changing speed at -5 miles per hour every hour. A television announcer's statement that an astronaut being launched is experiencing 5 g's means that the rocket and its occupant are experiencing acceleration at five times the force of gravity—thirty-two feet per second per second. Gravity (g) is acceleration, the rate of increase in speed of a free-falling object with no air resistance at the earth's surface.

For an injury to occur, it makes no difference whether the energy is generated from a vertical fall or the semi-horizontal movement of a motor vehicle, a moving bullet, or any other object. If the same rate and amount of energy is concentrated at the same angle of impact on the same area of a given human body, the resulting damage will be the same. The laws of physics and biomechanics can be used to predict the forces and resultant damage, given the variety of forces, their concentrations, and the elasticities of the objects, animate and inanimate, involved.

Newton's first law of motion states that an object will remain in a state of rest or uniform motion unless subjected to some unbalanced force. The second law states that momentum is changed at a rate proportional to the resultant force acting on the body. These laws do not hold when bodies are moving near the speed of light, but for present purposes they can be considered invariant. The reader should consult a good physics textbook[4] for a complete exposition of the laws of mechanical energy.

A few important equations and examples of their application will suggest the usefulness of this knowledge in practical injury-control problems. For example, how can we predict the energy with which a person will strike interior surfaces of a vehicle in a collision? The energy of a moving object (K) is expressed as:

$$K = \frac{w}{32} v^2/2 \qquad (2.2)$$

We already know how to calculate m (mass) from the object's weight, w, and v (velocity) by the distance moved in a period of time. When weight is measured in pounds and velocity is in feet per second, K is in foot pounds—the energy necessary to lift a given number of pounds one foot at the earth's surface.

Consider what this means when a ten-pound baby is held by a parent in a vehicle that crashes at thirty miles per hour (forty-four feet per second). The infant's mass seems tiny, 10/32 or 0.31. That mass, however, is multiplied in the equation by 44 squared and divided by 2. The result is 302 foot pounds of energy. A parent restrained by a lap and shoulder belt so that he or she did not continue to move forward in the crash would nevertheless have to have the strength equal to that required to lift 302 pounds one foot off the ground to be able to hold the child. Of course, virtually no one is anywhere near that strong. The child would leave the parent's arms in a fraction of a second and strike interior surfaces at a velocity fractionally reduced by what little retarding force the parent could exert.

The vast majority—85 to 90 percent—of parents would not be belted at current belt-use rates in the United States. In that case, the energy of the parent must be added to that of the child. A parent who weighed 150 pounds would crush the child with 4,537 foot pounds of additional energy as they both moved into the suddenly stopped interior surfaces of the vehicle.

A second very important equation relates acceleration to distance and velocity:

$$v_t^2 = v_0^2 + 2ad \qquad (2.3)$$

Velocity (v) squared at time t is velocity squared at time 0 plus two times acceleration (a) times distance (d) traveled. This equation has multiple uses. The calculation of human tolerance to mechanical energy and the absorption of energy in free-fall are excellent examples.[5]

If a person falls from a known height, the distance traveled is known and the acceleration during the fall is known to be about 32 feet per second per second (g). A person who fell from a window 100 feet from the ground would begin with zero velocity, so from equation 2.3 the calculation of final velocity squared would be 0 + 2(32)(100) or 6,400. The speed at impact would be the square root of 6,400, that is, 80 feet per second. If we find the person weighs 150 pounds, then the kinetic energy at impact can be derived from equations 2.1 and 2.2. Mass is 150/32 = 4.69 and velocity squared is 6,400. Therefore, from equation 2.2, the energy at impact would be approximately 15,008 foot pounds.

This calculation is approximate because of rounding and neglect of wind resistance, but considering these factors would change the result very little. The approximation is quite adequate for assessing the tolerance of the striking body surface and the energy-absorbing capability of the surfaces struck.

Newton's third law of motion states that for every force on a body, there is an equal and opposite force on another body. Force is expressed as a body's mass times its acceleration.[6] Experience with mechanical force should suggest that the extent of injury from such a force is related to the shape and size of the surface of the object contacted. A kitchen knife will do much more damage to a finger if the blade edge strikes the finger than if the blade face is the surface contacted, at the same speed. Technically, the difference is one of unit load, expressed in force per surface area exposed, such as pounds per square inch. The knife blade's edge does more damage than its face because the square inch equivalent of the finger surface to which the force is applied is much smaller.

The extent of damage is also a function of the structure of the part of the body affected. Contact with an energy source generates forces counter to the load, called stresses. These constitute the resistance of the bonds among tissue molecules to deformation. The same tissue may have different capacity for tension stress (pulling molecules apart), compression stress (pushing molecules together), or shear stress (from a tangential force).[7]

Strain refers to the extent of deformation and may also be classified as resulting from tension, compression, or shear stress. Tissue varies in elasticity—the extent to which strain is eliminated when the load is removed. It should be obvious that skin, muscles, bones, teeth, and soft tissues in vital organs vary with regard to these properties. For example, the track of a bullet through a body depends not only on its velocity, mass, and shape but also on the stress and strain of the tissues it encounters. Americans have become all too familiar with the details of bullet tracks in the human body from descriptions of the injuries of politicians and celebrities wounded by gunfire. Also, there are important interpersonal differences that result in varying severity of injuries given the same load. For example, someone with osteoporosis, which involves an increased bone brittleness, will suffer a bone break under loads that would produce only slight strain in someone without the disease.

To the extent that the object striking or struck by human tissue is less stressed than the tissue, the energy will be transferred to the inanimate object and the human tissue will be damaged less. DeHaven's classic study of people who survived falls of up to 150 feet found that no major injury was experienced in some cases where the deformation in the ground, car, or other object struck was as little as a few inches.[8]

With the exception of persons with diseases such as scurvy, osteoporosis, and hemophilia, which involve low injury thresholds, human beings are capable of experiencing substantial forces with little or no injury if they do not involve highly concentrated loads. Stapp conducted experiments with animals in rocket sleds and wind tunnels to test the limits of tolerance and then tested healthy human volunteers, including himself, within the estimated limits. Held in the sled only by three-inch-wide nylon webbed harnesses over the shoulders and legs and anchored to the sled, the volunteers experienced decelerations up to 35 g's with no damage and up to 45 g's with little damage.[9] The effective weight of a 160-pound person decelerating at 35 g's is 5,600 pounds.[10] Yet, because the accompanying load distributed over the surface of the restraining belts was mainly absorbed by the belts, the test subjects sustained no serious injury.

It was the work of DeHaven and Stapp in the 1940s and 1950s that led to the conclusion that much of the kinetic energy of occupants of transportation vehicles in crashes could be managed. Restraint or other systems that would prevent or reduce occupant movement into the interior structure during deceleration or that spread the extent of contact over a broader area, reducing the load, became possible strategies for the prevention of the harmful consequences of what had seemed to be uncontrollable mechanical energy.

Major Vehicles of Injurious Mechanical Energy

Motor Vehicles

As noted in chapter 1, the motor vehicles on our streets and highways are the most common vehicles of injurious energy. There is substantial variation in the incidence and severity of the injuries associated with the vehicles—variation that is predictable from the vehicles' physical characteristics.

The probability of a crash is associated with characteristics that make the vehicle more or less easy to handle.[11] For example, the instability in moderate-speed turns of so-called utility vehicles has been demonstrated in tests of remote-controlled vehicles and in analysis of crash and fatality rates. The high center of gravity (central point of the vehicle's mass) from the ground relative to the narrow distance between the wheels results in susceptibility to rollover. The 1980 Jeep CJ-5 was found the most extreme utility vehicle in this regard: it rolled over in a 90-degree turn at 22 miles per hour and at 32 miles per hour in a rapid lane change such as one might make to avoid hitting something in the road.[12] Fatal rollover crashes of Jeep CJ-5s in 1978 to 1979 were 11 per 10,000 registered vehicles, higher than the 8.2 rider deaths per 10,000 registered motorcycles,[13] and almost four times the 2.8 fatal crashes per year of all types of vehicles per 10,000 registered in 1979.[14] The high death rate of motorcyclists is related both to the problems of handling a relatively unstable two-wheeled vehicle and to the limited protection the vehicle affords its riders in energy exchanges with the environment in crashes.

The incidence and severity of injury in (or by vehicles that hit pedestrians) when they crash is a result of the velocity and physical characteristics of the vehicle, the biomechanics of the occupants, and the characteristics of the environment that the vehicles and people impact. If the occupants are restrained, they decelerate nearer the rate of the vehicle and seldom will be injured if peak deceleration is below 35 g's. Unrestrained occupants strike interior surfaces at about the speed of the vehicle before the crash (Newton's first law). The load on the human tissues then depends on the deceleration rate and the surface contacted. Any hard protrusions that are struck, such as knobs and edges, reduce the surface area of the body that experiences the forces and thus increase the load.

Surgeons in emergency rooms sometimes invent names for such vehicular surfaces. For example, the "karate-chop dashboard" refers to those dashboards with narrow edges pointed toward the occupants; in front crashes their necks tend to strike the dashboard, resulting in such swelling of the tissue that the trachea is closed and the person dies of lack of oxygen.[15] A flat-surfaced, energy-absorbing dashboard with knobs either recessed or missing would cause little or no injury when impacted at a force that can kill when concentrated on the front of the neck.

Two fundamental characteristics of motor vehicles with respect to incidence and severity of injury in crashes are size and weight; and these are often confused with one another. Although there is some variation among vehicles in the use of space and weight, in general greater size is more protective of occupants than weight. Weight is more aggressive to occupants of other vehicles in multivehicle collisions than it is protective to occupants of the heavier vehicle.[16] In slow-motion film of frontal crashes of light and heavy cars, one can see the lighter car reverse direction during the crash, which indicates that the occupants are experiencing much higher declerations.[17] In fatal collisions of cars and heavier trucks, death is three times as frequent in the car if the car is large (> 115-inch wheelbase), and six times as frequent if the car is smaller.[18]

Even if all vehicles were the same size, the death rate would be greater if all vehicles were small than it would be if all vehicles were large because of the greater space available for deceleration in larger vehicles. In single-vehicle crashes, cars with wheelbases (distance from front to rear axles) less than 101 inches have an average 60 percent higher death rate per vehicles registered than cars with wheelbases of 120 inches or more.[19] Smaller cars simply have less room for energy to be absorbed and occupants to decelerate in a crash.

Equation 2.3 can be applied to calculate the stopping distance necessary to decelerate from a given speed to 0 at a uniform deceleration of 30 g's. From 60 miles per hour (88 feet per second) to a total stop, for example, $0 = 88^2 + 2(32)(-30)d$ and, thus, $d = 4$ feet. Many vehicles do not provide sufficient energy absorption or deceleration space for survivable decelerations to belted front seat occupants in frontal barrier crashes at 35 miles per hour.[20] Figure 2-1 illustrates the approximate hazard for restrained persons

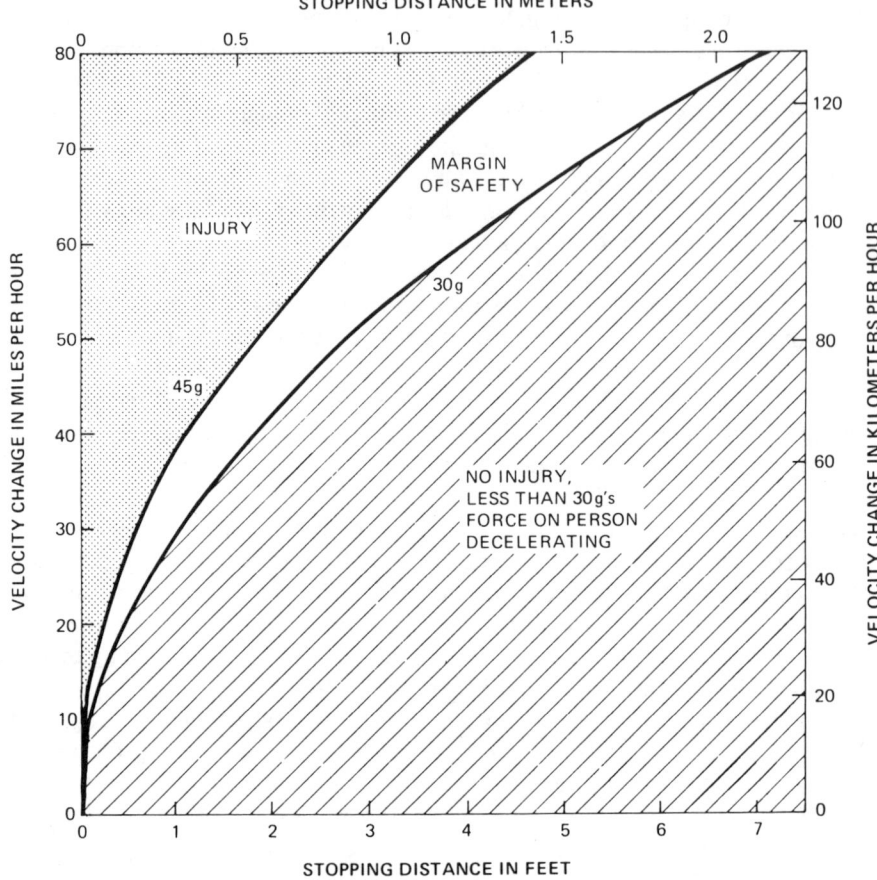

Figure 2-1. Stopping Distance, Velocity Change, and Injury for Seated, Properly Packaged Normal Adults Decelerating Forward

without debilitating conditions (that make them more susceptible to injury at less than 30 g's) for combinations of velocity change and stopping distance at a uniform maximum deceleration.[21] Of course, uniform deceleration is not absolutely achievable.

It should also be noted that the theory that small cars are less hazardous because of their crash-avoidance capabilities is not supported by data on their overall crash frequencies. On average, subcompacts have slightly higher crash-insurance claim frequencies than larger cars.[22]

The maximum braking capability and the maximum speed capability of vehicles are important factors in their crash velocities. The maximum sustained deceleration capability of most car brakes is −15 feet per second per

Agents and Vehicles of Injury

second. If no object (for example, another vehicle or fixed object) is encountered, a car braked at that capacity from 100 miles per hour requires about 717 feet to stop while the same car braked at that capacity from 50 miles per hour requires only about 170 feet to stop. Notice that doubling the speed of the vehicle quadruples the necessary stopping distance. Also, these distances do not include reaction time of the driver before braking, slick roads, or poor tire gripping capacity, any one or all of which would increase the total stopping distance. While vehicles are not driven at their maximum speeds all the time, they often fail to stop before striking people, other vehicles, or objects at these and at much lower than capacity speeds.

The nature of injuries to a pedestrian struck by a motor vehicle is determined by vehicle speed at the time of impact, the shape and elasticity of the material striking the pedestrian—usually the material on the front of the vehicle, which is often sharp, pointed, and relatively inelastic sheet metal—and the strain on the pedestrian's tissues.

Simulated pedestrian impacts have been tested with adult cadavers arranged so that their weight is on the right leg, as would be the case for an adult pedestrian stepping from a sidewalk. At impact speeds of eleven to twenty-eight miles per hour and bumpers twenty-five or more inches from the road surface, the shearing force not only broke bones in the leg but also in hip and knee joints, and vital organs in the abdomen were lacerated. Bumper heights less than twenty-one inches from the road produced only fractures.[23]

Data on injuries to pedestrians truck by bumpers of varying height reveal the same result: higher bumpers are associated with more severe injuries.[24] In the same study, when the ratio of hood height to pedestrian height was 0.46 to 0.5, the percentage of hip fractures was twice as high as those at other ratio intervals. It should also be noted that bumpers at heights that would strike adults in the legs or hips strike children more often in the head or chest.

Firearms

The most common means of suicide and homicide in the United States are firearms. These deaths, combined with the unintentional deaths from this source, comprise the second most frequent cause of death associated with mechanical energy.

Bullets are accelerated by the expanding gases that result from the explosion of gunpowder in guns. Their muzzle velocities commonly range from 1,200 to 2,700 feet per second (818 to 1,841 miles per hour). At close range, despite their small mass, bullets with these velocities have energy varying from 124 to 4,440 foot pounds. Bullets at the higher range of muzzle velocities generate so much energy that bones are sometimes broken by the bullet as it passes through nearby soft tissue. The cells impacted by the bullet are pushed aside at rates and amounts that greatly damage structure not directly impacted.[25]

A slogan, popular in some circles, claims "guns don't kill people—people kill people." That slogan is not supported by the evidence. The Federal Bureau of Investigation reports that although 23 percent of assaults are committed with firearms, 63 percent of deaths from assaults occur from firearm injuries.[26] Greater mechanical energy is generated by guns as compared to cutting instruments, fists, and so on. Since nonfatal injuries from assault are less likely to be reported to the police, particularly those that do not involve the public disturbance generated by gunshots, the discrepancy between those percentages could be substantially larger.

The Geneva Convention requires, for military use, fully jacketed bullets that retain their approximate dimensions while moving through human tissue. On the other hand, bullets commonly used for purposes such as hunting and target shooting are designed to expand or fragment; and they form wounds in tissue of much greater volume than do those used by the military. The size of the wounded area caused by such bullets, whether the victim is an animal or human, averages more than twenty-seven times that created by military bullets.[27] It is, of course, the nonmilitary bullets that injure in most nonwar firearm incidents.

The potential for death or disability from bullet wounds depends on the nature of the tissue directly or indirectly impacted, the extent to which the damage is reversible, and the prevention or control of infection in the wound. Shotguns that spray pellets rather than a single bullet are less often involved in human shootings than handguns and rifles, but they usually produce a larger wound area. At a range of ten yards, 95 percent of the pellets from a shotgun will enter the skin in a circle approximately nine inches in diameter. At a range of forty yards, the circle's diameter is about thirty-six inches.[28] The muzzle energy is inversely related to the number of pellets per shell. At a muzzle velocity of about 1,300 feet per second, the muzzle energy can vary by a factor of forty depending on the number and weight of the pellets.[29]

Plastic ammunition, which is sometimes used for target practice with handguns and rifles and for riot control in European countries, is unlikely to produce a serious wound except in the eye. Tests using cadavers resulted in failure to penetrate the skin when such ammunition was fired at a range of twenty feet.[30]

Elevation

It is perhaps pushing the concept of vehicle to refer to elevation as the vehicle of the mechanical energy that kills people in falls. In some cases the host

Agents and Vehicles of Injury

is no more elevated than his or her own height at the time of a fatal fall. And, in the fall, it is the potential energy of the host converted into kinetic energy that results in injury if it is not sufficiently absorbed by any material impacted at the end of the fall. Nevertheless, given that velocity due to the acceleration of the body will be greater the higher the point from which a body falls, perhaps the concept is appropriately applied.

The Consumer Product Safety Commission uses a sample of emergency room visits in hospitals around the United States to estimate the number of injuries associated with particular kinds of products. In 1978, there were about 572,000 treated injuries that involved stairs, steps, ramps, or landings[31]—about one such injury for every 400 persons in the country.

Fatal injuries in falls are highly concentrated among the elderly, in part because impairments in perceptual and motor skills, as well as medical conditions, increase their likelihood of falling; furthermore, their frailty increases their vulnerability to energy exchanges that would not seriously injure younger persons. Children, on the other hand, sometimes fall to their deaths from windows, fire escapes, or outside landings. Epidemiologists in New York City found that these deaths were concentrated in areas with high-rise buildings. Of 132 deaths from falls to children under five years of age during 1965 through 1969, 85 percent came after falls from windows and an additional 4 percent came after falls from fire escapes.[32]

Asphyxiation

Any matter that blocks intake of oxygen into the lungs for more than a few minutes will result in permanent brain damage. Lack of oxygen for a few minutes beyond the point of brain damage results in death. Water in the lungs is the most common form of asphyxiation: drowning accounts for about 6,500 deaths annually.

Because of the fragmented way in which national data are collected, a systematic attribution of drowning and other forms of asphyxiation to specific vehicles is not possible. While water is the obvious vehicle in drowning, no national data have been collected on the circumstances bearing on the incidence. The Coast Guard reports fatalities[33] related to boating—about 1,400 in 1979—but not all boating deaths are drownings.

In a study of 117 drownings in Maryland, 52 percent were in rivers or creeks; 17 percent in lakes, ponds, reservoirs, and the like; 14 percent in the Chesapeake Bay, including its harbors; and 11 percent in swimming pools. Waters of such disparate sizes and degrees of human exposure as the ocean, bath water, and collections in ditches and holes were each involved in less than 3 percent of the drownings.[34] The extent and type of exposure to the various bodies of water is unknown and poses an interesting problem for epidemiological study. The large involvement of rivers and creeks, where water is more likely to be moving swiftly, suggests that the kinetic energy of the water is an important contributor to drownings.

Watercraft were involved in 29 percent of the drownings studied in Maryland. More than two-thirds of the watercraft were small rowboats or outboard motorboats and 15 percent were canoes. Nationally, boating-related deaths reported to the Coast Guard were mainly associated with outboard motorboats (56 percent) or those propelled by oars or paddles (21 percent), where the means of propulsion was known. Since boats without motors do not have to be registered in most states, the numbers in use are not known precisely.

The incidence of deaths associated with sailboats is low, less than 3 percent of boating deaths in Maryland, where sailing is popular, and 2 percent nationally. One suspects that the kinetic energy of the boats propelled by motors and/or of the fast-moving waters when they are used in rivers and creeks (where few would attempt sailing) is a prime factor in drownings and other deaths from boating. The Coast Guard does not use mutually exclusive categories in its classification of "causes," so it is not possible to say that the 17 percent of boating deaths in rapid or rough water are all of this kind, or that those attributed to operator error, falls, and so on were not related to the speed of the water or of the involved boats.

Not counted in the Maryland data were an additional sixteen deaths from drowning in hurricane-generated floodwaters. Floods may drown or injure by the mechanical energy of swift-moving objects in the water. In cases in which dams or piles of waste with water behind them give way suddenly, injury may also occur from explosions, fires, and downed electric lines caused by the wall of water moving "everything in its path."[35] Floodwaters may also impede rescue efforts or damage medical facilities so that treatment of injuries is delayed.

Recent studies of asphyxiation in children, excluding cases of drowning, smoke inhalation, and aspiration of vomitus, indicate the involvement of a variety of objects that lodge in the throat or trachea, strangle through pressure on the throat, or cover the mouth and nose. Flexible, round objects such as hotdogs, pacifiers, balloons, and candy were particularly evident; but hard objects such as small wooden balls, rattles, and nuts and bolts were also found. Strangulation occurs most often when children's throats are either trapped between crib slats or beds and mattresses or hanged on ropes and cords, including cords holding pacifiers around their necks. Somewhat less common are entanglements between pieces of furniture, including parts of high chairs, in clothing, and in closing windows.[36,37] Old refrigerators that cannot be opened from the inside by children also kill.

Children's asphyxiations result from a combination of exposure to objects and their developmental stages that determine their use of or move-

Agents and Vehicles of Injury

ment in relation to these objects. Infants (less than one year old) are more often smothered or strangled by objects around the face and neck, while older children are more often asphyxiated by ingested objects.

Heat Energy

Too much heat exposure for too long or too little heat exposure for too long will damage human tissue. Most such damage to residents of the United States is from too much heat, the inhalation of the by-products of combustion, or the depletion of oxygen. The physics and chemistry of combustion are complex and vary according to 1) the concentration and type of heat source; 2) the chemistry, shape, and size of a combustible; 3) oxygen concentration; 4) the vaporization of gases; and 5) the presence or absence of catalysts.[38] Combustion of some materials under certain conditions is so rapid that the accompanying shock waves or pressures can injure directly or indirectly through the generation of mechanical forces. These injuries are usually attributed to "explosion" rather than to "fire."

As students of the energy crisis are well aware, many materials are not easily converted into heat energy. Nevertheless, the everyday environments of home, transportation vehicles, work places, and schools contain materials that are easily ignited when exposed to ignition sources. While most heat-related deaths occur from incineration or asphyxiation from smoke and other by-products of burning materials, severe but usually nonfatal burns also occur from contact with water and space-heating devices that are heated beyond human tolerance.

Any time there is a heat differential among solids, liquids, or gases in proximity to one another, including those that make up the human organism, there will be heat transferred from the medium at higher temperature to the medium at lower temperature. Heat is transferred by a mixture of conduction, radiation, and convection. Substances that conduct heat rapidly are often used for that purpose, while substances that conduct heat slowly are used for insulation where heat transfer is undesirable. Radiant heat is energy in the form of electromagnetic waves of various lengths from sources as distant as the sun. Heat in this form can be concentrated or diffused by various means, such as prisms or reflectors. Finally, convection is the transfer of heat by the flow of a gas or liquid.

Burns usually occur first to the skin or in the mouth as these surfaces are exposed to sufficient heat. The heat is conducted to deeper tissue depending on the temperature and length of exposure. Irreversible epidermal injury occurs at temperatures of sixty-five degrees Celsius in one second, but as low as at forty-five degrees Celsius for an exposure of 10,000 seconds. Necrosis of tissue below the epidermis begins at temperatures a few degrees higher in the same periods of time.[39]

Recovery from burns is a function of the area of the body surface, the depth of penetration, and the degree of infection that commonly occurs in necrotic tissue. A satisfactory index that predicts the probable outcome as a function of a combination of these factors has not been developed. In addition, clinical classifications of burns vary somewhat from one burn center to another. The probability of loss of life or permanent disability increases exponentially as a function of the surface area burned. The vital nature of the organs affected by deep burns determines their loss or reduced function. In one series of 1,683 hospitalized burn cases, 241 (14 percent) died. Of these, 27 percent died from tissue incineration, 16 percent from septicemia (infection spread in the bloodstream), 14 percent from pulmonary damage, 14 percent from fluid imbalance, and the remainder mostly from cardiopulmonary complications.[40]

The study of hospitalized cases probably results in underestimation of the importance of asphyxia due to smoke and reduced oxygen in fires. A detailed study of about half of the fire injuries in Ohio in 1976 revealed that asphyxia was involved in 69 percent of fatal fire injuries compared to 40 percent of nonfatal fire injuries.[41]

The Ohio research and a similar investigation of California fires in 1975 included data on ignition sources and the materials that burned in home fires. In these fires, the most frequent ignition source was cigarettes (29 percent), followed in order by cooking units (9 percent), space-heating systems (8 percent), "incendiary/suspicious" causes (6 percent), and electrical systems (4 percent). These sources were similarly ranked for nonfatal injuries, with cigarettes somewhat less involved (18 percent) and the others somewhat more involved. In 31 percent of fatal fires and 14 percent of nonfatal injury, the ignition source was undetermined.

In fires ignited by cigarettes, the material first ignited was predominantly bedding or mattresses (31 percent), upholstered chairs and sofas (29 percent), and newspapers (14 percent). Materials primarily ignited by cooking units were fat and grease (57 percent) and food starches (14 percent).

Fires related to transportation were mainly in motor vehicles. Three-quarters of deaths and 92 percent of injuries in transportation fires were in motor vehicles. Automobiles accounted for 46 percent of the transportation-fire deaths and 56 percent of the injuries in the Ohio and California data. In front-to-rear crash tests of six 1973 model cars at speeds of thirty-six to forty miles per hour, fuel spillage from ruptured gas tanks occurred in every case and a spontaneous fire was ignited in one. The fire filled the passenger compartment of the struck car almost instantaneously.[42]

Chemical Energy

The interaction of a chemical compound with the chemistry of human cells may result in harmful changes to the cells. The variety of such chemical reactions and the toxicity of each are too complex to examine in detail in a general survey of agents of injury. The reader interested in such detail should consult a textbook on toxicology.[43]

The effects of chemicals are dependent on the characteristics of the cells or organs involved. They also vary according to the chemicals' concentrations and in relation to the age of the individual, genetic susceptibility, and the presence or absence of other chemicals. The effect as a function of concentration is called the dose-response curve, which may be a straight line or curvilinear. The LD_{50} is the median concentration at which 50 percent of people die. The extent of variation in lethal doses is determined by the other factors mentioned above.

If a chemical is used in human beings for therapeutic purposes, the ratio of the LD_{50} to the median dose necessary for therapy, called the ED_{50}, yields an index of potential harm relative to usefulness. Where fully developed dose-response curves are known, variations of the therapeutic index give a more precise comparison of risk to benefits. For instance, one would like to know whether LD_1, the lethal dose for 1 percent of the population, is well above ED_{99}—the effective therapeutic dose for 99 percent of the population. Similar knowledge of nonfatal effects is available for some chemicals, but not for many others.

Toxicologists divide the process of harm by a chemical into three phases: exposure, toxokinetic, and toxodynamic. Most exposure to acutely poisonous substances occurs through swallowing or breathing the chemical. The toxokinetic phase refers to the chemical's absorption through the membranes of the alimentary canal or in the lung sacs and the distribution, metabolism, and excretion in the vascular and waste disposal systems. The interaction of the chemical with receptors in target tissues constitutes the toxodynamic phase.

The most frequent exposures to acutely toxic concentrations of chemicals occur when drugs—most commonly analgesics, antipyretics, sedatives, and hypnotics—are ingested in greater than therapeutic doses. Alcohol, presumably used mostly for nontherapeutic reasons, is consumed in amounts sufficient to account for about one in seven poisoning fatalities. Finally, carbon monoxide generated by cars parked with the motor running is the chemical most often inhaled in fatally toxic concentrations.

The form of a chemical—liquid, crystalline, and so on—may effect the speed of absorption and distribution when ingested. In some cases, enhancement of or antagonism to toxicity is also a function of form. The presence or absence of other materials in the alimentary canal, blood stream, and organs may interact chemically with the substances or lengthen the time of absorption and distribution. In the case of inhaled gases, the concentration in the air is the primary determinant of absorption. The absorption of inhaled droplets or dusts is moderated by the size of the particles.

When movement of a chemical in an organism is primarily through simple diffusion across membranes, the concentration in the organism increases as the concentration ingested or inhaled increases. If the chemical's movement depends on carrier molecules, it will increase to a saturation point and level off. Elimination of the substance may also be limited by the presence of carriers or factors in the metabolic system that can process only so much of the chemical in a given period of time. The relative acidity or alkalinity of urine in combination with the ionization of a substance can result in absorption through the walls of the renal tubules and thus slower elimination.

Toxicologists often refer to the half-life of a substance, meaning the period of time it takes for half of the substance to be eliminated. There is enormous variation in the half-life of chemicals, from a few hours in the case of alcohol to years in the case of fat-soluble pesticides such as DDT, aldrin, and dieldrin. Persons who have damaged livers, kidneys, or deficiencies in certain enzymes will retain chemicals longer than individuals in good health.

Damage is effected when the chemical produces a lesion; it may also result if the substance interfers with a process necessary for normal function. There is substantial disagreement as to whether or not chemicals that are known to be toxic above certain concentrations are totally benign at lower concentrations. Carbon monoxide, for example, competes with oxygen for positions on hemoglobin molecules and wins. At a sufficient concentration of the chemical, an exposed person will die from lack of oxygen. The acute effect is reversible if the carbon monoxide is removed before anoxia causes damage. We do not know however, whether relatively low concentrations of carbon monoxide impair nervous system functioning, thus increasing the risk in driving or other hazardous activities.

For purposes of regulatory standards, a certain concentration of a chemical in the environment or in an individual—such as the level of alcohol in the blood or breath of drivers—can be designated as legally permissible. Less than 0.10 percent alcohol by weight in blood or breath is allowed for driving, even though lower concentrations increase the risk to the driver and to others. Solvents, lead, and other toxic substances may have similar effects.

Electrical Energy

Electrical energy is inherent in matter and is generated in large, concentrated quantities in economically developed areas. Use of shields and automatic cutoff devices results in substantial control of electricity such that its potential exposure in damaging amounts to human beings is less than that of the forms of energy previously discussed. Nevertheless, where controls are inadequate or unused by electrical workers or other users, electrical injuries occur. Concentrated electrical energy in storms is also an occasional source of human damage.

Agents and Vehicles of Injury

Atoms are made up of electrons (negatively charged), protons (positively charged), and neutrons (neutrally charged). Gain or loss of electrons in orbit about the nucleus determines whether the atom is positively or negatively charged. The flow of electrons is electric current. The atoms of different materials, including human tissues, vary in their tendency to hold an electrical charge.

The term *amperes* refers to electrical current flow in a unit of time and varies as a function of the electromotive force (volts) divided by the resistance to conductivity (ohms) that characterizes the materials and situation involved. The extent of damage to human tissues in contact with electrical energy increases with amperage. Muscular paralysis occurs at about 0.02 amperes, ventricular fibrillation at 0.10 amperes, and ventricular paralysis at 2.0 or more amperes. The resistivity of skin varies one hundred fold as a result of its wetness—100,000 ohms when dry but 100 ohms when soaked. The water serves as a low-resistance conductor if the water is in contact with the ground.[44] Thus, a 120-volt electrical current will have low amperage (0.001) in contact with dry skin, but will be high enough (0.12) to cause ventricular fibrillation if the skin is soaking wet and in contact with the ground.

In a study of sixty-four individuals hospitalized with electrical injuries, 76 percent were injured by contact with more than 100 volts. Two-thirds contacted the electricity with one or both hands; it exited to the ground through one or both legs or feet in 69 percent of the cases. Thirty-two amputations were performed on nineteen patients, involving loss of seventeen fingers or toes, eight arms, three legs, two feet, and one hand. The remaining case was a shoulder disarticulation. Cardiac complications were found in twenty-three patients (36 percent), and sixteen (25 percent) suffered neurological complications.[45]

A study of 220 deaths attributed to electricity during twenty-two years in Dade County, Florida, included vehicles of the electricity. More than two-thirds of the ninety-three high-voltage (>1000) cases were workers who touched a power line (27 percent) or were in contact with objects that contacted a power line, such as a derrick or crane (41 percent). In twenty-six nonwork cases of high-voltage electrocutions, touching a downed or defective line (31 percent) or an antenna in contact with a line (23 percent) were most common.

Only 45 percent of the low-voltage cases were workers, and their deaths were mainly due to energized tools, electrical equipment, and wiring. Appliances accounted for 40 percent of electrocutions of nonworkers. Only sixteen (7 percent) of the total deaths were caused by lightning. The authors noted that death from electrical energy is sometimes attributed to other causes unless there is careful investigation of potential sources of electrical conduction.[46]

Ionizing Radiation

Acute injury from ionizing radiation has been rare, with the exception of the bombings of Hiroshima and Nagasaki during World War II. Whether the prevailing fear and care that has thus far been taken to prevent exposure to radiation at such huge rates and amounts could have been generated without that horrible experience is unknown.

The nuclear reactions involved in weapons and nuclear power plants depends on nuclear fission. Fission occurs when unstable uranium isotopes are bombarded with neutrons to begin a chain reaction of particle exchange. The amount of energy thereby released in heat, light, and charged particles or "rays" from small amounts of fissionable material is almost beyond human comprehension. In weapon form, the resultant, uncontrolled reaction is called an atomic explosion. When the heat from the reaction is used to promote fusion of hydrogen isotopes, as it is in hydrogen bombs, the energy released is multiplied.

Despite supposedly fail-safe procedures and mechanisms to prevent unintentional nuclear detonation, in at least one case a nuclear weapon was dropped to earth from an airplane and only one of the six mechanisms to prevent a nuclear reaction remained intact. Numerous other weapons have been jettisoned or were in planes that crashed.[47] In the generation of electricity from nuclear power, the probability of nuclear explosion is of less concern; but workers in generating plants and people in close proximity to the plants could be exposed to acutely injurious concentrations of radiation under certain conditions.

A hydrogen bomb has not been used against human populations, but knowledge of the Hiroshima-Nagasaki atomic bomb blasts and of the energy released in tests has led to estimates of the potential effects on populations concentrated in cities. The Hiroshima bomb generated the energy equivalent of fifteen kilotons (15,000 tons) of TNT and killed about 100,000 people, not counting the long-term health effects due to radiation exposure. A sixty-kiloton bomb killed approximately 100,000 people in Nagasaki. The destructive capacity of these bombs was tiny compared to the bombs and warheads now deployed in the strategic arsenals of the United States, Soviet Union, United Kingdom, and France.

Hydrogen warheads that have the energy-equivalent power of up to twenty-five megatons (one megaton is a million tons) of TNT that can be delivered by missile between continents are currently deployed. The United States and Soviet Union, by the mid-1970s, had more than 10,000 tactical nuclear weapons deployed in Europe, each as large as the Nagasaki bomb. Some smaller tonnage weapons are delivered by field artillery over distances shorter than fifteen miles. Total deployment of nuclear weapons by the nuclear powers is estimated to contain the destructive power of about sixty tons of TNT for every person on the earth.

The actual consequences of a nuclear detonation used against human populations would depend on the concentration of the populations relative to the point of detonation and the structures and vehicles in which they were located. Also, most of the deaths would occur from the mechanical force of the blast (50 percent) and the heat energy generated (35 percent). About 5 percent would die from the injurious effects of ionizing radiation and an additional 10 percent from its long-term effects. A one-megaton nuclear warhead would destroy apartment houses, killing most of the people in them over an area of some thirty-nine square miles. Most people in wooden homes in an area of some ninety-eight square miles would die.[48]

An exchange of weapons up to twenty-five megatons, each targeted on the major cities of any two countries, would destroy the civilization of those countries and render them uninhabitable. Not only would tens of millions of people die, but those who survived would be faced with virtually no medical facilities or personnel to treat the immediate wounds and burns that would number in the millions.[49] Disease would probably become rampant because of the complete breakdown of sanitation, the absence of medical care, and the suppression of bodily resistance by radiation exposure. The destruction of communication and supply systems, as well as the fear of radiation by potential suppliers of food and shelter, would very likely result in shortages of food and shelter for survivors. Many experts believe that the proliferation of nuclear weapons of ever-widening variety with their diversified delivery systems will result in their eventual use. Thus, this currently most uncommon source of acute injury has the potential to be our most common destroyer.

References

1. J.J. Gibson, "The Contribution of Experimental Psychology to the Formulation of the Problem of Safety," *Behaviorial Approaches to Accident Research* (New York: Association for the Aid of Crippled Children, 1961).

2. W. Haddon, Jr., E.A. Suchman, and D. Klein (eds.), *Accident Research: Methods and Approaches* (New York: Harper and Row, 1964).

3. National Center for Health Statistics, *Vital Statistics of the United States, 1975, Volume II, Mortality* (Washington, DC: U.S. Department of Health, Education and Welfare, 1976).

4. F. Bueche, *Principles of Physics*, 3d ed. (New York: McGraw-Hill, 1977).

5. R.G. Snyder, D.R. Foust, and B.M. Bowman, *Study of Impact Tolerance Through Free-Fall Investigation* (Ann Arbor: University of Michigan Safety Research Center, 1977).

6. R.J. Stephenson, *Mechanics and Properties of Matter* (New York: John Wiley and Sons, 1952).

7. H.M. Frost, *An Introduction to Biomechanics* (Springfield, Illinois: Charles C. Thomas, 1967).

8. H. DeHaven, "Mechanical Analysis of Survival in Falls from Heights of Fifty to One Hundred and Fifty Feet," *War Medicine* 2(1942): 586-96.

9. J.P. Stapp, "Human Tolerance to Deceleration," *American Journal of Surgery* 93(1957):734-40.

10. Haddon, et al., *Accident Research*, p. 562.

11. R.N. Janeway, "Vehicle Design Aspects of Safe Handling," *Passenger Car Design and Highway Safety* (New York: Association for the Aid of Crippled Children and Consumers Union, 1962).

12. "Jeep CJ-5 Rollover Tendencies Demonstrated," *Insurance Institute for Highway Safety Status Report* 15(December 22, 1980):2-4.

13. "CJ-5's Have Higher Fatality Rate than Motorcycles," *Insurance Institute for Highway Safety Status Report* 15(December 22, 1980):5-8.

14. National Highway Traffic Safety Administration, *Fatal Accident Reporting System, 1979* (Washington, DC: U.S. Department of Transportation, 1980).

15. N.R. Olson, "Dashboard Injuries of the Larynx," *Proceedings of the 14th Annual Conference of the American Association for Automotive Medicine* (Ann Arbor, Michigan, November 12-20, 1970).

16. B. O'Neill, H. Joksch, and W. Haddon, Jr., "Relationships Between Car Size, Car Weight, and Crash Injuries in Car-to-Car Crashes," *Proceedings of the Third International Congress on Automotive Safety* (Washington, DC: U.S. Government Printing Office, 1974).

17. Insurance Institute for Highway Safety, *Small Cars and Crashes* (New York: Harvest Films, Inc., 1972).

18. L.S. Robertson and S.P. Baker, "Motor Vehicle Sizes in 1440 Fatal Crashes," *Accident Analysis and Prevention* 8(1976):167-75.

19. B. O'Neill, M. Ginsburg, and L.S. Robertson, "The Effects of Vehicle Size on Passenger Car Occupant Death Rates," Society of Automotive Engineers Paper Number 770808, 1977.

20. National Highway Traffic Safety Administration, *The Car Book* (Washington, DC: U.S. Department of Transportation, 1981).

21. W. Haddon, Jr., "A Logical Framework for Categorizing Highway Safety Phenomena and Activity," *The Journal of Trauma* 12(1972): 193-207.

22. *Percentage of Collision Coverage Claims with Associated Injury Claims for 1974 and 1975 Models* (Washington, DC: Highway Loss Data Institute, 1977).

23. E.B. Weiss, Jr., H.B. Pritz, and C.R. Hassler, "Experimental Automobile-Pedestrian Injuries," *The Journal of Trauma* 17(1977):823-28.

24. S.J. Ashton, "Vehicle Design and Pedestrian Injuries," *Pedestrian Accidents*, ed. A.J. Chapman, et al. (London: John Wiley & Sons, 1982).

25. W.E. DeMuth, Jr., "Bullet Velocity and Design as Determinants of Wounding Capability: An Experimental Study," *The Journal of Trauma* 6(1966)222-32.

26. Federal Bureau of Investigation, *Uniform Crime Reports* (Washington, DC: U.S. Department of Justice, 1980).

27. W.E. DeMuth, Jr., "Bullet Velocity," p. 224.

28. E.A. Luce and W.O. Griffin, "Shotgun Injuries of the Upper Extremity," *The Journal of Trauma* 18(1978):487-91.

29. W.E. DeMuth, Jr., G.G. Nicholas, and B.L. Munger, "Buckshot Wounds," *The Journal of Trauma* 18(1976):53-7.

30. V.J.M. DiMaio and W.U. Spitz, "Variations in Wounding Due to Unusual Firearms and Recently Available Ammunition," *Journal of Forensic Sciences* 17(1972):377-86.

31. *Consumer Product Safety Commission 1979 Annual Report: Part Two* (Washington, DC: U.S. Government Printing Office, 1979).

32. L. Bergner, S. Mayer, and D. Harris, "Falls from Heights: A Childhood Epidemic in an Urban Area," *American Journal of Public Health* 61(1971):90-6.

33. U.S. Coast Guard, *Boating Statistics 1979* (Washington, DC: U.S. Department of Transportation, 1980).

34. P.E. Dietz and S.P. Baker, "Drowning: Epidemiology and Prevention," *American Journal of Public Health* 64(1974):303-12.

35. K.T. Erikson, *Everything in Its Path* (New York: Simon and Schuster, 1976).

36. S.P. Baker and R.S. Fisher, "Childhood Asphyxiation by Choking or Suffocation," *Journal of the American Medical Association* 244(1980):1343-46.

37. K.W. Feldman and R.J. Simms, "Strangulation in Childhood: Epidemiology and Clinical Course," *Pediatrics* 65(1980):1079-85.

38. G.H. Tryon and G.P. McKinnon, *Fire Protection Handbook*, 13th ed. (Boston, MA: National Fire Protection Association, 1969).

39. A.R. Moritz and C.F. Henriques, Jr., "Studies in Thermal Injury II. The Relative Importance of Time and Surface Temperature in the Causation of Cutaneous Burns," *American Journal of Pathology* 23(1947):695-720.

40. W. Rutowski, et al., *Burn Therapy and Research* (Baltimore, MD: Johns Hopkins Press, 1976).

41. U.S. Fire Administration, *Fire in the United States* (Washington, DC: U.S. Department of Commerce, 1978).

42. A.B. Kelley, *Cars That Crash and Burn* (film), (New York: Harvest Films, Inc., 1973).

43. J. Ariens, et al., *Introduction to General Toxicology* (New York: Academic Press, 1976)—the source of most of the discussion of toxicology.

44. R.K. Wright and J.H. Davis, "The Investigation of Electrical Deaths: A Report of 220 Fatalities," *Journal of Forensic Sciences* 25(1980): 514-21.

45. L. Solem, R.P. Fischer, and R.G. Strate, "The Natural History of Electrical Injury," *The Journal of Trauma* 17(1977):487-91.

46. R.K. Wright and J.H. Davis, "The Investigation of Electrical Deaths," pp. 519-521.

47. Stockholm International Peace Research Institute, *Armaments and Disarment in the Nuclear Age: A Handbook* (Atlantic Highlands, NJ: Humanities Press, Inc., 1976).

48. Stockholm International Peace Research Institute, *Armaments and Disarmament.*

49. H.J. Geiger, "Addressing Apocalypse Now: The Effects of Nuclear Warfare as a Public Health Concern," *American Journal of Public Health* 70(1980):958-61.

3 Human Vectors and Hosts

Human beings themselves can be vectors, or animate carriers, of damaging energy—for example, in contact sports or as assailants toward self or others; or they can indirectly deliver the energy by operating vehicles, using fire, or participating in other activities in which exposure of themselves and others to potentially damaging energy is increased. Most of the research on human behavior has been concentrated on persons immediately involved in such activities. Little scientific attention has been paid to the behavior of persons whose decisions regarding design, manufacture, and supply of energy systems, vehicles, and other environments place people at greater or lesser risk. In this chapter, human factors in immediate proximity to injurious energy exchanges are examined. Some evidence about and needed research on the decisions that determine the product designs that greatly influence the outcomes of such incidents will be discussed in chapters 6 through 9.

For purposes of injury control, research into the human factors in injurious processes would comprise answers to questions such as the following: To what extent is the factor inherent in the species or in age and sex groupings? If intrinsic, to what extent is there interperson variation? What is the evidence that the factor is modified by environmental influences? What are the limits to such modification? These questions are fundamental in the behavioral sciences and, to say the least, the answers for most human behaviors are in dispute. Enough is known, however, to suggest some implications for injury control.

One human characteristic that is very much in evidence is a misconception of human abilities. Advocates of one or another behavior-change program often sound as though they believe that human beings have infinite potential capabilities to handle hazardous energy and its vehicles, if only their programs were fully and appropriately implemented. The serious student of injuries should begin the study of human factors by considering human limitations.

Human Limitations

The limited ability of human beings to detect and react to movement of vehicles, other moving objects that they are operating, or moving objects in their immediate environment is crucial to understanding why kinetic energy—the energy inherent in *all* moving objects, animate or inanimate—is the most frequent cause of injury. In the discussion of motor vehicles in chapter 2, it was noted that the inherent nature of velocity and the limits of braking systems result in the approximate quadrupling of stopping distance as speed doubles. Additional factors are time lags in the mechanical system and the distance that the vehicle travels from the time the driver perceives the need to stop to the time the foot is firmly on the brake.

Studies of reaction time have found a wide variation in time of response under varying conditions. A few people in a simulated driving situation are able to perceive a changing stop light and move their foot from accelerator to brake in about half a second. Others take as long as two seconds, depending on the available visual stimuli. About 50 percent of the drivers in such experiments react in 0.9 seconds or more.[1] Consider what these times imply at various speeds. Table 3-1 presents the distance traveled while reacting in 0.5, 0.9, and 2 seconds, and total stopping distance at initial speeds of fifteen, thirty, and sixty miles per hour at a breaking deceleration of minus 15 feet per second ^{2}, the maximum braking capacity of most vehicles. At the median reaction time of 0.9 seconds, a driver traveling at fifteen miles per hour will move twenty feet from the initial stimulus to the point at which brakes are applied. If a child darted from between parked cars less than twenty feet in front of the car, the child would be struck at fifteen miles per hour. Avoidance by steering may take slightly less time since the hands are usually already on the steering wheel when a hazard is perceived; but space for the vehicle to move sideways may not be available.

In the average to slower cases, whether reaction time is a permanent characteristic of a person or can be improved with practice, training, corrected vision, and the like remains to be demonstrated. Even if all drivers performed to the best of their abilities, human beings, as a species, are limited in their capability to react. These bounds are an inherent part of human perceptual processing, motor functioning, and coordination. At the speeds people commonly drive vehicles and at the distances available to perceive hazards and avoid them, collisions are sometimes inevitable.

Table 3-1
Stopping Distance of Motor Vehicles Braked at −15 Feet Per Second^2
(feet)

Speed (mph)	0.5 sec		0.9 sec		2 sec	
	While Reacting	Total	While Reacting	Total	While Reacting	Total
15	11	27	20	36	44	60
30	22	87	40	105	88	153
60	44	302	79	337	176	434

Slower speeds would reduce the number of inevitable collisions, but speed perception is itself problematic. Apparently our ability to correctly estimate the speed of either our own and/or another vehicle under a variety of conditions is restricted. A randomized experiment has illustrated these limitations. While traveling in the right front passenger seat with the speedometer out of sight, experienced drivers were asked to estimate speed under four conditions: (1) under normal circumstances, (2) while blindfolded, (3) with sound excluded, and (4) with both sight and sound masked. These estimations were gathered at five-mile intervals from ten to sixty miles per hour—each change from one speed to the next coming at random.[2]

For conditions 3 and 4, the estimated speed, on average, was lower than the actual speed over the range of speeds, indicative of the importance of sound in estimating speed. Perhaps more important was the pattern of responses at different speeds and the interperson variation. For each experimental condition, actual speed was underestimated at each speed, on average, from ten to twenty-five miles per hour—in most cases by four to six miles per hour. At all speeds, the estimates of about 35 percent of the participants under normal circumstances were different from actual speeds by ten miles per hour or more, as often as not on the low side.

While this experiment was conducted under unusual conditions in the sense that the speedometer could not be seen, the participants were probably more attentive to speed than they usually were as drivers. No one can continuously monitor the speedometer while driving, and undoubtedly a substantial proportion of drivers depend on their senses rather than the speedometer to adjust their speed most of the time. To the extent that they often underestimate speed, as the experiment suggests, their ability to stop or to take other appropriate action in emergencies would be misjudged.

One type of misjudgment of speed results from adaptation. Anyone who has glanced at the speedometer sometimes after leaving a high-speed freeway, and who thought the speed to be much lower than it was in actuality, has noticed the phenomenon. In one experiment that studied speed adaptation systematically, drivers who could not see the speedometer were asked to maintain a relatively constant high speed to which they accelerated for varying periods and then to slow until they thought they had reached 40 miles per hour. The high speed was about 70 miles per hour. The actual speeds, thought by the drivers to be 40 miles per hour, averaged 44.5 miles per hour after five seconds at 70, 50.5 miles per hour after twenty miles at 70, and 53.4 after accelerating for another stint of twenty miles at 70 and again being asked to slow to 40.[3] Such overestimates would result in an exponentially longer-than-expected stopping distance should the driver have to stop.

In addition to handling his or her own car, a driver must judge the speed of other vehicles in the vicinity. This judgment is particularly crucial in decisions to overtake and pass a vehicle on a two-lane road, which necessitates moving into the lane of approaching vehicles. Research on drivers' decisions regarding the distance necessary to complete a passing maneuver indicates that, on average, they underestimate the necessary distance and that the underestimation is worse at higher speeds.

In an experiment on an airport runway set up to simulate a two-lane road, drivers were told to follow a lead car and press a button to place a chalk mark on the road when they thought they had reached a minimum distance for passing and safely returning to their lane before reaching a designated point down the runway.[4] A line was drawn at that point and the drivers were then asked to pass the lead vehicle, beginning their maneuver at that line. In the actual passing runs, the drivers were found to have underestimated the distance necessary to complete the passing maneuver by 10 percent at eighteen miles per hour, 35 percent at thirty miles per hour, and 78 percent at fifty miles per hour.

In on-road driving, many drivers would not attempt the pass at the least possible distance, or would have time to retreat to their lane if they perceived their misjudgment in time. Because of these factors the head-on crash rate is not as high as the degree of underestimation would suggest. Nevertheless, the ability to make judgments regarding speed is limited to such an extent that the number of collisions with vehicles, roadside objects, or pedestrians caused by the misjudgment of speed should not be surprising.

Drivers' estimation of the speed of other vehicles—or perhaps their seeing them at all—is related to the size of the other vehicle. Comparisons of the maneuvers of cars and motorcycles in collisions are indicative of the difficulty. Only 4 percent of car-motorcycle collisions occur when a motorcyclist turns left into the path of a car approaching from the opposite direction; but 39 percent of such collisions involve a car turning left into the path of a motorcycle approaching from the opposite direction.[5]

Some motorcycle organizations interpret these results to counter the argument that motorcycles are inherently unsafe. It is the "fault" of the auto drivers, they say, that results in the high involvement of motorcycles in severe crashes. This argument assumes that the auto drivers have the ability to perceive and judge the speed of smaller vehicles in the variety of environments in which they encounter them. Surely some drivers are not as alert as they could be; but it is also possible that there are limits to perception of objects as a function of their sizes and speeds that result in inevitable collisions. The only fault of the drivers involved may be that they are human.

Furthermore, since 46 percent of motorcycle deaths occur in crashes that do not involve other vehicles,[6] the possible fault of drivers in multiple-vehicle collisions is not a sufficient explanation of motorcyclists' death rates. In fact, motorcyclists' deaths per registered motorcycle or per mile of motorcycle travel in single-vehicle crashes alone are higher than the total (single- and multiple-vehicle) death rates for occupants of all but a few cars and trucks. The relatively higher involvement rate of inexperienced compared to experienced motorcyclists has been interpreted as proof of the importance of training.[7] An alternative explanation is that the safe operation of a motorcycle for any length of time is beyond the limits of the perceptual and motor capacities of a significant proportion of the population. These novice motorcyclists are perhaps divisible into the quick and the dead, though such an identification before the fact is not possible with any known technology. And, if the means of identification of a group with a high probability of crash involvement were available, its use in licensing would not necessarily reduce the problem. About 48 percent of fatally injured motorcyclists less than eighteen years old have no license to operate a motorcycle.[8]

The focus here is on motor vehicle injuries because of their prominence in the overall injury problem and the fact that drivers have been studied more adequately than persons involved in other injuries. The substantial evidence that human limitations are an important element in motor vehicle injuries suggests that analogous research should be undertaken in other areas. For example, a recently reported study of correlates of worker injuries in munitions plants found a moderate correlation with lack of worker understanding of how to do the job. Elsewhere in the report it was noted that some workers had literacy problems in responding to a questionnaire.[9] Were the people who had literacy problems more frequently injured? Were these workers expected to learn how to do the job solely or substantially by written instructions? Were the literacy problems correctable or the result of permanent retardation?

These are the kinds of questions that usually are not asked. Yet the answers could alter fundamentally the approaches that we take to injury reduction.

Temporary States and Permanent Traits

One important aspect of human attributes relevant to injury control is their existence in time. A psychological or physical condition may prevail from a fraction of a second to a lifetime. Conditions of individuals that contribute to injury-related behaviors can thus be placed along a continuum from very temporary to permanent. The relatively temporary conditions are called states and the more permanent conditions are called traits.

An individual's capacity for perception of changing conditions and his or her judgment regarding adapting to them can be altered by a large variety of factors. Because of the speeds involved, adaptation by drivers must occur in fractions of seconds. The precise extent to which transient states of drivers contributes to crash incidence is unknown. Some likely candidates for involvement are psychological stress, anger, fatigue, sleepiness, preoccupation with matters other than driving, distraciton by people or other factors in or out of the car, and confusion by signs or other supposedly helpful guides to driving. Many if not most of these states are probable contributors to other types of injuries as well, but the continuous alertness needed in driving makes them particularly dangerous in that situation. Some estimates of psychological and physical states have been made in studies of drivers after crashes, but post-crash recall is notoriously unreliable and, because of their very transience, there are no precise objective measures of such states.

The capacities or limits of individuals for learning, sustained alertness, and judgment are not understood to the same extent as our understanding of the physical characteristics of energy and vehicles. A few minutes of honest self-reflection by the reader will probably suggest that relatively frequent lapses in attention are the rule rather than the exception. As one careful thinker noted, "people do not usually know their limitations until they reach them, and when they are in charge of weapons and other contrivances with an almost infinite capacity to do harm, the probabilities that the future will be marked by periodic disasters are certainly increased."[10]

If they persist long enough, relatively transient conditions can sometimes be measured after an injury. One of the more commonly measured factors is blood alcohol concentration (BAC). The rate of elimination of alcohol up to six hours after ingestion is known. Thus, if the time of injury is known and the BAC is measured within a few hours of the injury, the BAC at the time of the injury can be inferred.[11] The time of injury is often not established, however, and the BACs considered important vary from one researcher to the next. Classifications of BAC vary from study to study. Also, those who are not fatally injured may consume alcohol between the time of injury and measurement.

In a study of persons sixteen years of age or older who agreed to give a breath sample for alcohol analysis when they appeared in an emergency room, 11 percent of those injured claimed to have used alcohol after the incident. These persons had a positive BAC more often than those who did not claim post-injury alcohol use. Of the people who claimed to have not consumed alcohol after the injury and who came to the emergency room within three hours, 19 percent had a positive BAC, compared to 8 percent of the patients who presented a variety of symptoms other than injuries. The number of positive BACs varied by where the injury occurred: work place—12 percent, home—27 percent, transportation—32 percent, and fights or assaults—64 percent.[12]

It should be noted that these results probably underestimate alcohol involvement. In addition to the possibly overstated claims of post-injury drinking, the estimates excluded 26 percent of injured patients, including those who refused a breath test, diagnosed alcoholics, persons with known psychiatric complications, and those who were dead on arrival. The latter are known from other research to have consumed alcohol more often than persons with nonfatal injuries (see chapter 1).

In jurisdictions where blood alcohol is assayed routinely in persons who die violently, the involvement is frequent. A study of all violent fatalities in Washington, D.C., during six months found that 28 percent of those murdered by firearms had blood alcohol concentrations of 0.03 percent by weight or higher, while 37 percent of all persons murdered had similar BACs. In general, alcohol was found to be present or implicated in one-third to one-half of all types of violent death.[13]

In a five-year period in Baltimore, white males who died by homicide had positive BACs in 78 percent of the cases where the man killed had been involved recently in an altercation or dispute with his assailant that led up to the homicide, compared to 14 percent of persons killed where there was no evidence of such prior involvement with the assailant.[14]

The causal role of alcohol in driver deaths has been specified by comparison of blood alcohol concentrations of fatally injured drivers to those of drivers stopped by police and tested for alcohol at the site of the fatal crash, at the same time of day, the same day of week, and moving in the same direction of traffic. About half of the fatally injured drivers had blood alcohol concentrations of 0.10 percent by weight or above at the time of the crash compared to less than 5 percent of the comparison group.[15] Of adult pedestrians fatally injured by motor vehicles, 42 percent had such blood alcohol concentrations, compared to 8 percent of a sample of adult pedestrians stopped and tested for alcohol at the same site and time of day, on the same day of week, and moving in the same direction.[16]

A study comparing drivers in crashes mainly of nonfatal severity with other drivers who did not crash under similar circumstances found only 15 percent of those in crashes with blood alcohol of 0.10 percent by weight or higher. Both the probability of being in a crash and the severity of the crash increased as alcohol concentration increased. Drivers are six times more likely to crash at blood alcohol of 0.10 percent and 25 times more likely at 0.15 percent by weight than at zero concentration.[17]

Laboratory research on the effect of alcohol on individual abilities has demonstrated minor impairment of single abilities at relatively low alcohol concentrations, where crash risk increases substantially. Some of the faculties tested were vision, audition, visual acuity, reaction times, or motor skills related to driving. Alcohol in these relatively low concentrations, however, has a substantially impairing effect on performance of tasks that require divided attention, which is certainly required on most trips while driving.[18]

For example, in a driving simulator, drivers given specified amounts of alcohol have little trouble keeping their "car" on course if they only have to watch the road in front of them. When lights were introduced in the area of peripheral vision, to which the driver had to react in addition to keeping the car on course, there was an average 30 percent increase in reaction time to the lights when blood alcohol was increased from 0 to an average 0.085 percent by weight. Such a decrement in reaction time in actual driving would greatly increase the stopping distances in situations where braking is necessary to avoid crashes and, to the extent that braking is delayed, the speed of any impacts would be higher and the decelerations exponentially higher, multiplying the severity of impacts.

Driving after drinking, at least at lower blood-alcohol concentrations, could be at least partly the result of a driver's awareness that his or her single abilities are not noticeably impaired. It is also likely that judgment regarding these abilities decreases as blood alcohol increases. Unfortunately, judgment is more difficult to measure accurately than factors such as reaction time; and the degree to which drinking and driving is a reasoned choice is unknown. Also, aggressiveness and other emotions may be altered by alcohol in ways that affect behavior.

The frequent involvement of alcohol in injuries related to altercations could be a consequence of an impairment that results in the injured person being less able to defend himself or judge when to cease an argument. Whether the assailant in such instances has a similar or worse BAC has not been evaluated. Additional possibilities that must be considered are: (1) factors that contribute to drinking also contribute to aggressive behavior, (2) drinking contributes to aggressive behavior, or (3) there is a synergistic effect of alcohol and other factors.

Differences in agonistic aggression between males and females in a variety of animal species suggest that there are sex-linked propensities to such behavior. The sex hormones have been studied to some extent in this regard. Among the most promising research is that finding a high abnormal concentration of luteinizing hormone (LH) in blood of persons who died violently.[19] Those who had high LH also had high blood alcohol, and it is known that alcohol stimulates the secretion of LH. It is also possible that some persons increase their drinking in an attempt to cope with aggressive or other impulses that are provoked by high LH. This hypothesis or a similar feedback of cause and effect could explain binge drinking that ends in violence, or loss of consciousness from alcohol's depressive effect on the nervous system.

Such inferences are highly speculative in the absence of more data, but another possible link between fluctuation in hormones and injury has been found among women. Among women in high schools and colleges, visits to the school nurses for treatment of injuries are twice as frequent in the 14-percent segment of the cycle preceding and during menses than during the other segments of the menstrual cycle.[20] A study of female psychiatric patients found more than half of suicide attempts were in the four days preceding or during menstruation.[21]

The parallel in a possible factor contributing to suicide attempts and other injuries should not be interpreted as an indication that a significant proportion of injuries not classified as suicidal are the result of suicidal tendencies. The best available test of that hypothesis was conducted by comparing drivers hospitalized after motor vehicle crashes and persons who were recovering from appendectomies at the same time. Psychiatric examinations revealed no greater suicidal tendencies in the motor-vehicle group than in the appendectomy group.[22]

Only a few drugs other than alcohol have been researched to any extent with regard to injury risk. Any substance inhaled, ingested, injected, or otherwise introduced into the body that affects cognition, emotion, perception, or motor performance can potentially affect driving and other behaviors that place the individual and others at greater risk of injury. Commonly used drugs such as marihuana and tranquilizers are known to have such effects on simulated driving singly and in combination with alcohol.[23]

Barbiturates and alcohol in combination are fatally toxic in sufficient dosage and the depressant effect on the nervous system of the two together probably increases the impairment that contributes to injury to a greater extent than either alone. Commonly used tranquilizers and antihistamines impair skills needed in driving, especially when they are used in conjunction with moderate amounts of alcohol.[24]

Although the young may view adolescence as a seemingly interminable period, youth is a relatively temporary state. The high rate of most types of injuries among adolescents and young adults is sometimes attributed to a greater penchant for risk taking in those age groups. This characterization implies a deliberate toying with dangers that are known to the individuals at risk. The assumption of foreknowledge and deliberation before acting is dubious at best.

Use of alcohol and drugs in adolescence is known to be influenced by peer pressure and could be augmented by rapid hormonal changes, among others, that occur in that period of life. A study of 500 cases of drug use that came to the attention of courts or hospitals in New York revealed that only 10 percent had taken the drug solely at their own initiative. Three-quarters had been offered the drug by peers and 15 percent by adults. One-third did not know the drug they had been given.[25]

The subjective states that can lead to alcohol and drug use or other behavior that increases physical risk—boredom, need to prove oneself to parents or peers, reaction to pressures and frustrations in school or jobs—are difficult to measure accurately after the fact. The incidence of injury in the mid- to late teens is relatively high: about one in five youths licensed to drive on their sixteenth birthdays will be in a crash that injures or does property damage of $400 or more before their eighteenth birthdays.[26]

These are sufficient numbers so that prospective studies, including measures of some of the potential precursors to involvement before the fact, could be undertaken.

Substances that are not used voluntarily should also be considered in future research. For example, persons exposed to a fire retardant (PBB) that was mixed into cattle feed, apparently inadvertently, in Michigan reported fatigue, need to sleep fourteen to eighteen hours per day, muscle weakness, problems with memory and judgment, as well as "a lot of accidents."[27] While psychological distress resulting from knowledge of the exposure and the social and economic consequences could have contributed to these incidents, the fact that PBB is lipid soluble and that nerve tissue has high lipid content suggests the possibility that cognition and behavior were affected by the chemical.

A known toxin to the nervous system is lead, which is found in the air, in food and water where it settled from motor vehicle exhausts and smelter emissions, and in old paint and plaster chips that children put in their mouths. The strong association of lead in shed baby teeth with academic performance and behavioral problems in school, as well as reaction time,[28] suggests that environmental lead exposure at less than poisonous concentrations contributes to problems that could impair driving and other abilities later in life. The fact that substances such as PBB and lead are retained and can be measured in human tissue opens the possibility for epidemiologic investigations of their association with injuries, certainly in the fatally injured and possibly in other persons involved as well.

Developmental Stages

One of the important research problems regarding human factors in injury is separation of the effects of experience from other correlates of age. Age, in and of itself is not a cause. It does not act on anything. Age is indicative of such factors as increased frequency of physical and mental impairments in the elderly, and developmental stages and hormonal changes in children and adolescents—all three age groupings that are disproportionately involved in certain injuries (see chapter 1). For example, about 75 percent of pedestrian fatalities in a Baltimore study were less than ten years old, sixty-five years old or older, or under the influence of alcohol.[29] In general, the abilities of children to comprehend hazard are related to their age. When four age groups—five to six, seven to eight, nine to ten, and adult—were compared in their ability to judge the time of approach of a car viewed on film, each group overestimated the actual time of arrival. The accuracy of judgment increased with age.[30]

Studies of children's behavior in areas of motor vehicle traffic and their knowledge of appropriate action reveal substantial potential for harm.

Children as young as three and four years of age were seen unaccompanied by adults in areas where a short, playful run would place them in the paths of vehicles. In models of traffic intersections and road crossings, six to nine year olds did not remember the rules for looking in all the directions from which vehicles might approach. Children have difficulty discerning the direction of auditory cues of approaching vehicles and misinterpret the meaning of road signs. One sign displaying children running as a warning to drivers was interpreted by some of the children as a place where they should run across the road to avoid being struck.[31] These results suggest a substantial need for investigation of children's behavior in proximity to hazards of all sorts, with particular emphasis on correlating the extent of their abilities to perceive and avoid danger with developmental stages.

Surveillance of emergency rooms by the Consumer Product Safety Commission revealed approximately 13,000 injuries to children less than fifteen years of age associated with small, two-wheeled motorcycles called minibikes. These vehicles can be driven up to fifty miles per hour. A pediatrician active in efforts to control children's injuries reported one case in which an eight year old fell from a minibike at night and used an ignited match to examine himself and the vehicle. The gasoline exploded, delivering substantial third-degree burns to his legs.[32]

When consumer products other than motor vehicles and guns that contribute to head injuries were studied, striking differences by age were observed. Head injuries from furniture and fixtures around homes were high among children up to age six (3 to 5 percent annually) but decline to less than 1 percent in those seven and older. Similar injuries from home structural materials such as window and door glass and stairs annually involve 4 to 4.5 percent of infants and toddlers, 2 to 2.5 percent of three to twelve year olds, and less than 1 percent of those thirteen and older. Toys account for head injuries to 2 percent of toddlers but less than 0.5 percent of older children, while sports and recreational equipment were implicated annually at a rather steady rate of 1.5 to 2.5 percent of children from the toddler state to eighteen years of age.[33]

In a study of almost 900 bicycle-motor vehicle collisions reported to police, the assignment of "probable responsibility" for the collisions was strongly related to age. Responsibility was assigned to the bicyclist in 92 percent of cases where the bicyclist was less than age twelve, but to only a third of bicyclists more than twenty-five years old.[34]

The available studies also find great differences by age in types of injury and products involved. Because good data on exposure of different age groupings to a large variety of vehicles of injurious energy are not available, in some cases it is not possible to infer that developmental factors are involved independent of differential exposure to various vehicles at particular ages. It is obvious that children continue to be exposed to home furnishings, fixtures, and structures as they grow older. The high rates of injuries associated with them among young children are undoubtedly a function of the children's development of mobility without a similar growth in perception of hazards. Data organized by age on the frequency and conditions of use of certain toys, sports equipment, bicycles, and the like are needed to specify the ages at which children can handle them without risk of serious injury.

The data on motor vehicle use by adolescents indicate that exposure and experience do not explain age differences in crash involvement. In one study, 14.2 percent of drivers licensed at sixteen had crashes reported to the police in their first year, compared to 13.4 percent in their second year and 11.5 percent in their third year at age eighteen. Among those who waited until eighteen to be licensed, 11.9 percent reported crashes in their first year, about the same percent as eighteen year olds with two years of experience.[35] Nineteen-year-old-drivers licensed since they were sixteen had 10.2 crashes per 100 drivers compared to 10.5 per 100 newly licensed nineteen year olds. Apparently, correlates of age other than experience contribute to most of the higher crash involvement of drivers less than eighteen years old.

Fatal crashes per licensed driver are similar among those aged sixteen to twenty-four. The miles driven per licensed driver, however, are substantially fewer among younger adolescent drivers. Table 3-2 presents by age and sex the number of fatal crashes,[36] fatal crashes per licensed driver, and fatal crashes per 100 million miles[37] in 1978 in the United States. Sixteen year olds have two and a half times the fatal crashes of eighteen year olds per miles driven and more than ten times the rate of middle-aged persons. Males have about twice as many fatal crashes as females per miles driven in the younger age groups, but sex differences narrow in middle to old age. Since the elderly are more likely to die given the same injury pattern as a younger person, the increase in fatal crashes of elderly drivers cannot be entirely attributed to impairment of driving skills associated with age. The highest fatal crash rates still occur to drivers in the age group that is physically the most fit.

Details of the type of exposure of teenage compared to older drivers could partly explain their greater involvement in crashes as well as the sex differences, but data on specific times and places that they drive are not available. It is clear, however, that on the basis of percentage of an age group's total fatal crashes, teenage drivers are more often involved in fatal crashes at night, particularly weekend nights, than are adults. About 25 percent of fatal crashes of sixteen- to seventeen-year-old drivers occur between 8 P.M. and 4 A.M. on Friday and Saturday nights; and about 30 percent of those in which eighteen-year-old drivers are involved occur during those hours—a period that comprises only 9.5 percent of the hours of a week. About 18 percent of crashes of adults occur in the same hours.[38]

Table 3-2
Drivers in Fatal Crashes[a] Per 10,000 Licensed[b] and Per 100 Million Miles Driven,[c] United States, 1978

	Age														
	16	17	18	19	20-24	25-29	30-34	35-39	40-44	45-49	50-54	55-59	60-64	65-69	70+
Male															
Fatal crashes	1266	2032	2695	2717	11435	7674	5355	3816	2980	2613	2378	2020	1558	1111	2000
Per 10,000 licensed	11.9	12.5	14.7	14.0	11.5	8.0	6.5	5.7	5.2	4.8	4.3	3.9	3.6	3.2	4.1
Per 100 million miles driven	48.9	24.6	19.9	12.6	8.3	5.1	4.0	3.3	3.1	3.1	2.9	2.8	3.3	4.0	7.1
Female															
Fatal crashes	329	465	547	549	2218	1514	1119	885	613	536	587	472	425	369	591
Per 10,000 licensed	3.8	3.6	3.6	3.3	2.5	1.8	1.5	1.4	1.2	1.1	1.2	1.1	1.2	1.4	1.8
Per 100 million miles driven	19.8	12.8	9.0	5.4	3.8	2.7	2.3	2.0	1.8	1.7	2.0	1.9	2.7	3.6	5.6

[a]From the Fatal Accident Reporting System computer tape (Washington, DC: National Highway Traffic Safety Administration, 1978).
[b]Federal Highway Administration, *Driver Licenses—1978* (Washington, DC: U.S. Department of Transportation, 1979).
[c]Federal Highway Administration, *Highway Statistics* (Washington, DC: U.S. Department of Transportation, 1978).

Alcohol use is higher among drivers in those hours because of the increased number of parties and bar hours on Friday and Saturday nights. Total miles driven are probably less then than during several other hours of the week. The exact extent of alcohol use, driving time and other correlates of age and sex as an explanation for differences in fatal crash involvement by age and sex at different times of day and day of week remains to be investigated.

Although the age and sex distributions of persons killed generally parallel those of involved drivers, the frequent, synonymous reference to the dead and drivers is inaccurate. Approximately two other persons are killed in fatal crashes for each driver killed when the driver is a teenager, and about one other person is killed per driver killed when the driver is more than twenty-five years old.[39]

As noted in chapter 2, fatality probabilities are associated with vehicle size. Commenting on the strong correlation between car size and fatal crash rates in the press, auto executives have often tried to exonerate the cars by claiming that small cars are driven by young drivers.[40] There are no national data on miles driven by age of driver and size of car combined, much less when and where the miles are accumulated. When fatal crashes involving drivers less than twenty-five years old are removed from the analysis, the correlation of car size and death rates per vehicle is nevertheless found. Thus, age of driver does not explain a correlation that is to be expected from simple physics (chapter 2). If younger drivers do more often drive small cars, their higher severe crash involvement may be partly a result of the more severe injuries that occur in smaller cars rather than vice versa. Good data on exposure by car size and age of driver are needed to test this hypothesis.

The elderly are more frequently injured than the middle aged because of their failing vision, hearing and mobility as well as the lowered resistance of their tissues to energy exchanges. Research relating injuries to age seldom makes the distinction among contributions of these factors.

Screening Traits

A rather elaborate research effort has sought for decades to establish the existence of relatively permanent psychological characteristics that can be used to identify individuals at great risk of injury. The persistence of the effort is most remarkable in view of the paucity of evidence of such traits.[41]

In one mistitled study of eighteen psychological traits as well as attitudes toward driving and a number of indicators of conditions under which drivers operated the vehicles, only the latter were correlated significantly to driving record. Rural driving, annual miles driven, car condition, and years driven were related to crash record, but none of the eighteen psychological traits showed a correlation that would not be expected from random variation in sampling.[42] Demographic characteristics such as age and sex are predictive of injury, at least partly because of differences in exposure; but there are no known psychological traits that predict interpersonal probability of injury with any accuracy for practical use.

Comparison of drivers less than twenty-one years of age who were involved in crashes with an age- and sex-matched comparison group indicates background characteristics that are significantly different in the groups. Crash-involved drivers had more often failed an elementary grade, were more often enrolled in a vocational course in high school, were more frequent smokers of cigarettes regularly before age sixteen, were more often employed full-time before age seventeen, and had more often been charged with a criminal offense.[43] Although some degree of involvement of nonconformity and, perhaps, lower intelligence is indicated by these results, other factors such as pattern of consumption of alcohol, drug use, and self-ratings on aggressiveness, irresponsibility, social conformity, and frustration tolerance were not different between the two groups.

The investigative pursuit of permanent traits that lead to injury includes the assumption that a large proportion of "accidents" are caused by a small group of people. In fact, a number of studies dating from the 1930s have found that the vast majority of motor vehicle crashes in any period (a year, two, or three) involve a substantially different set of drivers from those involved in the prior period.[44] In a random sample of 17,769 California drivers in the 1960s, 70 percent who crashed in a three-year period had no crashes in the prior three years.[45] Furthermore, one cannot assume that some personality or other kind of characteristic of the repeaters was responsible for their worse records without knowing whether the quantity and quality of their driving exposure remained constant in time and accounted for their extra crashes.

The same principle applies to all injuries: repeat involvement could follow from living or working in a hazardous environment and is not, in itself, an indicator of behavioral proneness. Indeed, given that most people live in the same environment, keep the same job, or drive about the same miles over the same routes for periods of years, it is rather remarkable that there is not a greater correlation of injury involvement from one period to the next, simply on the basis of relatively constant exposure to environments of high or low hazards.

There is no doubt that certain traits are involved in increased probability of injury. The correlation with use of addictive substances, such as alcohol in the case of most injuries and cigarettes at least in the case of fires, is well documented. While the use or nonuse at any given time is a state rather than a trait, frequent and heavy use means that the individual is more often at risk.

In the case of alcohol and tobacco use, there is evidence that the trait tends to be congenital—probably genetic—in origin. A genetically identical twin is more likely to use alcohol to a similar extent as the other twin than are nonidentical twins or other pairs of siblings. Abstinence from use of tobacco, though not extent of use among users, is also more often conjoint in pairs of twins than in other pairs of siblings.[46]

From the injury-control perspective, the presence of a trait does not necessarily mean that the vulnerable population can be easily identified and treated. Because of the involvement of heavy alcohol use and the possible association of other deviant behavior with fatal crashes, these crashes have been studied for evidence of prior violations that would predict such involvement. In 1,447 fatal crashes in the state of Maryland, the total prior violation record was not predictive of fatal crash involvement. Persons with eight convictions had about the same rate of fatal crash involvement per number licensed as those with one prior conviction, although both were more frequently involved than persons with no convictions.

When records for only the three years prior to the fatal crash were examined, higher fatal rates were found more often as prior violations increased (fig. 3-1). However, from the point of view of screening out large proportions of drivers who have a high fatal-crash probability, the results are disappointing. More than half the drivers in fatal crashes had no convictions in the prior three years. And, if one screened, for instance, those with more than one conviction in three years, the behavior of 6.5 percent of licensed drivers would have to be successfully changed to reduce 23.2 percent of the fatal crashes. That may seem worthwhile until one realizes that 145 million drivers were licensed nationally in 1980. Screening 6.5 percent would mean that 9.4 million would had to have been enrolled in some sort of behavior-change program. Only a fraction, if any, would be successfully changed (see chapter 5). In the group with the highest involvement in fatal crashes—those less than twenty years old with one or more convictions—157 drivers would have to be screened out and successfully changed for each fatal crash prevented.[47] And, nationally, three-quarters of the fatalities in the sixteen- to seventeen-year-old age group involve drivers with no prior convictions.[48]

A subsequent study claimed that the study just discussed was in "serious methodological error" because it claimed that crash involvement is more frequent when legal culpability is taken into account. It reported legally culpable drivers in fatal, two-vehicle collisions had about three times the average convictions in the prior three years as those not legally culpable.[49] The authors neglected the fact that average differences do not necessarily lead to efficient screening before the event, of drivers who will be involved. Of the forty-one legally culpable drivers in their study, eighteen (44 percent)

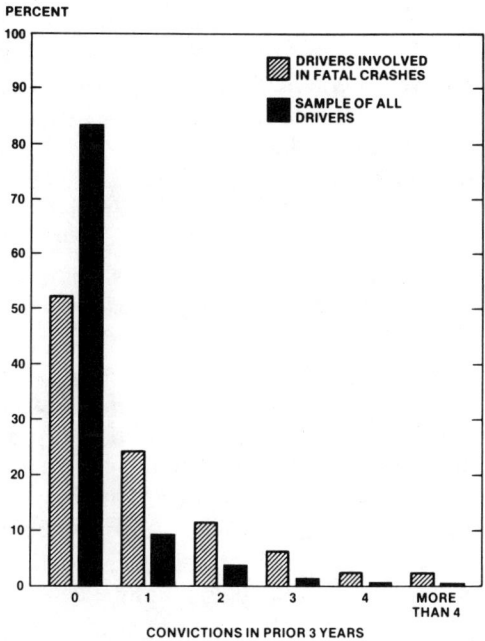

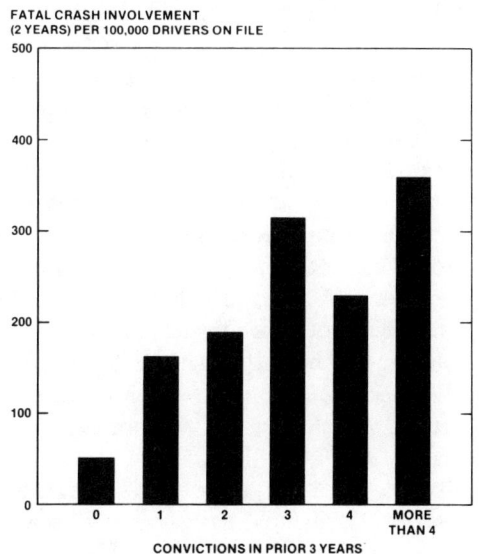

Source: Reprinted with permission from *Accident Analysis and Prevention*, vol. 7, L.S. Robertson and S.P. Baker, "Prior Violations of 1447 Drivers in Fatal Crashes," 1975, Pergamon Press, Ltd., p. 124.

Figure 3-1. Conviction Records and Fatal Crashes

had no convictions for prior violations and nine (22 percent) had only one such conviction. The average for the group was skewed upward by the two (5 percent) who had seven convictions and one who had six. Inference of large differences based on averages calculated from severely skewed distributions is a serious methodologic error. Had the ten drivers who had more than two convictions in the prior three years been put in jail for the year of the study, thirty-one of the forty-one fatal crashes would have nevertheless occurred.

Perhaps more surprising is the fact that physical impairment that would seem to increase the likelihood of crash involvement is not strongly related to motor vehicle crash records. One would expect a strong association with impairment of visual acuity, for example. In a study of 17,769 drivers licensed in California, seven different aspects of vision were measured and correlated with subsequent crash records. Difficulty in dynamic visual acuity—the perception of objects when there is relative motion of the object and the observer—was found to be more related to crash records than static visual acuity. Nevertheless, when the seven measures of vision were analyzed in combination with driver age, annual mileage, and three-year conviction records, only 8 percent of the differences among crash records of males and 6 percent of those of females were accounted for by the best predictive equation.[50]

Using more sophisticated methods, recent testing of 10,000 drivers obtaining new licenses or license renewals in two California communities revealed abnormalities in perception of the visual field in 3.3 percent and severe problems in 0.5 percent. Persons older than sixty-five had loss of part of the visual field in 13 percent of those examined. If the loss occurred in only one eye, the records of crashes and violations in the prior three years were no different than in drivers with no loss of visual field; but those with such problems in both eyes had twice the incidence of crashes and violations. The latter group included only 1.4 percent of the total tested and, thus, their excess crashes and violations accounted for no more than 1.5 percent of the totals in the population tested. While it certainly makes sense to screen for such problems and require corrected vision where possible—and perhaps refuse licenses where there is excessive risk—it is clear that the vast majority of motor vehicle crashes are not attributable to abnormal perception of the visual field.[51]

Other potentially hazardous traits, such as chronic physical ailments that can result in death while driving, have actually been found to create little if any danger for others. Studies of persons who have died of causes other than trauma while driving, combined with autopsies of drivers in fatal crashes that examined evidence of such illnesses as coronary occulsions and ruptured aneurysms, have failed to prove that trauma to others resulted from death at the wheel.[52] Apparently, either there is time to stop the vehicle or else the crashes these drivers are involved in usually do not produce much injury to others.

Physical condition is an important contributor to falls in the elderly. Compared to persons of the same age, fractures in falls occur more frequently among those who had experienced stroke, partial sightedness, and undetected visual problems. Motor abnormalities and generally poor physical condition were also associated with injuries.[53]

Sociocultural Environment

Among the most powerful influences on people's behavior are the culture and behavior of other individuals in their social settings. These cultural and social factors range from whether people should take action or be fatalistic about their environments to sets of beliefs about what kinds of information should be formally taught and what is learned by example. Few studies of behavior that contributed to injuries have considered this larger sociocultural context. Mention of a few examples of the phenomena will serve to highlight the types of questions and research that could lead to better understanding of these influences on probability of injury.

An investigation of differences in death rates from tornados among areas of the country found that, adjusted for population density relative to tornado activity, the South had much higher numbers of deaths than the North. Factors such as structure of housing and time of day that the tornados occurred could not have accounted for the size of the difference. Surveys of beliefs about personal control over life and confidence in sources of information, although based on small samples, suggested cultural differences among the populations that can contribute to behavior that increases or decreases risk of injury. Respondents in the South more often thought their lives were controlled by God or luck than those in the North. The southerners put less faith in technological identification of "tornado weather" or in the ability of the weather bureau to forecast tornados. Some combination of this fatalism, passivity, and distrust of authority could be a factor in the South's death rates.[54]

Another significant phenomenon is the variation in cultural patterns from one part of the country to another. The historical origins of these patterns are often difficult to trace, but the resulting behavior, when frequent and public, is easily observed. People who have lived in more than one city often comment that driver and pedestrian behavior varies markedly from one city to another. Certain maneuvers of drivers may be commonplace in one city and seldom seen in others. More frequent in Boston than elsewhere in the author's experience is a feint maneuver in which a driver at an intersection will begin to turn across the path of another vehicle and stop or go depending on whether the other driver applies the brakes. At heavily congested merge points in Boston, drivers jockey for position in an attempt to get ahead of other drivers. Drivers in Washington, D.C., in contrast, usually wait at the former and take turns at the latter points.

Drivers in California are said to stop quickly when a pedestrian shows any indication of entering a crosswalk. This behavior is allegedly because of stricter enforcement of laws regarding pedestrian right-of-way in that state. No study has yet demonstrated that driver behaviors toward pedestrians or pedestrian injuries are related to the enforcement of laws regarding pedestrians. Systematic observation of the behavior of drivers in response to pedestrians has found it to vary in relation to pedestrian behaviors and their numbers. Drivers approaching pedestrians decreased their speeds to a greater extent when pedestrians were not looking toward the driver than when apparent eye contact was established. Drivers also slowed more when a group of pedestrians began to cross in front of them than they did for a single pedestrian.[55]

A possible factor, though very difficult to document, is the effect on driving of almost nightly television viewing of car chases and crashes in which people seldom get injured. Occasional cases of assault in which children and adolescents acted out a scene that they saw on television suggest that the effects of frequently showing violence with cars, guns, fire, and other vehicles of mayhem may contribute to behaviors that result in violence, either directly or by subtle misinterpretation of the potential hazard. Research on the correlation of aggressive behavior of children and adolescents with television viewing has produced mixed results—some suggesting increased aggressive behavior and some none or less.[56,57]

In some belief systems the taking of risks is thought to be character building or a contribution to creativity and innovation. Unfortunately, advocates of such views do not distinguish between physical risks and the risk of wealth, reputation, and the like.[58] There is no reason to believe that contact sports or other activities that risk life and limb, if they contribute to stronger character at all, cannot be replaced by less physically risky activities that have the same effect. (The "punch drunk" boxer's character is hardly improved by the experience.) Is the competitive edge that is supposedly developed by activities such as children's minibike races any less well developed in spelling bees or talent contests? Besides, the competition of adults that contributes to creativity and innovation in complex, modern societies is psychological, social, and economic, not physical.[59]

Nevertheless, beliefs about the efficacy of physical risk persist and raise some questions worthy of research. Are the beliefs indigenous in the U.S. culture or only in identifiable groups? Is the supply of commercial products that increase such risk merely a response to existent demand, or do purveyors of those products cultivate the beliefs of the efficacy of physical risk to create demand? Are particular groups highly involved in physically risky activities more inclined to hold the beliefs and perpetuate them, or are these groups more susceptible to persuasion by those who gain from the risky activities?

One of the more remarkable phenomena in behavioral responses to risk is denial on the part of many individuals that the risk applies in their individual lives. The behavior can be easily demonstrated. When asked whether their risk of being injured or killed in a car crash is greater than, the same as, or less than "people like yourself," respondents in a random national sample of new car buyers chose "less than" six times as often as "greater than."[60]

Such denial can begin early in life. In a sample of boy and girl scouts aged seven to seventeen, the children were asked about the likelihood of various events, some health-related and some not. Responding on a scale from 1 (low expectancy) to 7 (high expectancy), the expectation of "accidents" averaged 2.04 among boys and 2.67 among girls. These were the lowest averages of the 10 health-related items that included flu, fever, colds, and missing school because of sickness.[61] Not only is the expectation unrealistically low relative to the incidence of injury in that age group, the sex difference in expectation is the opposite of that in incidence. We do not know the extent to which such responses represent a tendency not to admit vulnerability because of mutual expectations among peers (although the responses were anonymous) or a defense mechanism that contributes to the control of anxiety about real hazards.

Conclusion

In view of the ubiquity of hazardous agents, the human limitations in dealing with them, and the apparent beliefs regarding personal invulnerability, the incidence of injury and death is not surprising. Despite the evidence of the deadly combination of these factors, a chorus of "experts" continues to insist that the injury problem is essentially a problem of errant human behavior. Some of these responses are deliberately self-serving—coming from manufacturers of hazardous materials who do not want to be regulated or held culpable; or from the educators, behavioral scientists, police, and other purveyors of "human services" who benefit from labor-intensive behavior-change programs.[62]

The widespread acceptance of the premise of correctable human error cannot be entirely attributed to brainwashing by those with obvious self-interests, however. The assumption that human beings are for the most part rational actors in complete control of their actions is imbedded in our mores and laws. To question that assumption is to question both a cultural theme and a basis for personal self-esteem. It is true that in many contexts this cultural myth is harmless. Where split-second decisions mean the difference between life and death or health and disability, however, as is frequently the case in handling highly concentrated energy, reliance on the myth of the rational, fully informed, constantly alert, lightning quick human being is, paradoxically, an irrational act.

As a final and ironic note, in situations requiring evacuation of large populations the assumption that human beings will not be rational and will panic is common—no doubt fed by disaster movies and sensationalized press reports. The fear of mass confusion if people are warned about potential disaster has resulted in public officials sometimes waiting too long to order evacuations, with higher casualty rates as a result. In fact, panic is the exception, not the rule, in most disasters.[63] Such false assumptions about human abilities and behavior are at the core of many injury-control efforts. If control efforts are to be successful, the full range of the injury process, and particularly those factors that can be changed irrespective of human behavior, must be considered.

References

1. G. Johansson and K. Rumar, "Drivers' Brake Reaction Times," *Human Factors* 13(1971):23-7.

2. L. Evans, "Speed Estimation from a Moving Automobile," *Ergonomics* 13(1970):219-30.

3. F. Schmidt and J. Tiffin, "Distortion of Drivers' Estimates of Automobile Speed as a Function of Speed Adaptation," *Journal of Applied Psychology* 53(1969):536-39.

4. D.A. Gordon and T.M. Mast, "Drivers' Judgment in Overtaking and Passing," *Human Factors* 12(1970):341-46.

5. L.I. Griffin III, *Motorcycle Accidents: Who, When, Where, and Why* (Chapel Hill: University of North Carolina Highway Safety Research Center, 1974), p. 40.

6. National Highway Traffic Safety Administration, *Fatal Accident Reporting system, 1979* (Washington, DC: U.S. Department of Transportation, 1980), p. 20.

7. P.Z. Barry, "The Role of Inexperience in Motorcycle Crashes," *Journal of Safety Research* 2(1970):229.

8. L.S. Robertson, "Patterns of Teenaged Driver Involvement in Fatal Motor Vehicle Crashes: Implications for Policy Choices," *Journal of Health Politics, Policy and Law* 6(1981):303-14.

9. D.S. Edwards and C.P. Hahn, "A Chance to Happen," *Journal of Safety Research* 12(1980):59-67.

10. K.T. Erikson, *Everything in Its Path* (New York: Simon and Schuster, 1976).

11. W. Haddon, Jr., et al., (anonymously), *1968 Alcohol and Highway Safety Report* (Washington, DC: Committee Print, Committee on Public Works, U.S. House of Representatives, 1968).

12. H. Wechsler, et al., "Alcohol Level and Home Accidents," *Public Health Reports* 84(1969):1043-50.

13. L. Riddick and J.L. Luke, "Alcohol-Associated Deaths in the District of Columbia—A Postmortem Study," *Journal of Forensic Sciences* 23(1978):493.

14. S.P. Baker, L.S. Robertson, and W.U. Spitz, "Tattoos, Alcohol and Violent Death," *Journal of Forensic Sciences* 16(1971):219-25.

15. J.R. McCarroll and W. Haddon, Jr., "A Controlled Study of Fatal Motor Vehicle Crashes in New York City," *Journal of Chronic Diseases* 15(1962):811.

16. W. Haddon, Jr., et al., "A Controlled Investigation of the Characteristics of Adult Pedestrians Fatally Injured by Motor Vehicles in Manhattan," *Journal of Chronic Diseases* 14(1961):655.

17. R.F. Borkenstein, et al., *The Role of the Drinking Driver in Traffic Accidents* (Bloomington: Indiana University Department of Police Administration, 1964).

18. H. Moskowitz, "A Behavioral Mechanism of Alcohol Related Accidents," *Proceedings of the First Annual Conference of the National Institutes of Alcohol Abuse and Alcoholism* (Washington, DC: U.S. Department of Health, Education and Welfare, 1971).

19. J.H. Mendelson, P.E. Dietz, and J. Ellingboe, "Postmortem Luteinizing Hormone Levels and Antemortem Violence," *Pharmacology, Biochemistry and Behavior* 17(1982):171.

20. N.E. Liskey, "Accidents—Rhythmic Threat to Females," *Accident Analysis and Prevention* 4(1972):1-11.

21. K. Dalton, "Menstruation and Acute Psychiatric Illness," *British Medical Journal* 1(1959):148.

22. N. Tabachnick, et al., *Accident or Suicide?* (Springfield, IL: Thomas, 1973).

23. O.J. Rafaelson, et al., "Cannabis and Alcohol: Effects on Simulated Car Driving," *Science* 179(1973):920-23.

24. H. Moskowitz and M. Burns, "The Effects of Alcohol and Valium," *Proceedings of the Twenty-First Conference of the American Association for Automotive Medicine* (Morton Grove, IL, 1977).

25. I. Chein, et al., *The Road to H: Narcotics, Delinquency and Social Policy* (New York: Basic Books, 1964).

26. L.S. Robertson, "Crash Involvement of Teenaged Drivers When Driver Education Is Eliminated from High School," *American Journal of Public Health* 70(1980):599-605.

27. E. Chen, *PBB: An American Tragedy* (Englewood Cliffs: Prentice Hall, 1979).

28. H.L. Needleman, et al., "Deficits in Psychologic and Classroom Performance of Children With Elevated Dentine Lead Levels," *The New England Journal of Medicine* 300(1979):689-732.

29. S.P. Baker, L.S. Robertson, and B. O'Neill, "Fatal Pedestrian Collisions: Driver Negligence," *American Journal of Public Health* 64(1974): 318.

30. E.R. Hoffman, A. Payne, and S. Prescott, "Children's Estimates of Vehicle Approach Times" (abstract), *Journal of Safety Research* 12(1980):43.

31. S. Sandels, "Young Children in Traffic," *The British Journal of Psychology* 40(1970):111-16.

32. L.R. Berger, "Childhood Injuries: Recognition and Prevention," *Current Problems in Pediatrics* 12(1981):30.

33. F.P. Rivara, "Epidemiology of Childhood Injuries." A.B. Bergman (ed.), *Preventing Childhood Injuries* (Columbus, OH: Ross Laboratories, 1982).

34. A.F. Williams, "Factors in the Initiation of Bicycle-Motor Vehicle Collisions," *American Journal of Diseases of Children* 130(1976):370-77.

35. J.A. Pierce, *Drivers First Licensed in Ontario, October 1969 to October 1975* (Toronto: Ontario Ministry of Transportation and Communications, 1977).

36. Counts from computer files of the Fatal Accident Reporting System, National Highway Traffic Safety Administration, Washington, DC.

37. Federal Highway Administration, *Highway Statistics* (Washington, DC: U.S. Department of Transportation, 1978).

38. L.S. Robertson, "Patterns of Teenaged Driver Involvement," pp. 306-07.

39. R.S. Karpf and A.F. Williams, "Teenage Drivers and Motor Vehicle Deaths," *Accident Analysis and Prevention*, in press.

40. A. Salpukas, "Japanese Cars Held Less Safe, But the Report Is Criticized," *New York Times* 131(January 31, 1982):12-1.

41. W. Haddon, Jr., E.A. Suchman, and D. Klein, (eds.), *Accident Research: Methods and Approaches* (New York: Harper and Row, 1964), p. 387ff.

42. D.H. Schuster and J.P. Guilford, "The Psychometric Prediction of Problem Drivers," *Human Factors* 6(1964):393-421.

43. A.S. Kraus, et al., "Pre-driving Identification of Young Drivers with a High Risk of Accidents," *Journal of Safety Research* 2(1970):55.

44. T.W. Forbes, "The Normal Automobile Driver as a Traffic Problem," *Journal of General Psychology* 20(1939):471-74.

45. A. Burg, "The Stability of Driving Record Over Time," *Accident Analysis and Prevention* 2(1970):57-65.

46. J. Partenen, K. Bruun, and T. Markkanen, *Inheritance of Drinking Behavior* (Helsinki: The Finnish Foundation for Alcohol Studies, 1966).

47. L.S. Robertson and S.P. Baker, "Prior Violation Records of 1447 Drivers Involved In Fatal Crashes," *Accident Analysis and Prevention* 7(1975):121-28.

48. L.S. Robertson, "Patterns of Teenaged Driver Involvement," p. 310.

49. W.W. Banks, et al., "The Relationship Between Previous Driving Record and Driver Culpability in Fatal, Multiple-Vehicle Collisions," *Accident Analysis and Prevention* 9(1977):9.

50. A. Burg, "Vision and Driving: A Report on Research," *Human Factors* 13(1971):79-87.

51. C.A. Johnson and J.L. Keltner, "The Incidence of Visual Field Loss in 20,000 Eyes and Its Relationship to Driving Performance," mimeo (Davis, CA: University of California, Davis, no date).

52. S.P. Baker and W.U. Spitz, "An Evaluation of the Hazard Created by Natural Death at the Wheel," *New England Journal of Medicine* 283(1970):405-9.

53. J.C. Brocklehurst, et al., "Fracture of the Femur in Old Age," *Age and Aging* 7(1978):2-15.

54. J.H. Sims and D.D. Baumann, "The Toronado Threat: Coping Styles in the North and South," *Science* (1972):1386-91.

55. A. Katz and A. Elgrishi, "An Experimental Study of Driver and Pedestrian Interaction During Crossing Conflict," *Human Factors* 17(1975):514-27.

56. S. Feshbach and R.D. Singer, *Television and Aggression* (San Francisco, Jossey-Bass, 1971).

57. National Institute of Mental Health, *Television and Behavior* (Washington, DC: U.S. Department of Health and Human Services, 1982).

58. H. Fairlie, "American Desire to Build a Risk-Free Society," *Washington Post* (July 22, 1979):D8.

59. D. Klein, "Societal Influences on Childhood Accidents," *Accident Analysis and Prevention* 12(1980):275-81.

60. L.S. Robertson, "Car Crashes: Perceived Vulnerability and Willingness to Pay for Crash Protection," *Journal of Community Health* 3 (1977):136-41.

61. D.S. Gochman, "Children's Perceptions of Vulnerability to Illness and Accidents," *Public Health Reports* 85(1970):69-73.

62. H.L. Ross, "Little Men, Big Machines," *American Behavioral Scientist* 15(1972):381-402.

63. E.L. Quartantelli, "Panic Behavior: Some Empirical Observations." In D.J. Conway, ed., *Human Response to Tall Buildings* (Stroudsburg, PA: Dowden, Hutchinson and Ross, 1977).

4 Injury-Control Options Analysis

What can we do? We know the agents of injury and understand much of their nature. The vehicles that convey the agents to susceptible hosts have been identified and their characteristics and distributions in human environments are, for the most part, evident. Studies have evaluated the capacities of the human organism to withstand interactions with various forms of energy. Human abilities and limitations in coping with day-to-day and, in some cases, moment-to-moment encounters with the hazards are substantially defined. Yet we have not been able to control the slaughter and maiming associated with a large-scale injury rate.

Sporadic efforts at injury control have a poor record, with only an occasional success, partly because they are often based on assumptions at variance with available knowledge. Important success and failures in attempts to reduce injuries will be reviewed in the subsequent three chapters. This chapter focuses on progress in thinking systematically about the choices available to reduce or eliminate injuries.

The groundwork for most of the ideas in this chapter was generated by William Haddon, Jr., who, more than anyone else, has produced or strongly influenced the thinking that is central to understanding of the field. Haddon's division of the injury problem into factors and phases involved in injury events focuses attention on interactions of aspects that were previously neglected. His ten strategies for intervention force the consideration of a far richer variety of options than has been evident in past injury-control efforts.

Factors and Phases of the Injury Process

The Haddon matrix consists of the possible combinations of factors involved in an injury event—human, vehicle, and environment—and the phases in time of the event—before, during, after, and ultimate outcome.[1] The basic matrix is presented in figure 4-1. A more elaborate form of the matrix can include subdivisions of human factors into such categories as abilities and limitations. Vehicle factors might be divided into injury-enhancing versus protective characteristics and the environment can be separated into physical and sociocultural aspects.[2] Interactions among the contents of different cells should also be considered.

	Factors		
Phases	Human	Vehicle	Environment
Preevent	1	5	9
Event	2	6	10
Postevent	3	7	11
Results	4	8	12

Source: Reprinted with permission from W. Haddon, Jr., "A Logical Framework for Categorizing Highway Safety Phenomena and Activity," *Journal of Trauma* 12 (The Williams and Wilkins Co., 1972):197.

Figure 4-1. Factors and Phases in Injuries

A useful exercise for understanding the state of knowledge of a relatively homogeneous set of injuries is to review the studies of those injuries and list in each cell of the matrix what is known on the basis of good evidence. Such an exercise can lead to the development of important research questions as well as expand or narrow the consideration of alternatives for amelioration. It can also serve as a tool for resource allocation and the management of those resources.

Consider some of the major factors that we would list if our concern were severe injury to motor vehicle occupants. In the human, pre-event cell (numbered 1 in fig. 4-1), the effects of alcohol on drivers would be listed as well as—if our literature review were thorough—the limited ability of sober drivers to judge the speeds of their own and others' vehicles. The cell for human factors during the event (cell 2) would focus our attention on human tolerance of crash forces. Type and extent of injury in the post-event phase (cell 3), such as hemorrhage or multiple trauma, are important factors in eventual outcomes. Those outcomes (cell 4) include the deaths, disability, and other adverse effects to human beings noted in chapter 1.

Prominent among pre-event, vehicle factors (cell 5) would be defects in essential equipment such as brakes and tires. The energy-absorbing capability of components peripheral to the passenger compartment, as well as those that would be struck by moving bodies in the passenger compartment, would be listed in the vehicle-event cell (no. 6). Fuel leakage that could result in a conflagration after an otherwise minor crash would be listed in the vehicle, post-event cell (no. 7). The ultimate outcome in the case

Injury-Control Options Analysis

of vehicles (cell 8) includes the large cost in vehicle repairs that occurs in even minor collisions.

Environmental factors before the event (cell 9) would include physical features of the road that increase crash frequencies and the sociocultural patterns that contributed to major dependence on automobiles as a form of transportation, rather than on less hazardous forms such as trains. During the event, the most prominent environmental factor (cell 10) would be unyielding roadside objects such as trees, utility poles, and bridge abutments placed a few inches or feet from the roadside. These structures often destroy vehicles that leave the road at common traveling speeds, killing and maiming the occupants. Post-event factors that contributed to the promptness and competence of the emergency medical system would be environmental (cell 11). Cell 12 would include the foregone income of social security recipients that results from the lost productivity of the killed and maimed in the working population.

Once can quibble about where particular factors should be classified. The decision to place a utility pole on the edge of the road is obviously made before a vehicle strikes it. The damage to human beings occurs during the crash into the pole. The point is that the matrix is to be used as an analytical and management tool, not as the center of pedantic arguments about classification.

During the first sixty years of motor vehicle use, research and ameliorative efforts were almost exclusively directed at pre-crash, human factors, that is, at the behavior of vehicle operators. This orientation seems particularly odd when one considers that the basic physics of vehicle crashes had been known for two centuries when the automobile was invented, while the science of human behavior remains of doubtful use in changing behavior even today. Injuries are a major health, social, and economic problem, not because of our lack of knowledge, but because of failure to recognize where the knowledge fits and can be used in a large schema. The Haddon matrix is a tool for such a fundamental reorientation.[3]

The Ten Strategies For Injury Control

Having identified the factors that contribute to a set of injuries and the phases of the injury process in which the factors interact, a more refined set of strategies is needed to point to specific tactics that can be employed toward amelioration. In his "tigers paper,"[4] Haddon outlined ten logically distinct strategies and illustrated their use in analysis of a variety of damaging energy exchanges. More recently, the use of the ten strategies was expanded to yield a set of closely parallel, generic strategies that apply to all hazardous agents—including infectious agents and others that substantially, but not exclusively, cause harm that is not usually considered as injury.[5]

In the cases of injuries, the ten strategies are mainly directed at the necessary and specific conditions for injuries—damaging energy exchanges—and the vehicles of such energy. Specific tactics considered for each strategy include those that have been applied, those that could be easily applied, and those that appear to be difficult or impossible to apply and are too easily dismissed for that reason. It is important, however, to consider all possible options at the outset of such an analysis without initially worrying about the practical problems that each might pose. Feasibility and practicality are issues for consideration when the mix of choices available is arrayed.

The ten strategies, as Haddon defines them, are:

1. prevent the creation of the hazard in the first place
2. reduce the amount of the hazard brought into being
3. prevent the release of the hazard that already exists
4. modify the rate or spatial distribution of release of the hazard from its source
5. separate, in time or space, the hazard and that which is to be protected
6. separate the hazard and that which is to be protected by interposition of a material barrier.
7. modify relevant basic qualities of the hazard
8. make what is to be protected more resistant to damage from the hazard
9. begin to counter the damage already done by the environmental hazard
10. stabilize, repair, and rehabilitate the object of the damage.[6]

The reader who is not familiar with the work of Haddon or other writers who have followed his lead in suggesting specific tactics that apply to particular aspects of injuries, may find it useful to compile a list of possible applications of the strategies to a given set of injuries. In the author's experience, the availability of the ten strategies provides a focus for systematic consideration of alternatives that otherwise never would have been contemplated. In the following discussion of applications, the number of a given paragraph refers to the corresponding number of a strategy in the above list. The injuries discussed are, in order, those that account for most of the fatal injuries experienced in the United States.

Applications to Motor-Vehicle Injuries

Motor vehicles account for about a third of all fatal injuries and about half of unintended injuries. The ten strategies suggest many interventions, not just those that apply to driver behavior.[7]

1. The hazards of motor vehicle use would never have occurred had we never built them in the first place. Their manufacture could be discontinued,

the production and importation of fuel could be stopped, or the use of those in existence could be prohibited. These options no doubt appear ludicrous to those who grew up and live in a society where many basic needs and services have been made largely dependent on transportation in motor vehicles. Human beings managed, nonetheless, to enjoy useful lives for thousands of years before the invention of motor vehicles—and perhaps will do so long after any conceivable fuel supplies for their use have been exhausted. The diminution of those fuels, however, makes the latter proposition problematic if alternative fuels for presently competing use (such as keeping warm) are not available. Prohibited manufacture or use of especially hazardous vehicles such as minibikes, motorcycles, and certain utility vehicles would have a positive effect disproportionate to any inconvenience thus caused.

2. Short of completely discontinued use, reduction in manufacture of vehicles and/or the fuel supply is likely, even without deliberate planning. The increased cost of vehicles and fuels, as raw materials are diminished, puts their use out of reach of greater proportions of the population.

The kinetic energy in motor vehicle crashes would be reduced by decreasing mass or speed. It is important to note, however, that reducing mass by decreasing the size dimensions that are protective in crashes, as manufacturers have frequently done to increase fuel economy, is not appropriate. Vehicles made of light-weight materials that would better absorb energy in crashes (strategy 6) would increase fuel economy *and* crash protection.[8] Furthermore, vehicles capable of high speeds are less fuel-efficient and generate disproportionately greater and potentially more damaging kinetic energy. Limitations on maximum speed capability would reduce injuries and increase fuel economy.

3. Options to prevent kinetic-energy release in rates and amounts that damage people include increased skid resistance of road surfaces, improved visibility of vehicles and road signs, more efficient handling and braking capabilities of vehicles, and improved driver knowledge and skills or prohibited use of vehicles by high-risk drivers. While driver-based measures are theoretically manipulable, the limits in human abilities and the transient variation in human responses to particular stimuli make the optimization of most of the possibilities that depend on human behavior problematic.

4. The rate and spatial distribution of damaging energy in motor vehicle crashes can be modified by the use of child restraints or seat belts that increase the uniformity of deceleration of occupants with vehicles. The physical principles of such deceleration were discussed in chapter 3. Failure of voluntary use of seat belts diminishes the usefulness of this strategy.

5. The separation in time and space of potentially harmful energy from susceptible hosts is especially relevant to pedestrians and bicyclists. The obvious fact that pedestrians and bicyclists would not be struck by motor

vehicles if their paths did not intersect is largely ignored, as shown by the lack of over- and underpasses or removal of pedestrian paths and bikeways from roads. Vehicle crashes would also be less severe if vehicles of widely varying masses were assigned to separate roads, or use of roads were allocated to vehicles of different mass at different times. Removal of proximate utility poles and trees from roadsides is also an important element of this strategy.

6. Possible material barriers between energy and a susceptible host include increased energy-absorbing material in the vehicle's exterior components, particularly the front end and doors. Inside the vehicle, cushions that inflate automatically when sensors detect crash forces have been developed and tested successfully for a decade but in recent years have not been available in the marketplace. These so-called air bags spread the load over larger surfaces of the bodies moving forward in frontal crashes than do seat belts. Use of crash helmets, particularly by motorcyclists and bicyclists who have no protection from exterior vehicle structure, is also a good application of this strategy. Structures in the medians of roads that prevent vehicles from crossing into the path of oncoming vehicles is effective, especially when the design facilitates the guidance of a vehicle back into its lane without turning it over or sharply forcing it into a second lane or off the road. Energy-absorbing materials can be placed between the roadway and rigid objects where vehicles are likely to leave the road and hit them.

7. The basic design of motor vehicles can be modified to reduce the abrupt energy exchanges in crashes. Hard surfaces, pointed knobs and edges can be eliminated. Energy-absorbing materials can be used in the interior to protect occupants and on the exterior to reduce severity of impacts to anyone struck. As for objects involved in crashes, some of these can be modified so that they do not concentrate energy loads. Utility, light, and sign poles and posts can be made to detach so that they do not injuriously decelerate impacting vehicles.

8. Any attempts to increase resistance to damage by changing body structure are limited by the complexity of the human organism. Treatment of diseases that lower the threshold of injury to the organism by mechanical energy, such as hemophilia and osteoporosis, may reduce susceptibility somewhat. Strengthening of fuel tanks and containers for hazardous cargo can limit fuel spillage in crashes and any resulting damage by fire or explosion.

9. The effectiveness of initial response to trauma is determined by the rapidity of reaction in some cases and the quality of action taken in others. Training the population in stopping hemorrhages and recognizing potential spinal cord injuries, which can be exacerbated by avoidable movement, is important. Emergency roadside telephones and well-situated, trained, and

equipped professionals ready to respond quickly can make a difference in crash outcomes.

10. The repair and rehabilitation of survivors depend on the nature of the injury and the availability of trained professionals and resources. Plastic surgery can alleviate some superficial scars and bone destruction. Prosthetic devices for amputees and specially designed wheelchairs, beds, and equipment used in work and other activities allow the more severely injured to live a closer approximation of normal lives than would otherwise be possible.

Applications to Firearm Injuries

One of the remarkable characteristics of the debate about gun control is its narrow focus on registration and licensed use. Consider the far wider range of options suggested by the ten strategies:[9]

1. The cessation of the manufacture of guns, particularly handguns, and the destruction of those extant is not given consideration because the gun is perhaps more sacred in some circles than the automobile, despite its questionable usefulness for any purpose but recreational target shooting and killing. One option would be the prohibition of the manufacture of ammunition. Target shooters and hunters could substitute bows and arrows. Once the supply of ammunition was exhausted, people so inclined could "bear arms" to their hearts' content.

2. The firearm hazard could be reduced by restricting the sale of guns and/or ammunition to police departments, military units, or particular groups that could demonstrate a specific and necessary use.

3. Accelerated transformation to the "cashless society," in which identification not easily transferable to other persons would be used in transactions that now involve cash, would decrease the use of guns in robberies. Guns used in hunting and target shooting could be kept locked up at supervised hunting and target ranges, with use only authorized on the premises.

4. This kind of strategy led to the rare ownership and use of submachine guns by the public. A further reduction in the rate of the hazard's release could be effected by the prohibition of the manufacture, distribution, or use of any gun that can fire more than once without reloading.

5. Separation of the hazard in time and space could be substantially accomplished by restricting hunting and target shooting to unpopulated areas.

6. People who are likely targets or in dangerous areas, and others who so desire, can use physical barriers that include bulletproof vests, glass, and armor to reduce firearm injury.

7. Guns and bullets can be modified to reduce dangerous aspects of their design. A maximum restriction on muzzle velocity is one option. Requirements that all guns have devices that lock triggers and that cannot be

released by children would reduce injuries from their finding and playing with guns, sometimes shooting themselves and others. Application of the Geneva Convention to ammunition sold domestically would reduce the damaging effects of flattening and fragmenting in victims. Finally, restricting the sale of ammunition to plastic bullets that will not penetrate skin at short distances is also a possibility.

8-10. See the tactics for motor vehicles. These also apply to firearms.

Applications to Falls

The application of the ten strategies to falls, particularly among the very young and elderly, has been explicated. A few of the strategies are not applicable to falls but a wide variety remain viable.[10]

1. The transfer of mechanical energy to human tissue at the end of falls from high structures would not occur if no such structures were part of our environment. This option applies to everything from multifloored buildings to beds. While the construction of tall buildings is born of some necessity by population density, the height of a bed from the floor is mainly a matter of custom—one that is particularly hazardous to children and the elderly.

2. The energy potential involved can be substantially reduced by housing the most vulnerable populations in buildings that have only one floor or those in which there are no stairs or inclined surfaces. Making well-stabilized wheelchairs available to persons with osteoporosis is an illustration of this strategy.

3. Existing energy can be contained by removing objects that trip people. Coefficients of friction of floors, bathtubs, sidewalks, and other surfaces, as well as the bottoms of shoes, can be improved. Canes, walkers, and handrails would help protect the elderly, while cages and safety belts would perform a similar function for workers who must be elevated.

4-6. Since the source of the energy is the mass and speed of the falling person, neither can the rate and spatial distribution of energy be separated from the person nor can the person be separated from the energy in time, space, or by a physical barrier.

7. Basic qualities of the energy exchange can be modified, however, by changing the surfaces that are likely to be impacted. Furniture does not have to be constructed with pointed corners, edges at right or even sharper angles, and hard materials on their surfaces. Floors can be surfaced with appropriately padded carpet or other material. The surface of playgrounds can be softer than asphalt, concrete, or crushed stone. Similarly, bathroom fixtures can be recessed in the wall in some cases or made of soft, yielding materials.

Heightened structures such as buildings and bridges can be modified so that it is difficult if not impossible to fall or jump from them. Well-placed nets along their sides are one possibility, and energy-absorbing materials on the ground another.

8. Exercise programs for the elderly to retain musculoskeletal strength may reduce the frequency of falls. In one study, use of estrogen for six or more years by postmenopausal women was associated with a 50 to 60 percent lower frequency of hip and lower forearm fractures. Since estrogen use is also associated with endometrial cancer, its usefulness for reduction of fractures is problematic;[11] but for women who have had a hysterectomy, it is certainly an option. The principle that bone can be made more resistant to damage is worthy of continued research.

9-10. Important elements of these strategies that were mentioned in regard to motor vehicles also apply here.

Applications to Asphyxiation

The materials that can block the flow of oxygen to body cells are of enormous variety. Here use of the ten strategies to ameliorate some of the more common forms of asphyxiation, such as drowning, is illustrated.[12]

1. Prevention of any accumulation of water that can drown, such as in private swimming pools and baths, and prohibition of the manufacture of any object that can lodge in the trachea are logical options; but in practice they are unachievable in an absolute sense.

2. Reductions in these bodies of water, either in number or depth, and restricted manufacture of choking-size objects (such as strings and ropes on children's rattles, toys, and cribs) are, however, possible. The horsepower of boats relative to their size could also be reduced, thus lowering the risk of occupants falling overboard at high speeds and drowning or swimmers being struck in the water.

3. Recall of toys with components that can lodge in the trachea or education of the public in how to remove such objects from children's environments can be undertaken.

4. Sensors in dams and levees can be used to release water at a controlled rate to avoid dangerous buildup. Bathroom faucets can be modified to avoid the rapid filling of bathtubs that may increase children's risk of drowning. Swimming pools could be emptied when not in use. Flotation gear could be worn when on or near bodies of water. A flotation belt that is inflated by a concentrated gas when a button is pushed has been invented for swimmers who tire or are disabled in deep water.

5. Separation of populations from drowning or choking hazards in time and space includes evacuation of populations when hurricanes or flash floods are anticipated. Playgrounds could be constructed at a distance from

streams, or streams could be rerouted away from playgrounds. Ropes, wire, and similar materials that can encircle children's throats could be locked up when not in use by adults.

6. Barriers such as unscalable fences and locked gates can be constructed around swimming pools, water-filled quarries, and docks. Wells, irrigation and drainage ditches, and culverts could be covered in such a way that children cannot enter them.

7. Objects that could potentially choke could be modified in design or size so that they could not be put in the mouth. Children's food could be prepared to a consistency that precludes lumps that block the trachea. Slats on cribs could be placed close enough together that infants cannot get their bodies between them. Mattresses for cribs could be designed so that gaps between the mattress and crib cannot occur.

8. It is not known whether proficiency in swimming reduces drowning to an extent that would offset the increased exposure from exercising that skill. Since swimmers as well as nonswimmers drown, the option of training more people to swim strictly for the purpose of injury control should be considered with caution.

9. Immediate response to imminent asphyxiation is an important strategy. The population could be trained in techniques to dislodge pieces of food or other objects lodged in the upper trachea[13] and in artificial respiration. Lifeguards trained in extricating people from possible drownings could be placed in more areas of potential water hazard. Rapid identification of persons in trouble in water could be augmented by more visible swimwear, underwater lights in pools, and lights on boats. Availability of auxiliary equipment such as life preservers and lifeboats could lower the risk to the rescuer.

10. Special rehabilitation of persons with brain damage from anoxia would help them adapt more readily to their disability.

Applications to Heat and Related Damage

As noted in chapter 2, damage associated with heat energy is largely an issue of asphyxiation. Potential tactics to counter such damage, however, have been reserved for this section because of the overlap with reduction in the damage done by heat itself.[14]

1. Because one source of heat that can damage is the sun, prevention of its creation is not an option. Some important vehicles of heat as a hazard, though, can be controlled and their manufacture prohibited. If cigarettes were not manufactured, substantial numbers of burns and asphyxiations would be prevented, along with large numbers of cancers and cardiovascular diseases. Open-flame cookstoves could give place to appropriate substitutes.

2. The flammability of materials and the release of toxic gases when they burn in dwelling units, furniture (particularly chairs, sofas, and bedding), and clothing could be greatly reduced. Maximum temperature in hot water heaters could be lowered. The size of cans and tanks of flammable liquids, in storage and particularly when transported, could be limited, as could the size of the portals through which they are poured. Use of fewer fats and other flammables in cooking would decrease the hazard from that source.

3. Reduction of heat release could be effected by tactics such as the use of child-proof matches, lighters, and containers of flammable materials. Spillage of hot liquids occurs less often from bowls and cups with large bottom surfaces that increase their stability. The minimum depth of cooking utensils could be increased. Thermostats linked to valves in gas-fired heaters could turn off the gas when pilot lights are not burning to prevent gas accumulation.

4. The rate or spatial distribution of heat and smoke can be reduced by the use of flame-retardant materials that do not produce toxic by-products when heated in homes, institutions, and vehicles. Wool and modacrylic fibers burn more slowly than cotton and most plastics. In general, fabrics that are lightly woven and smoothly finished usually burn slower. Smaller spouts on containers for hot or flammable liquids and faucets that require more turns to release large amounts of hot water are good possibilities. Automatic sprinkler systems should also not be neglected.

5. Illustrations of separation in time and space include transportation of flammable liquids during periods of least traffic, cooking while children are not in the kitchen, use of cooking units that children cannot reach, and use of implements with long handles or remote controls for heated materials.

6. Use of physical barriers such as firewalls in vehicles and buildings, insulated clothing in high-heat environments, insulated covers over fireplaces, and gates to keep children from the kitchen during meal preparation could be increased. Furnaces and other units that generate heat to warm buildings could be housed separately from the occupied buildings.

7. Basic qualities of vehicles of heat can be modified to reduce heat transfer. Cigarettes that self-extinguish, matches with short burn time, pot and pan handles made of materials that are low conductors of heat are good examples. Windows on broilers and ovens provide for earlier detection of grease fires.

8. Suntans developed in moderate exposures may improve resistance to sunburn, but the probable increased rate of skin cancer from sun exposure makes this a questionable tactic.

9. Initial response to countering damage can be enhanced by use of smoke and heat detectors, fire extinguishers, and increased numbers of fire alarm systems. The public's knowledge of how to smother fires from various sources and the use of cold water on burns can possibly be improved.

10. Treatment of burns and use of grafts and plastic surgery in specialized burn treatment centers are important elements of recovery and rehabilitation from burn injuries.

Applications to Chemical Injuries

Most people probably think of exploding containers of toxic chemicals in reference to chemical injury. But toxic chemical exposure is as common as the weekend party where excess exposure to alcohol is frequent. Some of the ten strategies are possibly applicable to that ubiquitous custom as well.[15]

1. Prevention of the extraction or synthesis of poisonous chemicals may be possible in some cases. Fat-soluble chemicals that have chronic effects—DDT, aldrin, dieldrin—have been banned. Where adequate substitutes for therapeutic drugs, such as aspirin, that are frequently involved in poisonings exist, their continued manufacture is highly questionable.

2. The amounts of hazardous chemical energy in the environment can be reduced by changing the incentives for extraction and synthesis, such as adding depletion allowances to the tax code. Reducing the maximum number of pills per bottle sold to less than lethal dosages is an application to therapeutic chemicals.

3. Prevention of release of extant hazardous chemicals would include impounding those distributed in harmful concentrations.

4. The rate of exit and spatial distribution of carbon monoxide in vehicle passenger compartments can be modified by automatic air blow mechanisms that are active when the engine is running. It may be possible to modify the rate and spatial distribution of alcohol and other ingested drugs. For example, an emetic has been placed in certain drugs that is inactive at therapeutic doses but that causes vomiting at hazardous doses. Potential choking on vomitus is a disadvantage of this approach. Development of an additive to alcoholic beverages that would begin to taste bad after a couple of drinks might keep consumption to noninjurious amounts.

5. Transportation of hazardous chemicals on routes used only for that purpose or only on routes away from populated areas illustrate the separation of hazards in time and space. Substances that increase the rate of elimination of alcohol and other drugs as their concentrations increase have been tested, but a practically useful substance has not been found.

6. One can imagine a barrier to the transport of alcohol or other drugs from the gut to the bloodstream, though no such substance is apparently in use. Absorption is known to be reduced by the presence of food. Theoretically at least, something could be added to a drug that would block its passage in harmful amounts.

7. A number of these suggestions for additives to drugs exemplify a combination of this strategy and the one under which they are listed. The

compositions of chemicals are manipulable and, to the extent that we know their hazardous components, it may be possible to modify them without destroying their nonharmful uses.

8. Changing individual resistance to damage from chemicals is likely to be difficult. One attempt, in a sense, is the use of disulfiram in the treatment of alcoholics. This drug interacts with alcohol, causing discomfort and sometimes reducing alcohol consumption.

9. Increasing public knowledge of antidotes for common poisons and the awareness of poison information centers is the effort most commonly employed to counter hazardous exposures to chemicals. Installation of detectors that sense release of toxic chemicals and give warning is possible in some settings.

These lists should be more than sufficiently suggestive of the usefulness of Haddon's approach. They are not exhaustive. Their variety as well as application both to other vehicles of mechanical energy such as sports and to electricity and ionizing radiation could be expanded. It is clear from the variety of choices considered here, however, that the continued harm experienced from hazardous energy in the environment is not experienced for lack of choice of ameliorative actions. In some cases the array of choices is even too large and should be narrowed by consideration of other public-health principles.

Public-Health Principles

Knowledge of available options for the amelioration of injuries does not necessarily lead to application of the knowledge. Several barriers to implementation are common in attempts to protect the public's health. These range from emphasis on a single cause to lack of consideration of individual or organizational resistance to change.

To reiterate, one of the most important principles in considering ameliorative choices is avoidance of emphasis of a single "cause" of injuries to the exclusion of others.[16] The notion of primary cause implies that greater prominence should be given to one particular factor in the interaction of agent, vehicle, and host. The most common fallacy in this genera is the statement that human behavior is the cause of the vast majority of injuries; therefore, human behavior must be changed to prevent injuries. It should be obvious by now that such a focus excludes many options that would effectively alleviate the human damage.

Historically, public-health problems have often been reduced markedly without complete knowledge of their causes. In 1854, John Snow compared the incidence of cholera in populations using separate water supplies and discovered that the source of the water was strongly related to incidence.

The microorganism that damages human tissue diagnosed as cholera was not isolated until 1883; but Snow's discovery led to changes in water supplies in some communities. The 1866 cholera epidemic in the United States was much less severe than those of 1832 and 1849.[17] As one epidemiologist has noted, the search for ultimate causes can be a "long cut to prevention."[18]

Each discipline has its nihilists who believe any intervention is untenable until all the causes are known: epidemiology is no exception. Since perfect knowledge of causal processes will almost always be illusory, that position is a prescription for tragedy. Even apparently efficacious strategies, on the other hand, should not be adopted for general use without good research into their effects, at least in the laboratory and in field studies where the applicability or practicality of laboratory results remain in doubt.

In some cases, intervention could make matters worse. The attempts to eradicate bubonic plague produced a historical example. Even after the damaging microorganism was isolated, its ecology was not adequately understood. (The microbe is transmitted by fleas that live in the fur of rodents.) Disinfectants were poured into drains in an effort to kill the microbes; but, rather than kill the fleas or microbes, this course of action drove the rats into homes. Human exposure was increased and the rate of human infection and death rose.[19]

To avoid such consequences, an intervention should be tested experimentally in the laboratory where possible to be sure that it controls the damaging agent. If laboratory testing is not possible or leaves dangling questions, as in certain behavior-change programs, a field test should be conducted on a large enough scale to assure that the action is having the anticipated result, but on no larger a scale until the data have been examined for possible adverse effects. Unfortunately, this policy has not always been followed in injury-control efforts. Large-scale programs have sometimes been adopted willy-nilly, with no small-scale, experimental tests of the effects. Years later, when the programs are firmly entrenched and difficult to disassemble, their harmful, ineffective, or temporary nature is belatedly recognized. Resources that could have been applied elsewhere are thus wasted.

There is no magic formula for deciding when enough is known to adopt an intervention as general policy. One consideration should obviously be the reversibility of the decision. It is much easier to stop the use of a flame retardant that is found to be carcinogenic than it is to stop a labor-intensive activity with a large constituency advocating its continuation.

One very important constraint on the success of a public-health strategy is the number of people involved in its implementation. If large numbers of people must be persuaded or coerced into changing their behavior, the strategy is usually far more difficult to implement and, if implemented, to sustain effectively over the long run. Initial success by zealous program advocates may not be transmissible to those who subsequently staff a program

Injury-Control Options Analysis

as it grows. Individual behavior-change strategies have been labeled "active," in contrast to "passive" strategies in which agents, vehicles, or environments are changed to protect automatically the population at risk without each vulnerable individual having to take action.[20]

The nuclear power industry repeatedly assured the public that adequate precautions had been taken to prevent even the remote possibility of a catastrophe. In the aftermath of a near disaster at the Three Mile Island plant in Pennsylvania, however, we have learned that many such plants are not equipped with available automated control equipment, which would greatly lower the potential for the series of equipment failures and human errors that contributed to that incident. The plants generally are operated by relatively unskilled technicians who are expected to understand thick volumes of procedural instructions about what to do in all sorts of emergencies. They are not well informed of the overall picture. At Three Mile Island the technicians did not even know of prior problems with the system that contributed to the near meltdown of the reactor core. The operations center consists of row after row of dials and lights that no individual could reasonably be expected to monitor systematically and consistently. In the Three Mile Island case, the measurement of essential levels of cooling water was indirect, through instrumentation that confused the operators for hours and led to inappropriate actions that worsened the situation, while the nuclear core heated to near catastrophic temperatures.[21]

The implementation of approaches that protect people automatically can even be extended to intentional injuries. In Birmingham, England, when carbon monoxide was removed from the coal gas that was used for household cooking, and sometimes for suicide, the suicide rate from coal gas inhalation declined 86 percent. While some males, but not females, apparently substituted other methods, most did not; and the overall decline in the suicide rate was more than 50 percent.[22] Many, if not the majority, of homicides and suicides are impulsive acts that will not be repeated. It is the lethality of the means at hand more than the planned intent of the persons involved that results in death.

This is not to say that the implementation of passive strategies is easy. To the extent that even a few powerful people resist the change in agents, vehicles, or environments necessary to reduce or eliminate harmful effects, the implementation of the strategy may be long in coming. Once implemented, however, the results of passive strategies are usually permanent.

In addition to the numbers of people who must change, the frequency of action required by each individual for protection is an important factor in implementing a strategy. If an individual must do something every day, many times a day, for protection—such as buckle a seat belt—only a small proportion of the population will take the action. About 10 to 15 percent of car occupants in the United States are using seat belts, according to various surveys. If the individual must act only once or a few times for protection, such as by obtaining immunizations against certain diseases, the action is more frequent. The majority of people do in fact have their children immunized for polio, diphtheria, pertussis, tetanus, and rubella.[23]

Usually correlated but logically distinct from the frequency of action required is the amount of effort necessary to implement the protection.[24] The correct use of child restraints involves taking the time every trip to buckle or tether the restraint to the seat—in more than one place in some instances—as well as to buckle the child to the restraint. Parents must also deal with children who object to being restrained. In fact, in areas without child-restraint use laws, 93 percent of children were not restrained when observed in cars; and even in cars where the adult driver was using a belt, children were not restrained in 78 percent of observed cases.[25]

Similarly, discomfort, inconvenience, and costs are disincentives to protective behavior,[26] though of course individuals do not perform a complex risk-benefit calculation as they act or fail to act to protect themselves in their day-to-day lives. For example, the benefits of alcohol are very limited: imbibed in moderate amounts, it may reduce the risk of heart disease and it may help people cope with social situations and personal anxieties. The risks are substantial: motor vehicle deaths, homicides, suicides, drownings, falls, fires, some cancers, cirrhosis of the liver, child abuse, spouse abuse, and lost income from work due to absenteeism. Yet the majority of adults and many teenagers drink alcoholic beverages, with more than a few partaking in mind-numbing amounts. Such behavior is not simply for lack of knowledge, as observers of drinking at meetings of experts on the risks can attest.

Approaches relying on education and persuasion seek either to alter behavior by increasing knowledge of the risks or to alter habits that increase or decrease risks without changing incentives or disincentives. The manipulation of incentives and disincentives is usually attempted by enactment of a law or administrative rule. Some people obey laws and rules because of respect for authority or a general tendency toward conformity. The intent of most formal sanctions regarding injuries, however, is to offset disincentives for protective behavior or incentives for risky behavior by punishment for lack of compliance. Less frequent is the attempt to offset these disincentives by use of an incentive—a reward for increasing protection or reducing risky behavior.

The passive approach conveniently bypasses the complexities of human behavior and protects people irrespective of their behaviors and, usually, without any obtrusiveness whatsoever. (Fuses, sprinkler systems, and air bags are examples.) It removes the disincentives of frequency, effort, discomfort, and inconvenience to the individual being protected. The implementation of a passive strategy is often by law or administrative rule aimed at changing the relative incentives and disincentives to those who manufacture, supply, or otherwise control agents, vehicles, or environments of injury. These laws and rules too have most often prescribed punishment for lack of compliance rather than reward for compliance. Some passive approaches, on the other hand, have been adopted voluntarily.

The ultimate influence of a strategy depends on its effectiveness if used properly, the extent to which it is used properly, the contingencies that bear on its implementation, and the extent to which it can be sustained in the long run. The next three chapters examine some of the better empirical evidence on strategies that have been attempted to educate and persuade the population, to change its behaviors by law and administrative rule, and to change the agents and vehicles of injury by persuasion, laws, and administrative rules directed at those who manufacture, supply, or control these agents and vehicles.

References

1. W. Haddon, Jr., "The Changing Approach to the Epidemiology, Prevention, and Amelioration of Trauma: The Transition to Approaches Etiologically Rather Than Descriptively Based," *American Journal of Public Health* 58(1968):1431-38.

2. W. Haddon, Jr., "A Logical Framework for Categorizing Highway Safety Phenomena and Activity," *The Journal of Trauma* 12(1972):193-207.

3. For an application to a different set of injuries, see P.E. Dietz and S.P. Baker, "Drowning: Epidemiology and Prevention," *American Journal of Public Health* 64(1974):303-12.

4. W. Haddon, Jr., "On the Escape of Tigers: An Ecologic Note," *Technology Review* 72(1970):44. Also in part as an editorial in *American Journal of Public Health* 60(1970):2229-34.

5. W. Haddon, Jr., "Advances in the Epidemiology of Injuries As a Basis for Public Policy," *Public Health Reports* 95(1980):411-421 and W. Haddon, Jr., "The Basic Strategies for Reducing Damage from Hazards of All Kinds," *Hazard Prevention* 16(1980):1.

6. Haddon, "Advances in the Epidemiology of Injuries," p. 418.

7. This section mainly follows W. Haddon, Jr., "Reducing the Damage of Motor Vehicle Use," *Technology Review* 77(1975):53-9.

8. National Highway Traffic Safety Administration, *The Car Book* (Washington, DC: U.S. Department of Transportation, 1981), p. 56.

9. Some of the ideas in this section are from S.P. Baker and P.E. Dietz, "Injury Prevention." In: *Healthy People, The Surgeon General's Report on Health Promotion and Disease Prevention, Background Papers* (Washington, DC: U.S. Department of Health, Education and Welfare, 1979). Also see L.S. Robertson, "Environmental Hazards to Children: Assessment

and Options for Amelioration." In: *Better Health for Our Children: The Report of the Select Panel for the Promotion of Child Health, Volume IV, Background Papers* (Washington, DC: U.S. Department of Health and Human Services, 1981).

10. This section is based largely on W. Haddon, Jr., "Exploring the Options." In: *The Conference, Research Directions Toward the Reduction of Injury in the Very Young and Very Old* (Washington, DC: National Institute of Child Health and Human Development, DHEW Pub. No. (NIH) 73-124, 1973).

11. N.H. Weiss, et al., "Decreased Risk of Fracture of the Hip and Lower Forearm with Postmenopausal Use of Estrogen," *New England Journal of Medicine* 303(1980):1195-98.

12. P.E. Dietz and S.P. Baker, "Drowning: Epidemiology and Prevention," *American Journal of Public Health* 64(1974):303-12, and L.S. Robertson, "Environmental Hazards to Children," pp. 10-13.

13. S. Germaine, "Maneuvering Around Heimlich," *Paramedics International*, Fall (1979):35-37.

14. See, for a more complete list from which some of these examples were derived, G. Feck, M.S. Baptiste, and C.L. Tate, Jr., "An Epidemiologic Study of Burn Injuries and Strategies for Prevention" (a report prepared for the Centers for Disease Control by the New York Department of Health, Albany, 1977).

15. Some examples are from L.S. Robertson, "Alcohol, Behavior, and Public Health Strategies," *Abstracts and Reviews in Alcohol and Driving* 2(1981):1-3.

16. W. Haddon, Jr., "The Changing Approach to the Epidemiology, Prevention, and Amelioration of Trauma," pp. 1431-38.

17. C.E. Rosenberg, *The Cholera Years* (Chicago: The University of Chicago Press, 1962).

18. J.H. Renwick, "Analysis of Cause—Long Cut to Prevention?" *Nature* 246(1973):114-15.

19. L.F. Hirst, *The Conquest of Plague: A Study of the Evolution of Epidemiology* (Oxford: Clarendon Press, 1953).

20. W. Haddon, Jr., and J.L. Goddard, "An Analysis of Highway and Safety Strategies." In: *Passenger Car Design and Highway Safety* (New York: Association for the Aid of Crippled Children and Consumers Union of the U.S., 1962).

21. D.R. Ford, *Three Mile Island: Thirty Minutes to Meltdown* (New York: Penguin Books, 1982).

22. C. Hassall and W.H. Trethowan, "Suicide in Birmingham," *British Medical Journal* 1(1972):717.

23. L.S. Robertson, "Behavioral Research and Strategies in Public Health: A Demur," *Social Science and Medicine* 9(1975):165.

24. S.P. Baker, "Prevention of Childhood Injuries," *Medical Journal of Australia* 1(1980):466-470.

25. A.F. Williams, "Observed Child Restraint Use in Automobiles," *American Journal of Diseases of Children* 130(1976):1311-17.

26. S.P. Baker, "Prevention of Childhood Injuries," pp. 466-70.

5 Control Strategies: Educating and Persuading Individuals

A basic cultural theme in the United States, perhaps as widely shared as any in a diverse society, is that sufficient education will resolve almost any problem. Most behavioral and social scientists are also educators, and they are particularly prone to advocate educational programs. The behavioral-science and public-health literature is replete with studies of behavioral factors in various health problems, including injuries, that conclude with the statement "Therefore a health-education program should be launched . . . " to change whatever behaviors have been studied. These programs would attempt to change behaviors that contribute to injuries—driving skills, alcohol use, aggression, attentiveness—or behaviors that increase protection—use of seat belts, hard hats, safety glasses.

Such behavioral-change programs are called by a variety of names, from education, rehabilitation, motivation, behavior modification and anticipatory guidance to social support. Sometimes the stated goal is to influence factors like cognition, emotions, attitudes, and values; but the ultimate issue is whether the relevant behavior is changed and if change is sufficient and sustained enough to reduce injuries. Success is claimed more often than demonstrated, and failure is experienced more often than admitted.

Education

Education in its purest form aims only at conveying information or improving skills. Some writers use the term *training* to refer to the latter, but the purposes of this discussion allow them to be used interchangeably. In practice in this field, education programs are a mixture of information and skill training and in some cases attempt to change emotions, attitudes, values, and behavior. For education to change behavior that leads to injury or to induce increased protection, its assumptions must be valid. Following are four assumptions that are included, either explicitly or implicitly in educational efforts to reduce injury:

1. Persons informed of risk will retain the information and take recommended action to reduce the risk.
2. Persons skilled in a given hazardous endeavor are less likely to be injured than those less skilled.

3. The educator has the means available to teach information or skills, and to cause behavior change related to emotions, attitudes, and values.
4. The training of people to perform a hazardous activity will not result in an increase in the activity to the point that any injury-reducing effect of the training is more than offset by increased injuries resulting from use of the new skill.

Among the myriad educational programs aimed at injury reduction, the few that have been researched have not established the validity of each of these assumptions in each case. The evidence available suggests, rather, that often one or more of the assumptions is not valid. In some cases educational programs are even demonstrably harmful.

Among the most hazardous means of transportation is the motorcycle. Because motocycle crashes are more frequent among those inexperienced in their operation, motorcyclist education has been advocated. In England, however, motorcyclists trained in a special course had a greater average number of crashes per mile than a comparison group who learned to ride by other means. Some of the evidence pointed to the special training as an element in the creation of a greater-than-justified confidence in riding ability among the formally trained riders.[1] In the United States a study comparing motorcyclists with medically treated injuries and a sample of owners of registered motorcycles found a similar result: a greater proportion who acknowledged training were in the injured group.[2]

Research on drivers generally produces no support for the educational approach. A study comparing the crash records of drivers who had special advanced education in crash-avoidance techniques with ordinary drivers found a greater number of crashes per driver and per mile driven in the group with advanced training.[3] The specially trained drivers took the course to qualify for off-highway racing (Sports Car Club of America), so they may have been a self-selected group that overextended their abilities in cars generally, with or without special training. Nevertheless, their special training did not reduce their crash involvement per mile to that of drivers without such training; and one cannot rule out the possibility that the training increased the tendency to be overly confident in driving ability.

A bias in selection of high-school driver education courses by those who would have fewer crashes without the training has led to the unjustified conclusion that the training reduces injuries. For decades studies comparing the subsequent crash records of students who completed high-school driver education and those licensed without the course found fewer crashes among the high school-trained group.[4] When statistical controls were introduced for such factors as IQ, intellectual interests, and miles driven, however, the effect of a selection bias was discovered in studies that then produced little or no correlation of high-school driver education with crash records.[5] Apparently, parents who believe in education are more likely to have their children take the high-school driver education course to get a license but are also more likely to restrict the students' use of vehicles once licensed. Thus, their better driving record is mainly the result of less mileage driven.

The first controlled experiment on the effects of high-school driver education was done in England. No differences were observed in crashes per miles driven between students assigned to take the course and those assigned to a control group.[6] When voluntary selection into the course was replaced by student assignment, no effect on individual crash risk was found.

Preliminary results from a second experiment have found the same outcome. Students stating the intention of getting a driver's license were randomly assigned to a specially designed high-school course thought to be superior to those usually offered, or to a course more typical of those commonly taught in U.S. high schools, or a control group receiving no training in high school. No significant difference in crash rates has been found among the three groups in the two years following the courses.[7]

The experiment in England also discovered a net harmful effect of driver education due to earlier licensure of those students offered the course. Although the crashes per miles driven were the same as those in the control group, the crashes per person were higher in the trained group because of earlier licensure.[8]

Two studies in the United States have found a large impact of high-school driver education on early licensure of sixteen to seventeen year olds. Data from twenty-seven states of the United States during several years in the late 1960s and early 1970s revealed no correlation between the proportion of licensed sixteen- to seventeen-year-old drivers who had high-school driver education and the fatal crashes per licensed driver of that age. However, the licensed drivers per sixteen- to seventeen-year-old population increased at a rate of about eight new licenses for each ten persons completing high-school driver education. The results suggested that about 80 percent of sixteen to seventeen year olds completing high-school driver education would wait until age eighteen or older to be licensed if the high-school course were not available.[9]

That estimate proved very nearly accurate when nine Connecticut school districts dropped driver education from their curricula in the 1975-76 and 1976-77 academic years. Licensure after completing the high-school course declined by 7,580 with an offsetting increase of only 1,928 (25 percent) licensed after commercial or home training. The remaining 75 percent of those who would have been licensed after high-school driver education waited until they were eighteen or older to be licensed when the high-school driver education course was no longer available.

A comparison of the nine school districts that dropped driver education and nine others of similar population size that retained the course during the same period found that crashes per sixteen- to seventeen-year-old population declined commensurate with the net decrease in licensure. The decline occurred specifically in the high school-trained group. Three-fourths of the youngsters did not resort to licensure from home or commercial training and there was no increase in crashes of unlicensed sixteen- to seventeen-year-old drivers.[10]

The twenty-seven state study also considered the possibility that the effect of inexperience due to delayed licensure might result in a higher crash rate among eighteen to nineteen year olds. However, there was no significant correlation between the proportion of eighteen to nineteen year olds who had been licensed when they were sixteen to seventeen years old and their fatal crash involvement per licensed driver when they were eighteen to nineteen years old. As noted in chapter 3, the two-year experience of drivers licensed at sixteen does not make them any better drivers at eighteen than newly licensed eighteen year olds.

In sum, high-school driver education greatly increases exposure of the general population to driving by an age group that has the highest crash rate per mile without reducing the risk per miles driven. The assumptions that driver education can change information, skills, attitudes, and values sufficiently to reduce crashes and that teaching the course will not result in increase of a hazardous activity are not valid. And even if the 15 percent or so difference in crashes observed between those who take the course and those who do not, which is apparently due to self-selection rather than to the course, were actually a result of the course, it would hardly begin to offset the greater risk to the population resulting from increased licensure of sixteen to seventeen year olds.

Among older drivers who have been or would be licensed whether or not formal training is available, the potential for driver training as a reducer of crashes remains to be demonstrated by adequately designed research. Comparison of crash records of persons trained in commercial driver training schools[11] reveals no better records than among persons trained in high school. Claims have been made that the National Safety Council's "Defensive Driving" course reduces crashes,[13] but the research base for the claims was seriously flawed.[14]

One study of the defensive driving course that cleverly avoided the selection problem was done in Texas where those who complete the course receive a 10 percent insurance discount. The motivation for taking the course there is at least partly economic rather than based in concern about risk. In addition, the researcher compared the crash and violation records of persons who took the course to a group, with the same age and sex distributions, that took it two years later. At the time the first group took the course, their crash records before and after did not change significantly from the records of those who had not yet had the course. Thus, the course had no apparent effect on crash involvement when other factors were reasonably controlled.[15]

That study, along with studies of other educational programs, including the mentioned experiments in high-school driver education, found a significant reduction in subsequent convictions for violations that apparently resulted from the course. People seem to learn something about the laws and how to avoid being arrested in the various courses; but the factors that commonly lead to crash involvement are not changed to a significant extent in the courses that have been researched adequately. The limitations in human abilities and the low correlation of convictions and crashes noted in chapter 3 have not been considered by those who claim that reduced convictions is evidence of success.

The defensive driving course and other educational programs have also been used in attempts to change the behavior of persons convicted of particular offenses. Follow-up study of the conviction and crash records of two groups—one assigned to a defensive driving course and the other to the usual court treatment—found reduced convictions in the trained group but no difference in subsequent crashes.[16]

Other attempts to educate or counsel presumed high-risk drivers have shown little or no success when studied experimentally. In Nassau County, New York, individuals convicted of driving while impaired by alcohol were assigned randomly either to an education-rehabilitation program or to the usual court procedure. Subsequent driving records indicated no differences in convictions for alcohol-related driving but a significantly *higher* crash involvement of those in the education-rehabilitation program. Drivers in the program were allowed to keep their licenses, but some members of the comparison group had their licenses suspended for a time, possibly accounting for the difference.[17] The evidence suggests that a less effective or ineffective program was substituted for one of real impact.

A study in Texas compared drivers assigned to a rehabilitation-training program with a randomly selected group who were eligible but for whom no class was available. Eligibility was determined by four or more crashes and/or convictions for those twenty-one or older, and two or more crashes and/or convictions for those younger. The trained drivers aged twenty-five to thirty-four showed a slight improvement that was statistically significant in subsequent crash records compared to the control group; but among the younger drivers, the control group improved somewhat more than the trained group—a change that was not statistically significant, but the participants were fewer in number. The net effect for the entire group was not presented.[18]

An individual counseling program for drivers who accumulate demerit points for convictions during a certain period (twelve in twelve months, eighteen in twenty-four months, or twenty-four in thirty-six months) in Wisconsin was compared to a randomly selected control group without counseling. In the one year following the counseling, control drivers were significantly less likely to have a conviction, but there was no difference between the counseled and control groups in crash involvement.[19] The control group had a better crash record in three periods and the counseled group did so in one period, suggesting that different counselors or evolution in counseling techniques can have both positive and negative effects.

Various training schemes have been sold to operators of commercial fleets, but adequate studies of their effects on crashes have not been reported publicly. Surveys of fleet operators who have used such courses as an attempt to reduce crash losses find more claimed effect than is actually revealed in their fleet records. Before-after studies that show reductions in crashes after the training are inadequate unless factors other than the training that could have produced the change are taken into account.

One study has been reported in which certain drivers for a trucking company were assigned to a training course and compared to an untrained group matched for seniority and crash records. There was no statistically significant difference in crashes between the overall trained and untrained groups after more than four million miles of driving in each group. However, two trainers were involved; and the drivers taught by one of these trainers had significantly lower subsequent crashes per mile than those taught by the second trainer, or than the comparison group. The authors of the study commented that selection of trainers may be more important than selection of a particular training system.[20]

The issue, then, is not whether or not education can have an effect on crash rates under certain circumstances. Occasionally an especially good teacher may be successful; but we do not have sufficient knowledge to specify those circumstances or to guarantee that, if we had the knowledge, it could be administratively applied to large populations in such a way as to be uniformly effective. More evidence is needed on educational programs designed for hazardous activities (for example, swimming and skiing) and on behavior known to increase risk (such as alcohol use). We do not know the extent to which training people to swim or ski results in fewer injuries or in a greater amount of the activity without commensurate or greater reduction in risk per exposure.

There is some evidence that alcohol and drug education in high school increases use. A program designed to convey facts about alcohol, marihuana, and LSD to seventh and ninth grade students was administered in high schools. Self-reported drug use and selling of drugs by members of the educated groups and in control groups who had not received the education indicated greater use of all three drugs and increased selling of marihuana and LSD among students in the educated group. Answers to follow-up questionnaires suggested that the increased knowledge was accompanied by reduced fear of the drugs in the educated group, which at least partly explains their increased use.[21] The proliferation of drug-education programs in the public schools in response to increased use at some locations may have exacerbated the drug problem and contributed to its extension into areas where it would not have occurred.

The impulse to introduce new educational programs in the public schools has been extended in one case, at least, to the use of guns. In 1981, an elementary school principal in Houston announced that children in grades 2 through 5 would be trained in the use of BB guns and shotguns. A local attorney expressed concern that "[a]ll this does is enhance their fears and anxieties."[22] The news report did not mention whether anyone had considered that the training might result in greater use of guns with an accompanying increase in human injury.

Education of children requires even more care than education of adolescents and adults. Children less often interpret language, gestures, and direction as they are intended by the educator. A study of children taught a street-crossing drill including the phrase "look to the left, look to the right" found that children did not understand these as positional directions from the child's perspective. Many considered "left" and "right" as static states of the environment. Comparison before and after of children viewing a film about the drill with children who did not see the film revealed an increased static view of direction in those who saw the film—the opposite of the film's intent.[23] Other researchers have demonstrated success in training children in "pedestrian safety skills," but the number trained—fourteen children in one case and thirteen children of parents who were taught to reinforce safe behavior in another[24]—is small. The effectiveness of such techniques applied to large populations remains to be demonstrated.

Clinical Settings

Recently physicians have become more conscious of injury as the leading cause of death to children after infancy. Some effort has been taken to counsel parents in hospitals and physicians' offices regarding injury prevention. Such counseling is of interest because it carries the weight of medical authority and is on a more personalized one-to-one basis than most safety education. Experimental studies of continuous interest by physicians in patients' health—as opposed to episodic medical care—have found changes in some health-related behaviors.[25]

In a prepaid medical plan serving an upper-middle-class clientele, parents who brought children for medical visits (excluding those very acutely ill or with chronic debilitation) were divided into experimental and control groups. The experimental group received a discussion about household hazards to children, a booklet suggesting ten ways to reduce hazards in the home, and a follow-up phone call to discuss actions taken. Both groups were given free plastic covers for electric outlets and locking devices for cabinets. The control group was not contacted until a subsequent household survey of both groups.

A hazard survey of the homes was done by an unannounced home visitor eight weeks after the contact in the clinic visit. With the exception of the outlet covers, no difference was found between experimental and control groups in the incidence or number of hazards in eleven different categories.[26] Electric outlet covers were in somewhat greater use among the group that had been counseled on household hazards, but a slightly higher use of cabinet locks in the experimental group was not statistically significant.[27]

In an experiment attempting to increase use of infant restraints in cars, mothers of newborns, while confined in the hospital, were randomly selected to one of four groups:

1. those given literature on the importance of child restraints
2. those given literature along with a discussion with a health educator especially trained in persuasion techniques and demonstration of the use of infant carrier
3. those given literature and a free infant carrier
4. those in the control group who were not contacted

In addition to observation of infant-restraint use as they left the hospital, the children were observed while entering the parking lot in cars as they returned for a study of ear infection at age two to four months. At discharge, 11 percent of those given free infant carriers used them correctly, compared to 6 to 8 percent use in the other three groups. At the return two to four months later, 28 percent of those given free infant carriers used them correctly, compared to 20 to 22 percent use in the other groups.[28]

The literature alone and the education-persuasion-demonstration with literature had no apparent effect on infant-restraint use compared to the control group. Free restraints made a small but significant difference in use. A recent study duplicated the free-restraint treatment but gave the mother the seat at discharge. A member of the hospital staff conveyed the baby to the car in the carrier and demonstrated how to anchor the carrier using the car seat belt. This technique improved use on the trip home from the hospital to 66 percent, but only 28 percent were using the carrier correctly at a follow-up visit—the same percentage as in the earlier free-carrier study.[29]

These studies, although completed in the medical setting, did not involve physicians in the attempt at persuasion. A controlled study that included counseling by pediatricians regarding use of child restraints, a prescription for a restraint, and a demonstration by the pediatrician of how to use the restraint did find some effect. Compared to a control group that did not receive physician attention to restraint use—randomly assigned from the same physicians' practices—correct restraint use in the experimental group was higher by 23 percent in one month and 72 percent in two months, but only 9 and 12 percent at four and fifteen months, respectively.[30] Counseling by a physician, with the aura of medical authority and continuity of encouragement, has an effect when compared to that of health educators. When the behavior involved has all the disincentives associated with child-restraint use, however, even that effect is largely unsustained after an initial increase.

On the other hand, when people need take only a single action at relatively low cost to increase protection, as in the case of the use of electrical outlet covers noted above, physician counseling does have some effect. An experiment by two pediatricians demonstrated this principle in counseling parents regarding smoke detectors during a well-child visit. Parents in an experimental group were given a brochure in the waiting room offering the smoke detector for purchase at cost in the physician's office. During the examination, the physician briefly discussed the hazard to children of fire and the importance of early warning by smoke detectors. Nearly half of the parents without smoke detectors purchased them, and 35 percent were observed to have installed them correctly in a follow-up home visit. During a similar period, none of the parents in a control group that did not receive a brochure or counseling purchased a smoke detector.[31]

Falls of infants from elevated surfaces were also apparently reduced as a consequence of pediatric counseling. One series of parents received written material and counseling by the pediatrician regarding such falls during the first year of life. Signs reminding parents of the message were also placed over examining tables where the parents would see them during subsequent visits. A second series of parents, for whom data on medical contacts for falls were available in a prior period but who were not counseled or reminded about falls, reported falls among 17 percent of their infants compared to 10 percent in the counseled group during the first year of life. Although the specific actions taken by the parents to achieve the injury reduction were not specified, the bulk of the reduced incidents, in comparison to incidence in the control group, were children climbing over the side of cribs or rocking infant seats from table tops.[32]

Clinically based counseling in an attempt to prevent suicides had no apparent effect on suicide rates. Some 200 services were established during the 1960s in which troubled individuals could be counseled. Research comparing suicide rates per population in cities with these services before and after they became available with those of similar sized cities that did not have them found no change that could be attributed to the presence of counseling services.[33]

Whether the partially successful cases of counseling demonstrated by a few interested physicians will be adopted on a broad scale and be equally effective when persons perhaps less interested are doing the counseling remains to be demonstrated.

Health-Department Inspections

State-health-department projects directed at children's injuries are under way in several states. In one such project in Massachusetts, the state sanitary code was used as a basis for safety inspections of public housing in one community and residents of private housing in another were visited and asked to voluntarily allow inspections. The "inspection" involved a few items covered by the code—excessively hot tap water, stair and railing construction, and window screens—but as many as thirty-seven potential hazards noted by the inspectors were discussed with parents. A follow-up visit was made to determine the extent to which changes had been made. The average number of non-code hazards was reduced from 13.1 to 6.6 per household, and regulatory violations found in 17 percent of households during the first visit had been reduced to none by the second.[34] Apparently, counseling accompanied by the authority of the health department can be a substantially effective force in reducing household hazards, including those that do not fall under health codes.

Mass Media

In the changing of everyday behaviors, frequent reminders would seem to have some effect. The major means of delivering such a message in modern society is by advertising in mass media. Advertisers of commercial products seek to increase their share of the market, and new products are sometimes brought to market sucessfully through use of these means. Nevertheless, spectacular success is much less frequent than those who believe that people are easily manipulable by the media would have us think.

It is not unreasonable to attempt to change health-related behavior by advertisements. In order not to waste resources or perhaps even have a negative effect, however, such advertising should be demonstrated as effective on a small scale before transferal to a mass scale. As late as 1970, a review of the literature on safety campaigns found only two published studies that could be considered adequate evaluations, and these involved posters and letters rather than use of mass media. Most of the studies reviewed did not use control groups, and the outcome measured was familiarity with slogans rather than observation of behavior change or injury outcomes. In other cases the campaigns were mixed with legal enforcement efforts, to be discussed in the next chapter, so that the effect of media alone could not be distinguished.[35]

In the 1970s, studies were conducted to measure the effect of mass media campaigns on seat belt use in cars. This research raises serious doubts that a media campaign can be devised that will have a major impact in any

Educating and Persuading Individuals

change of daily behavior that involves even a slight inconvenience. One of the studies used a series of radio and television messages that had been used in campaigns by the National Safety Council, the American Safety Belt Council (an association of belt manufacturers), and the U.S. Department of Transportation. The messages were first shown to separate panels of communication experts and lay-persons. They disagreed on potential effectiveness. The experts emphasized entertainment value and avoidance of "the scare approach," while the lay panel rated scare content highly.

A mix of messages rated highly by the panels was selected for use in an experiment. Three communities with similar demographic characteristics were given intensive exposure, moderate exposure, and no exposure of the messages, respectively, in a five-week campaign on local radio and television stations. Belt use by drivers in their cars was observed and recorded before, during, and after the campaign at selected sites in the three communities. Belt use increased slightly in the intensive and no-exposure communities but not in the moderate-exposure community. Postcampaign belt use was about the same as precampaign use in all three communities.[36]

A second study was based on prior research on belt use. Preliminary to development of a new media campaign attempting to increase belt use, a team of researchers conducted a study to find correlates of belt use that might be useful in development of messages. Belt users and a random sample of nonusers observed at the same sites, times, and moving in the same direction were interviewed subsequently. Belt users were found to have more formal education. They rated belts as more comfortable and convenient than did nonusers; and they also claimed not to smoke while driving. Having had a friend killed in a crash made no difference in belt use, but users did say that they had a friend who was injured but not killed in a crash more often than nonusers. These factors were additively related to belt use—that is, inconvenience had an effect independent of smoking, for example—suggesting that reaching the ashtray while belted was not the inconvenience they had in mind.[37]

Wary of emphasizing the comfort-convenience problem lest that view be reinforced, and unsure about how to deal with formal education and smoking behavior as correlates of belt use, the campaign's designers emphasized the possibility of disfigurement or disability. This was done by creating filmed portrayals of surrogates for an injured friend: a woman and teenaged girl with facial scars attributed to a crash and a teenaged boy with leg braces on his way to a football game with his father. Parental responsibility for children and adolescents as well as physician endorsement were also used as themes. The convenience issue was addressed circumspectly in one message where children were urged by the "good car fairy" to tell their parents to use their belts that had been hidden between the seat and seatback by the "wicked car witch."

The messages were shown on one cable of a dual-cable television system used to research commercial campaigns. The two cables are distributed throughout a community in a checkerboard fashion. Subscribers to the cable television service did not know that different commercials were being seen in different households. The belt-use messages were substituted for those advertising commercial products or other public service announcements on the chosen cable. They were targeted to specific audiences: the children's message was aired on children's programs, the father-son on football games, the facial scars on soap operas. During a nine-month period, the messages were shown 943 times, which was the equivalent of a $7 million (1972 dollars) new-product campaign if done nationally.

Belt use of drivers in their cars was observed at sites throughout the community a month before the campaign, throughout the campaign, and a month after the campaign. License plate numbers were traced through the Motor Vehicle Administration files to identify addresses of the households of the observed drivers. Comparing these to the addresses on the cable television company's billing files, the driver observed was classified as being from an experimental, control, noncable, or out-of-town household.

This television campaign had no discernible effect on observed belt use. At no point before, during, or after the campaign was there a statistically significant difference in belt use in drivers from households on the experimental and control cables or between those and drivers from households not on the cables.[38]

In 1969, the Ontario Department of Transport developed a multimedia advertising campaign and attempted to persuade radio, television, and newspaper outlets as well as safety councils, businesses, schools, and police departments to use the materials. Study of employment of the materials by the media found only intermittent, unsystematic usage. Claimed belt use by drivers in collisions—as reported by the police—was unchanged by the campaign.[39] Without funds to implement and sustain a campaign, dependence on public-service outlets, irrespective of the adequacy of the campaign materials, is likely to result in haphazard implementation. Most media outlets will not provide prime time or space free of charge, or at rates substantially less than they receive for commercial products—and, even if they did, there is no reason to expect the advertising to have much, if any, effect.

In a three-community study of an attempt to reduce burn injuries, mass media in the form of television ads, newspaper articles and ads, and features on radio and television talk shows were used along with free booklets, programs for community groups in one community, and teaching materials in the public schools of a second community. The third community, on which no media or other efforts were expended, served as a control for comparison. The efforts were implemented during an eight-month period.

Based on epidemiological evidence on burns in the communities and surveys of the population and in the schools, the educational messages emphasized use of smoke detectors, home fire drills, and proper storage of matches, gasoline, and other highly flammable materials. Clothing design, electrical appliances and installations, and the particular hazards to children at various stages of development were included in the community group and school programs.

Data on burns in the three communities before and after the campaign revealed no effect in the media-school community and a slight effect in the media-community group effort. Interview data from adults and tests in the schools indicated that the campaign increased the knowledge of 44 percent of the test group and changed the behavior of 29 percent; only 19 percent persisted in that change, however, and only 13 percent applied any of the knowledge at the moment of need.[40] The assumption that knowledge has a large effect on behavior, particularly in an emergency, gains little support from such empirical evidence.

Posters aimed at a specific act that are prominently placed at the site where the behavior is relevant were found to have an effect on behavior in one experiment. Following a period of observation of the extent to which overhead chains used for moving materials in iron and steelworks were properly hooked above the head level of the workers, large posters admonishing the workers to hook the chains were placed in selected work places, but not in others, for a period of six weeks. A post-experimental count of hooked chains found an 8 percent increase in the experimental groups and no change in the control groups. In shops with low ceilings, a 13 percent increase in properly hooked chains was observed. Follow-up observations indicated that the behavior persisted after the posters were removed and even increased further in some shops.[41]

Behavior Modification

The principles of behavioral conditioning by manipulating rewards and punishment have been pursued for decades by experimental psychologists, mainly using rats, pigeons, and college student volunteers. In the laboratory, animals and people do modify their behavior in response to reward or punishment contingencies. Controlling such contingencies for a large population is another matter. An individual in the general population is subject to a large variety of rewards and punishments for acceptable and unacceptable behaviors both in informal groups and formal organizations. The measurement of these contingencies is difficult without disrupting the ongoing interaction. Also, there is substantial interperson variation in what is perceived as rewarding and what as punishing. Often individuals have the option to withdraw from a situation or alter it by countering with rewards or punishments directed toward those who would impose contingencies on them.

Application of conditioning to health-related behavior on a mass scale is a formidable task. The few attempts have brought results ranging from rebellious public reaction to substantial effects.

In an attempt to increase seat belt use in cars, the National Highway Traffic Safety Administration allowed automobile manufacturers, as an alternative to increased automatic crash protection, to install a buzzer and lighted belt-use reminder system in new cars manufactured from January 1, 1972, through the 1973 model year. If a driver or passenger in the front seat, excepting the middle seat, did not extend the belt from its stowed position, the buzzer sounded continuously and the lighted reminder remained on until the belts were extended. Many people reacted by extending and knotting the belts permanently, making them unusable. Others buckled them behind seats or had the system disconnected. Within six months of the system's introduction, a survey of belt use in ten cities found no statistically significant difference in belt use of 1972 model cars manufactured before the first of the year without the system (16 percent use) and those with the system (18 percent use).[42]

Two studies that claimed effectiveness of the buzzer-light system prior to its general adoption were seriously flawed. In one, five combinations of belts, lights, and buzzers were installed in General Services Administration cars used by governmental employees. On the basis of questionnaires distributed to drivers, the system was said to increase belt use.[43] It was known at that time, however, that claimed belt use was substantially in excess of actually observed use.[44] Furthermore, a number of agencies using the cars had rules requiring belt use in government cars.

A second study, conducted for Ford Motor Company, involved drivers in new cars on loan for a thirty-day test drive. None of these drivers had claimed in a telephone survey to use belts more than half the time. At the end of the thirty days, an interviewer went for a drive with each driver and observed that the majority used belts. The "intensive introduction to the vehicle, complete with test drive and a thorough explanation of the operation of all features which it contained,"[45] coupled with the prestudy telephone interview about seat belt use, could easily have created the perception of expectation that belts should be used. Also, in both studies, the drivers did not own the cars and were therefore probably reluctant to modify or dismantle the buzzer-light system.

In 1974 cars, the government allowed an interlock system as an alternative to increased automatic protection. This system would not allow the car to move in forward gear unless belts were extended from their stowed position or buckled when a certain weight was detected by a sensor in the driver's or right-front passenger's seat. A few months after the 1974 model cars were introduced, observations of belt use in six cities found a dramatic increase in use in these cars compared to earlier model years. About 59 percent of drivers were using belts—48 percent lap and shoulder and an additional 11 percent lap only—in contrast to 7 percent lap and shoulder and 21 percent lap only in 1973 cars seen at the same times and places.[46]

The effect of the interlock system on belt use was shortlived, as was the federal standard that allowed it. Letters to Congress complained of cars failing to start when cargo other than passengers was placed in the passenger seat. Mechanics did a brisk business in disconnecting interlocks. Soon after the beginning of the 1975 model year, legislation prohibiting the interlock provision in the motor vehicle safety standards was enacted by Congress and signed by the president. By 1977-79, belt use in 1974 model cars had declined to 15 percent.[47]

The use of rewards to belt users increases use when the rewards are sustained, but the effect does not last when the rewards are removed. Drivers offered a chance to win a prize if they were subsequently observed to use belts at a college campus parking lot were found to increase use from 15 to 40 percent during the period that prizes were given.[48] In another study, after the prizes stopped, belt use declined to the preexperimental rate.[49]

An industrial company has claimed 90 percent belt use of employees offered rewards of items worth $12 to $15 wholesale.[50] In a follow-up period during which the rewards were reduced to gifts costing the company $1 to $1.50, observations by independent observers found belt use ranging from 67 percent of the incoming morning shift to 39 percent of the outgoing night shift. These rates were substantially higher than the 10 to 15 percent use by drivers at other locations in the community where the plant is located.[51]

Experimental control comparisons of belt use by workers entering and leaving plants before and after being given fliers offering belt wearers a chance to win a prize found different effects in different groups. Those with the highest preexperimental belt use (18 percent) increased their use to 57 percent in the afternoons, when fliers were distributed, and 28 percent in the mornings. The increases were largely observed among salaried workers. The increase was only 2 percentage points among hourly workers in one plant and 7 percentage points in another.[52] This result is counter to economic theory that would predict greater response among those for whom the reward relative to overall income would be larger. Obviously there are factors other than a simple cost-benefit calculation by individuals that influences protective behavior.

It may be possible to use the principles of behavioral conditioning to optimize magnitude and frequency of rewards to obtain substantially higher rates of protective behavior than would otherwise be realized. The evidence suggests that the rewards do not have to be large but that they must be continued indefinitely. To implement reward systems for a wide variety of behaviors related to specific hazards would require lots of money and a large contingent of observers to identify those eligible. Also, the rewarded behaviors must be publicly observable to identify those eligible for rewards. The potential for corruption in such systems is obvious.

A variation on the use of rewards is applicable in special cases where the effectiveness in reduced damage can be easily illustrated to the persons at risk. In high-noise environments, it is possible to demonstrate temporary hearing loss in those affected immediately after it occurs. Following observation at randomly selected times of the use of earplugs by workers at noisy work stations, a team of researchers introduced a series of lectures on hearing protection to departments selected as experimental and control groups. In the experimental groups selected workers were then given audiometric tests before and after their work shifts. The results of these tests—showing marked decrease in hearing thresholds when earplugs were not used—were given to the workers tested and also placed on a bulletin board along with the worker's identity and whether or not earplugs had been used. For a period of time at the beginning of the study, someone was stationed at the bulletin board to explain the tests and their interpretation as other workers observed them. Not only did earplug use increase in the experimental group during the period that the workers were shown the results of the tests, it continued to increase in subsequent months. Five months after the experiment, earplugs were used by 85 to 90 percent of workers in the experimental group, compared to less than 10 percent of the control group.[53]

Where injuries are discrete instances spaced out in time, feedback in the form of information about outcomes is more difficult. In some cases, it may be possible to simulate the consequences of unsafe acts, particularly in training. Use of simulators to train beginning drivers is widely used, but there is no good evidence that drivers so trained have fewer crashes. Pilots are trained on simulators and periodically practice on them. It is not known whether the low crash rate of commercial air carriers can be attributed to such training, the strict selectivity of pilots for that occupation, or both. Few would advocate the abandonment of simulator training of pilots to find out the consequences.

A clever use of simulated injuries as a part of training in the use of machinery has been reported. A bench grinding machine was rigged to spray water on an operator who stood in front of the machine when turning it on, an act known to result in injury from flying metal fragments. College students who had not previously used such grinders were assigned to experimental and control groups. Each member of the control group was simply shown how to start and operate the machine, including directions to stand away from the front and use eye goggles. In the second group, the instructor also switched on the water spray to indicate the consequence of standing in front of the machine. Members of a third group were allowed to switch on the machine themselves and experience the spray. Both the demonstrated and experienced conditions were used in introducing the fourth group to the machine.

The students were told that they were testing the spark rate caused by grinding ten different metals and were taken through ten trials in which the machine was turned on anew for each trial. The average number of simulated injuries (the student being sprayed during the trial) was 5.5 in group 1, 2.75 in group 2, and 0.75 in groups 3 and 4. A week later the students returned for a second set of trials without the initial instructions and demonstration. The average simulated injuries in that session were 7.12 in group 1, 4.25 in group 2, 0.67 in group 3, and 0.38 in group 4. Follow-up studies indicated that the behavior was retained for up to six months among the groups that experienced the spray when operating the machine.[54]

This research suggests that where it is possible to simulate consequences of unsafe acts in a relevant manner, behavior change can be expected. It should also be noted that some machines could be equipped in such a way that they either could not be started or operated while the operator is in the line of flying metal or could not throw any metal at all.

In industry, rewards and punishment are more manipulable than among the public at large. Salaries, bonuses, promotions, special privileges, and vacation time are major means of attempting to influence productivity and could also be useful in changing injury-related behavior. Experimental evidence on this point is needed. Praise, recognition, and the like can also be used but are difficult to maintain systematically. To be successful, the behavior to be changed must be strongly related to injuries and must be precisely monitored. The more frequently that the desirable behavior is reinforced, the greater the compliance. Intermittent reinforcement must be maintained once the behavior is established to avoid reversion to old patterns of behavior.[55]

An example of the successful use of instruction followed by a system of monitoring behavior and praising workers for appropriate behavior has been reported. In a bakery with a high rate of injuries, descriptions of incidents during the previous three years were reviewed to ascertain those specific acts that contributed to injuries. Fifteen such acts were identified in one department and twenty in another, with only three instances of overlap. Checklists were prepared and observers recorded the frequency of the acts during a sequence of sampling periods. The behaviors observed were deemed unsafe about 30 percent of the time in one department and 22 percent in the second.

Meetings were held with the workers and slides of the behaviors comparing safe and unsafe acts were shown. A goal of 90 percent safe action was suggested and agreed to by the workers. Graphs of the incidence rate were posted and updated during subsequent observation periods. Supervisors were instructed to praise appropriate behavior and were asked to fill out a checklist when unsafe behavior was observed. During a period of eleven weeks in one department and three weeks in the other, the percentage of safe acts increased from 70 to 95 percent in the former and 78 to 99 percent in the latter. After five weeks, during which the graphs were not updated and no observations occurred, the behavior was found at the preintervention rates. Even during the intervention phase, the return of checklists from the supervisors was low, 15 percent in one group and 54 percent in the other.[56]

It appears that the workers responded mainly to the combination of observation and feedback of information on their performance by way of the graphs. When that process was no longer sustained, old patterns of behavior returned.

A similar study of worker behavior in a vehicle maintenance department of a city systematically compared conditions of training only with combinations of training and graphic display of worker performance. The training had little effect, but the combination of training and feedback of information significantly increased appropriate behavior. The authors of the study "concluded that training alone is not sufficient to substantially improve and maintain performance even though desired practices are objectively defined and examples are tailored to specific job situations."[57]

Altering Perception

A few experiments have been reported in which the environment is changed in an attempt to alter perception and subsequent behavior. Because of the distances covered between perception of environmental change and reaction by operators of motor vehicles at common traveling speeds, increase of perception of environmental change without an overload of the perceptual mechanisms could potentially reduce the injury rate. Attempts at increasing perception vary from use of somewhat exotic optical illusions to rather simple changes in road markings, vehicle signal lights, and lighting of roads.

As noted in chapter 3, drivers who have been moving at high speeds for a time tend to underestimate their current speed after having slowed from the higher speed. Such misperceptions are particularly hazardous at approaches to interesections, traffic circles, and toll booths as well as in curves in the road. The perception of speed is influenced by distance from the side of the road of vertical objects, the movement of vehicles both in tandem and in the opposite direction, and noise from the roadway. Placing vertical objects along a roadway would possibly reduce speed to some degree but would probably increase injury rates if the objects were rigid.

One of the more unusual experiments testing changes in the perception of speed was based on simulation of an optical illusion in a laboratory: placement of yellow lines twenty inches in width at exponentially decreasing intervals across the path of vehicles creates the illusion of acceleration when crossed by drivers at a constant speed.

Following measurement of speeds of vehicles approaching a traffic circle for thirty-eight days, a road approaching the circle was painted at exponentially decreasing intervals ranging from twenty to ten feet apart over a quarter mile of the approach, ending one hundred fifty feet before the entrance to the circle. Speed measurement continued for twenty-five days after the stripes were put in place. The average eighty-fifth percentile speed (that is, the speed exceeded by 15 percent of drivers) measured at a point between the last two stripes decreased from forty-seven to thirty-three kilometers per hour (twenty-nine to twenty-one miles per hour) from before to after the stripes were laid down.[58] Subsequently, the method was used at thirty-seven sites with mixed results. Twenty-nine sites had crash reductions; there was no change at six and an increase at two. The reductions were quite large, averaging about 66 percent.

Comparison of curves in roads with high and low crash rates suggests that perception of curvature is related to the apparent angle of curvature of the edge of the road. Road sections that have the same actual length and degree of curvature may be perceived as having greater or lesser curvature depending on road edge enhancement. A gradual increase in the marking of the inside (driver's side) edge increases the perception of degree of curvature. Another illusion that changes perception of road width is based on the Wundt illusion: stripes painted across the road in a herringbone pattern make the road seem narrower.

In a four-treatment experiment, speeds of drivers entering a modified curve and an unmodified curve further down the road were measured at three points in the approach zone. In addition to edge enhancement and the Wundt illusion, treatments included the cross road stripes spaced in an exponentially decreasing pattern, as described earlier, and one in which the only change was a sign saying "deceptive curve."

The treatments had different effects among drivers of different types of vehicles. Enhancing the inside edge of the road significantly decreased the speed of car drivers 97 meters before they entered the curve, but their speeds were little different at the curve than before; and the speed of truck drivers was not significantly influenced. The Wundt illusion significantly decreased the speed of car but not truck drivers at the entrance to the curve. The exponentially spaced stripes were the most effective for truck drivers—reducing speed at 195 and 97 meters before the curve as well as at the entrance—but car speeds were significantly lower only at the 97-meter mark. The sign indicating a deceptive curve had no significant effect on either group of drivers at any point in the approach.

Speeds at untreated curves further down the road were not influenced by the treatments. Thus, the effects are site specific and appear to depend on the angle of vision of the driver as determined by the size of the vehicle driven. The effects also tend to diminish over time, suggesting that frequent users of the roads adapted somewhat to the changes.[59] More experimentation with these and other patterns is necessary to specify the optimal patterns at specific sites and their effects on actual crash experience. Whether those who crash are frequent or infrequent users, are among those who are affected by the pattern, and if so in what way should be elements of such studies.

Research comparing the point at which a vehicle left the road and struck a fixed object to a site one mile back in the direction from which the vehicle traveled identified road curvature and grade as important distinguishing characteristics of the crash sites. Curves greater than six degrees on downhill grades of 2 percent or more were involved in 25 percent of single-vehicle fatal crashes, compared to 8 percent of points one mile back that were passed without mishap. Such crashes were also mainly on nonlocal roads, further narrowing the number of sites that should be given priority for modification.[60]

In Georgia, the state highway department used that study to identify sites disproportionately involved and placed reflectorized pavement markers on the center line to enhance the perception of curvature at night. Crashes at night, compared to daytime, were reduced about 20 percent at the marked sites.[61]

The monitoring of a vehicle's speed by the driver would be enhanced by placement of the speedometer readout in the driver's line of vision. Long used in some aircraft, such a display on the windshield would allow the driver to read the speedometer while viewing the road rather than looking away for what is sometimes a crucial one to two seconds.

A well-tested, but as yet unadopted method of perceptual enhancement is to place an additional brake light in the center of the rear of the car above the trunk lid. Three spearate experiments in which rear lighting was so modified have found about a 50 percent reduction in rear end collisions when the front vehicle is braking.[62] Other patterns, such as higher brake lights to the side, do not have the same effect, suggesting that it is perceptual enhancement rather than novelty that produces the reduced crash rate.

The shape, size, color, lettering, and placement of road signs have been the subject of some research and resultant improvement.[63] Nevertheless, road users in most communities can identify points where the directional signs are confusing for even frequent users and particularly misleading for strangers. The confusion is so common at some points that a filmmaker could go to one of them in daylight and, in a short period, record numerous instances of drivers having to switch lanes quickly to avoid fixed objects at turn-offs or to stay on the road they apparently intended to take.[64] Illumination is one obvious enhancement to perception, and it is not surprising that the nighttime vehicle crash rate is lower on lighted sections of roadway than on those without lights.[65]

Conclusion

Attempts to educate or persuade individuals to change behaviors that increase or decrease risk of injury or protective behavior have had results ranging from substantially increased harm in the case of high-school driver education to greatly reduced incidence in experiments where perception has been enhanced by changes in brake lights, reflectorization, and lighting of roads. The lack of recognition that behavioral approaches can be potentially harmful has resulted frequently in inadequate research before the approach is adopted for widespread use.

Behavioral-change programs, like pharmaceuticals, vaccines, and surgical procedures in the case of disease, can be studied in experimental-control trials before being put in use. Several examples of such research are cited in this chapter. It is time that proposed behavioral-change approaches were held to the same tests of prior proof of effectiveness as other approaches to public health. Instilling information and skills into people's brains has no more or less potential for good or ill as injecting materials or cutting into the brain or other body organs. We should evaluate a program's results on as small a scale as possible before consideration of adoption on a broader scale.

References

1. S. Raymond and S. Tatum, *An Evaluation of the RAC/ACU Motor Cycle Training Scheme—Final Report* (Salford, England: The University of Salford, 1977).

2. J.F. Kraus, R.S. Riggins, and C.E. Franti, "Some Epidemiologic Features of Motorcycle Collision Injuries I. Introduction, Methods and Factors Associated With Incidence," *American Journal of Epidemiology* 102(1975):74-97.

3. A.F. Williams, and B. O'Neill, "On-the-Road Driving Records of Licensed Race Drivers," *Accident Analysis and Prevention* 6(1974):263-70.

4. E.g., E. Allgaier, *Driver Education Reduces Accidents and Violations* (Washington, DC: American Automobile Association, 1964).

5. J.J. Conger, W.C. Miller, and R.V. Rainey, "Effects of Driver Education: The Role of Motivation, Intelligence, Social Class, and Exposure,"

Traffic Safety Research Review 10(1966):67-71; F.L. McGuire and R.C. Kersh, *An Evaluation of Driver Education* (Berkeley: University of California Press, 1969).

6. J. Shaoul, *The Use of Accidents and Traffic Offenses as Criteria for Evaluating Courses in Driver Education* (Salford, England: University of Salford, 1975).

7. H.W. Ray, et al., *Safe Performance Secondary School Education Curriculum* (Washington, DC: National Highway Traffic Safety Administration, 1982).

8. Shaoul, *The Use of Accidents and Traffic Offenses*, p. 3.

9. L.S. Robertson and P.L. Zador, "Driver Education and Fatal Crash Involvement of Teenaged Drivers," *American Journal of Public Health* 68(1978):959-65.

10. L.S. Robertson, "Crash Involvement of Teenaged Drivers When Driver Education is Eliminated from High School," *American Journal of Public Health* 70(1980):599-603.

11. M.H. Jones, *California Training Evaluation Study* (Sacramento, CA: California State Department of Motor Vehicles, 1973).

12. F.M. Council, R.B. Roper, and M.G. Sadof, *An Evaluation of North Carolina's Multi-Vehicle Range Program in Driver Education* (Chapel Hill, NC: University of North Carolina Highway Safety Research Center, 1975).

13. T. Planek, S. Schupack, and R. Fowler, *An Evaluation of the National Safety Council's Defensive Driving Course in Various States* (Springfield, VA: National Technical Information Service, 1972).

14. B. O'Neill, "Comments on 'An Evaluation of the National Safety Council's Defensive Driving Course in Various States,' " *Accident Analysis and Prevention* 6(1974):299-301.

15. T. Mulhern, "The National Safety Council's Defensive Driving Course As an Accident and Violation Countermeasure." Unpublished doctoral dissertation (College Station, TX: Texas A and M University, 1977).

16. P.S. Hill and B.D. Jamieson, "Driving Offenders and the Defensive Driving Course—An Archival Study," *The Journal of Psychology* 98(1978):117-27.

17. D.F. Preusser, R.G. Ulmer, and J.R. Adams, "Driver Record Evaluation of a Drinking Driver Rehabilitation Program," *Journal of Safety Research* 8 (1976):98-105.

18. M.L. Edwards and N.C. Ellis, "An Evaluation of the Texas Driver Improvement Training Program," *Human Factors* 18(1976):327-34.

19. C. Fuchs, "Wisconsin Driver Improvement Program: A Treatment-Control Evaluation," *Journal of Safety Research* 12(1980):107-14.

20. D.E. Payne and J.E. Barmack, "An Experimental Field Test of the Smith-Cummings-Sherman Driver Training System" *Traffic Safety Research Review* 7(1963):10-14.

21. R.B. Stuart, "Teaching Facts About Drugs: Pushing or Preventing?" *Journal of Educational Psychology* 66(1974):189-201.

22. "Sale of Guns in Houston and Shooting Class Assailed," *The New York Times* (May 7, 1981), p. A20.

23. K. Pease and B. Preston, "Road Safety Education for Young Children," *British Journal of Educational Psychology* 37(1967):305-13.

24. W.H. Yeaton and J.S. Bailey, "Teaching Pedestrian Safety Skills to Young Children: An Analysis and One Year Follow-Up," *Journal of Applied Behavioral Analysis* 11(1978):315-29, and D.D. Embry and J.L. Malfetti, *Reducing the Risk of Pedestrian Accidents to Preschoolers by Parent Training and Symbolic Modeling for Children: An Experimental Analysis in the Natural Environment* (New York: Safety Education and Research Project, Columbia University, no date).

25. L.S. Robertson, et al., *Changing the Medical Care System: A Controlled Experiment in Comprehensive Care* (New York: Praeger Publishers, 1975).

26. R.A. Dershewitz and J.W. Williamson, "Prevention of Childhood Household Injuries: A Controlled Clinical Trial," *American Journal of Public Health* 67(1977):1148-53.

27. R.A. Dershewitz, "Will Mothers Use Free Household Safety Devices?" *American Journal of Diseases of Children* 133(1979):61.

28. K.S. Reisinger and A.F. Williams, "Evaluation of Programs Designed to Increase Protection of Infants in Cars," *Pediatrics* 62(1978):280-87.

29. E.R. Christophersen, "Behavioral Approaches to Auto Safety Education." In A.B. Bergman, ed., *Preventing Childhood Injuries* (Columbus, OH: Ross Laboratories, 1982), pp. 33-7.

30. K.S. Riesinger, et al., "The Effect of Pediatricians Counseling on Infant Restraint Use," *Pediatrics* 67(1981):201-6.

31. R.E. Miller, et al., "Pediatric Counseling and Subsequent Use of Smoke Detectors," *American Journal of Public Health* 72(1982):392-93.

32. H. Kravitz, "Prevention of Falls in Infancy by Counseling Mothers," *Illinois Medical Journal* 144(1973):570-73.

33. D. Lester, "Effect of Suicide Prevention Centers on Suicide Rates in the United States," *Health Services Reports* 89(1974):37-9.

34. S.S. Gallagher, P. Hunter, and E. Hatch, "A Home Injury Prevention Program for Children." Presented at the annual meeting of the American Public Health Association, Montreal, Canada, 1982.

35. J.B. Haskins, "Evaluative Research on the Effects of Mass Communication Safety Campaigns: A Methodological Critique," *Journal of Safety Research* 2(1970):86-96.

36. G.A. Fleischer, *An Experiment in the Use of Broadcast Media in Highway Safety* (Los Angeles: University of Southern California Department of Industrial and Systems Engineering, 1972).

37. L.S. Robertson, B. O'Neill, and C.W. Wixom, "Factors Associated With Observed Safety Belt Use," *Journal of Health and Social Behavior* 13(1972):18-24.

38. L.S. Robertson, et al., "A Controlled Study of the Effect of Television Messages on Safety Belt Use," *American Journal of Public Health* 64(1974):1071-80.

39. Safety and Environmental Studies Section, "The 1969 Seat Belt Campaign," mimeo (Toronto: Ontario Department of Transport, 1970).

40. E. McLoughlin, et al., "Project Burn Prevention: Outcome and Implications," *American Journal of Public Health* 72(1982):241-51.

41. S. Laner and R.G. Sell, "An Experiment on the Effect of Specially Designed Safety Posters," *Occupational Psychology* 34(1960):153-69.

42. L.S. Robertson and W. Haddon, Jr., "The Buzzer-Light Reminder System and Safety Belt Use," *American Journal of Public Health* 64(1974): 814-15.

43. M. Perel and P.M. Ziegler, "An Evaluation of a Safety Belt Interlock System" (Washington, DC: National Highway Traffic Safety Administration, 1971), mimeo.

44. P.F. Waller and P.Z. Barry, "Seat Belts: A Comparison of Observed and Reported Use" (Chapel Hill, NC: University of North Carolina Highway Safety Research Center, 1969), mimeo.

45. D.J. Shaw, "Interim Results from Test Drive I Advanced Features Study." Transmitted to Docket 69-7, National Highway Traffic Safety Administration by Ford Motor Co., July 27, 1971, mimeo.

46. L.S. Robertson, "Safety Belt Use in Automobiles with Starter-Interlock and Buzzer-Light Reminder Systems," *American Journal of Public Health* 65(1975):1319-25.

47. B.M. Phillips, *Safety Belt Use Among Drivers* (Springfield, VA: National Technical Information Service, 1980).

48. D. Elman and T.J. Killebrew, "Incentives and Seat Belts: Changing a Resistant Behavior Through Extrinsic Motivation," *Journal of Applied Social Psychology* 8(1978):72-83.

49. E.S. Geller, E. Talbott, and L. Paterson, "A Cost-Effective Incentive Strategy for Motivating Seat Belt Usage," mimeo (Blacksburg, VA: Virginia Polytechnic Institute and State University, 1981).

50. Berg Electronics, "A Case Study of a Successful Employee Safety Belt Program," mimeo (New Cumberland, PA: E.I. DuPont de Nemours and Company, no date).

51. "Rewards Raise Belt Use; Fall-off Seen Later," *Insurance Institute for Highway Safety Status Report* 17(February 17, 1982):1.

52. E.S. Geller, "Development of Industry-Based Strategies for Motivating Seat-Belt Usage," mimeo (Washington, DC: U.S. Department of Transportation, 1981).

53. D. Zohar, A. Cohen, and N. Azar, "Promoting Increased Use of Ear Protectors in Noise Through Information Feedback," *Human Factors* 22(1980):69.

54. S. Rubinsky and N. Smith, "Safety Training by Accident Simulation," *Journal of Applied Psychology* 57(1973):68-73.

55. H.G. Fitch, J. Hermann, and B.L. Hopkins, "Safe and Unsafe Behavior and Its Modification," *Journal of Occupational Medicine* 18(1976):618-22.

56. J. Komaki, K.D. Barwick, and L.R. Scott, "A Behavioral Approach to Occupational Safety: Pinpointing and Reinforcing Safe Performance in a Food Manufacturing Plant," *Journal of Applied Psychology* 63(1978):434-45.

57. J. Komaki, A.T. Heinzmann, and L. Lawson, "Effect of Training and Feedback: Component Analysis of a Behavioral Safety Program," *Journal of Applied Psychology* 65(1980):261-70.

58. G.G. Denton, "The Influence of Visual Pattern on Perceived Speed," *Perception* 9(1980):393-402.

59. D. Shinar, T.H. Rockwell, and J.A. Malecki, "The Effects of Changes in Driver Perception on Rural Curve Negotiation," *Ergonomics* 23(1980):263-75.

60. P.H. Wright and L.S. Robertson, "Studies of Roadside Hazards for Projecting Fatal Crash Sites," *Transportation Research Record 609* (Washington, DC: National Academy of Sciences, 1976).

61. P.H. Wright, et al., "Effect of Pavement Markers on Nighttime Crashes in Georgia," *Transportation Research Record*, in press.

62. E.g., R.E. Reilly, D.S. Kurke, and C.C. Bukenmaier, Jr., *Validation of the Reduction of Rear-End Collisions by a High Mounted Auxiliary Stoplamp* (Washington, DC: National Highway Traffic Safety Administration, 1980).

63. OECD, *Hazardous Road Locations: Identification and Countermeasures* (Paris: Organisation for Economic Co-operation and Development, 1976).

64. A.B. Kelley, "Boobytrap" (film) (Washington, DC: Insurance Institute for Highway Safety, 1972).

65. P.C. Box, "Relationship Between Illumination and Freeway Accidents," *Illuminating Engineering,* May/June (1971):365.

Control Strategies: Laws and Regulations Directed at Individuals

An alternative strategy for changing individual behavior is to require or prohibit the behavior as appropriate, by law or administrative directive. Universal efforts have been made to codify such formal rules with respect to intentional injury to other persons; in addition, some jurisdictions have gone further by making suicide illegal. Laws specify when, where, and how transportation vehicles can be operated. Administrative rules commonly regulate the use of hazardous materials and protective equipment in work settings, an area of concern for which some jurisdictions have promulgated laws to require the use of protective equipment.

Despite the widespread use of formal rules attempting to reduce injury, the imposition of new rules or changes in old rules often result in acrimonious debate. Positions in the debate are usually based on ideological presuppositions regarding the right of the governmental or administrative authority to impose the rule and enforce it with sanctions. Discussions of the potential value and limitations of the rule for reducing injury, while extensive, are often only a buttress to a basically ideological argument about freedom.

The U.S. Constitution defines a set of fundamental freedoms that, theoretically at least, are not to be negated by any government or private organization. As long as this principle is adhered to, police power to impose and enforce rules that are directed at individuals is mainly delegated to state and local jurisdictions. Visitors to the United States have difficulty understanding why no national laws exist that deal with such issues as drunk driving and seat belt use. The reason is that the Constitution was written by representatives of states interested in preserving their prerogatives; and they intentionally left the police power of the federal government severely limited. The constitutional authority of the federal government allows regulation of interstate commerce and levying taxes; this power has been used to impose some rules directly and encourage others by tax or other funding incentives.

In addition to the issue of whose freedom to do what will be regulated by whom for what purpose, one must also consider the limits of such rules in reducing injuries. Changing individual behavior by formal rule involves meeting several conditions:

1. The behavioral change must lower the frequency or severity of injuries.
2. People must conform to the rule voluntarily or, if not, conformity can be accomplished by use of sanctions.
3. If sanctions are necessary and effective, the policing agencies and courts or private administrators must impose them.

In this chapter the research evidence regarding the extent to which these conditions can be expected to hold will be examined in cases in which the imposition of formal rules did attempt to curb injuries. The goal is to specify, as far as possible, general principles concerning the effectiveness and limits of this approach.

This evaluative research is sometimes less definitive than that involving approaches to injury prevention that can be studied by experimentally controlled designs. Legislators are unlikely to randomly enact a law merely in order to satisfy the rigors of a scientific experiment. A few attempts have been made to structure experiments around the imposition of enforcement and penalties, but police and judges have resisted the application of sanctions to randomly chosen offenders.[1] Researchers must therefore resort to before-after or quasi-experimental comparisons of jurisdictions with and without changes in law or enforcement that are more or less reasonably comparable on other factors that can influence behavior and associated injury rates.

A large set of laws, rules, and sanctions is aimed at deterring kinds of behavior, such as alcohol use, that increase the likelihood of injury. These laws tend to be more politically acceptable than laws directed at protective behavior, such as required seat belt use, at least partly because the behavior proscribed by deterrence-type laws is perceived as a greater threat to the public in general as well as to those persons whose behavior is proscribed by the laws. Few people oppose laws against drivers running red lights or driving while intoxicated or speeding, although the maximum speed limit acceptable on certain roads is controversial. Changing the law to allow right turns on red after stopping has also raised arguments in some states.

Alcohol

Because of the frequent involvement of alcohol in severe and fatal motor vehicle crashes (chapter 3), laws aimed at deterrence of use of alcohol above specified limits in association with driving have received increasing scientific scrutiny. Originally stated as proscription against imprecisely defined behavior—such as "driving while intoxicated" or "drunk driving"—these laws were revised in most jurisdictions to specify concentrations of alcohol in the blood that were not permissible based on correlation of those concentrations to severe crash involvement.[2] Although the probability of involvement in a severe crash increases exponentially as a function of blood alcohol, modern laws specify a point at or above which the driver is presumed impaired. In most U.S. jurisdictions, 0.10 percent by weight or above has been chosen, mainly to conform to federal standards for state safety programs. In many countries the laws indicate concentation above 0.08 percent by weight as per se evidence of impairment, and a few specify 0.05 percent.

The specification of such a limit theoretically reduces the ability of the accused to challenge the accusation because, with properly maintained instruments administered correctly, alcohol in blood or breath can be measured very precisely. Challenges to the accuracy of the instruments and their use occur on occasion, but these are small factors in the effective administration of the law.

The major problems in maintaining effectiveness of drunk driving laws are cultural patterns in the use of alcohol and motor vehicles, the difficulty police have in spotting illegally intoxicated drivers—or at least their failure to do so, and the lack of systematic imposition of sanctions on those violators who are apprehended. Apparently, few authorities who license establishments to sell alcoholic beverages pay any attention to the fact that many of them can only be reached by motor vehicle. There is as yet no evidence on the extent to which this placement stands as a tacit indication to drinkers that authorities are unconcerned about their use of vehicles after drinking.

Most alcohol users have no way of knowing their blood alcohol concentration; and, even if they did, the social norms promoting alcohol use, and its addictive nature, suggest that more precise knowledge might make little difference in behavior. The mutual expectation that each person in a group "buy a round" in bars increases the likelihood of impaired driving afterward. In some social circles, a good host does not limit the number of drinks served, and pressing guests to drink is often considered good form. Persons addicted to alcohol but who have not discontinued use either maintain continuously high blood-alcohol concentrations or drink in uncontrolled binges.

Police officers must have probable cause in the form of a crash, a traffic law violation, or suspiciously unusual driving behavior to stop a driver and administer a breath or blood test. Requesting tests from drivers at road blocks or chosen at random from passing vehicles has been attempted in a few jurisdictions but has been challenged in the courts as a violation of the constitutional prohibition of unreasonable search in the United States. A 1976 law in Victoria, Australia, allows the police to use random breath testing, but it has been little used other than during two short intensive patrol periods in 1977 and 1978. Claims of reduced crashes during those periods compared to the year before have been questioned because other factors that might have reduced crashes during the same period were not controlled.[3]

The State of Victoria, Australia also enacted a law in 1974 requiring tests of the blood alcohol concentrations of persons medically treated for injuries in motor vehicle crashes. A report on the legislation notes that 21 percent of casualties were found to have illegal blood alcohol concentrations and 60 percent of these were prosecuted. The numbers of illegal concentrations increased over time but, without controls for other factors, this fluctuation cannot be taken as evidence against some deterrent effect.[4] If there was an effect, it was not substantial. For such an effect to occur, the drinking drivers would have to admit to themselves that their probability of a crash was increased and alter their drinking or driving accordingly.

One of the primary hypotheses of deterrence theory is that greater probability of arrest will decrease the incidence of an illegal act.[5] Roadside surveys of drivers stopped at random and asked to give a breath sample have been compared to numbers of arrests for drunk driving in the same area. The highest estimate of probability of arrest found in such studies is 1 in 200.[6] Data on the correlation of incidence of felonies and arrest rates suggest that a much higher arrest rate for driving while intoxicated would be necessary to have a deterrent effect. When the arrest rate is less than 30 percent of reported felonies, there is no correlation between arrest and incidence rates. As arrests increase from a rate of 30 percent of reported incidence, the average incidence per capita declines.[7] Although it is possible that at least some violators of drunk-driving laws would respond differently to probability of arrest than those who commit felonies, it is doubtful that current arrest rates in the absence of publicity about special crackdowns have much, if any, general deterrent effect on violation of the drunk-driving laws.

Research on special efforts that apparently increased the perception of a greater probability of arrest has demonstrated temporary reductions in injury rates. The largest reported effect of such an effort occurred following the British Road Safety Act of 1967. That act established a per se limit of 0.08 percent blood alcohol concentration by weight for legal operation of a motor vehicle and gave the police power to test the breath of suspected drivers. The Parliament also considered allowing random testing but ultimately rejected the idea. The law was accompanied by an intense publicity campaign on television and other media that, for a time, created the impression that persons exceeding the specified limit were virtually certain of being detected by scientific means. Observers reported that the number of vehicles in parking lots of pubs declined substantially when the law initially went into effect.

Analysis of trends in the motor vehicle fatalities before and after the institution of the law and accompanying publicity found about a 25 percent reduction in the fatality rate during the first few months. Within three years, however, the death rate was near what would have been expected without the law. The reduction was found only during traditional night drinking hours and not at times of day when drinking and driving is infrequent, suggesting that it was specifically driving after drinking that was deterred.

Several reasons were given for the lack of sustained effect. There was no apparent increase in the actual probability of arrest and no change in the penalties of those arrested. Although the act may have temporarily reinforced the idea that driving after drinking is dangerous behavior, it was not designed to change the persistent societal norms that encourage alcohol consumption in situations that are likely to be followed by driving. Challenges to the act and its enforcement in courts were widely publicized. Claims that certain patent medicines could be used to fool the breath test for alcohol were advertised.[8] The end result was the erosion of the law's effect.

In 1969 the Criminal Code of Canada was amended to establish 0.08 percent alcohol by weight as the limit for driving legally and to authorize the police to use breath tests as evidence of violation of the code. This change occurred with less publicity than that accompanying the British Road Safety Act and with less effect. Research on trends in mortality rates indicated that deaths were reduced about 8 percent from what would have been expected during the first year following the change in the law. That effect was temporary, as in Britain. Within a year, the fatality rate returned to levels expected had there been no change in legislation.[9]

Temporary reductions in severe and fatal motor vehicle-related injuries have been found in other well-publicized crackdowns or blitzes against drunk driving by police.[10] The general rule seems to be that the drinking public's perception of the probability of arrest can be increased by publicity. After a time, however, the word gets around that the actual risk of arrest has changed little and former behavior with respect to drinking and driving is resumed. Thus, perceived probability of arrest does have some effect but not for long as the perception is learned to be incorrect.

Another hypothesis in deterrence theory receives less support in the research on alcohol and driving. The notion that threat of more severe punishment will decrease the behavior in question is shared by classical utilitarian theorists and writers of letters to newspaper editors. The threat of jail sentences for those convicted of drunk driving, long a policy in the Scandinavian countries, has been tried intermittently elsewhere, with little demonstrated success anywhere.

In Finland during 1950, the maximum sentence for violation of the drunk-driving law was doubled from two to four years' imprisonment for the simple offense and up to seven years' imprisonment in the case of severe injury or death. The fatal crashes per registered motor vehicles dipped only slightly below the trend in the subsequent period.[11] Visitors to the Scandinavian countries commonly are impressed that, at middle-class gatherings, one person in a group traveling together will often abstain from drinking and be designated the driver. This behavior is taken as evidence of the deterrent effect of the threat of jail sentences. Perhaps moderate social drinkers are deterred somewhat by the threat, but most such people in any case would not consume alcohol in amounts that would put them over the legal limit even in the absence of the threat. The measurable effect on severe injury rates is minimal.

A case of increased threatened severity accompanied by substantial publicity occurred in Chicago during 1970-71. A supervisory judge announced that all people convicted of drinking and driving would receive an automatic seven-day jail sentence. The Chicago crackdown was widely reported in local media and the policy was extended several months after the first two, again with extensive publicity, when great success in the form of reduced fatalities was claimed. Subsequent analysis found that, although a decline in deaths occurred during the period of the crackdown, it was not statistically different from general fluctuation in the rates in the past. Comparison of injuries in Chicago and Milwaukee, a city with similar climate but no crackdown, found a similar decline in motor vehicle deaths in Milwaukee during the same period.[12]

Motor vehicle-related fatality rates tend to decrease during economic recessions. The United States experienced such a recession in 1970, and the decrease in fatalities in both Chicago and Milwaukee was probably a part of the usual recession effect. Each of these recessions breeds an increase in the number of claims of effective law enforcement and other programs directed at motor vehicle injuries. Most such claims are based on simple before-after observations and need to be subjected to rigorous scientific comparisons before being accepted as successful efforts. Those launching programs during periods of economic prosperity are strangely silent about the effects of those programs.

During the Chicago crackdown, arrests for driving while intoxicated (DWI) did not increase, but convictions for DWI declined significantly in cases where blood alcohol was not tested. This phenomenon is illustrative of the tendency for social systems to adapt. When sentences become mandatory and more severe than in the past, the chances of conviction by sympathetic judges or juries are lessened. In fact, the probability of painful consequences of an illegal act are diminished at several points between the act and the imposition of sentence, which suggests that severe penalties should not be expected to have much effect on deterrence. For the severe sentence to be imposed, the illegal act must be observed or sufficient other evidence be gathered by police; the police must decide to arrest; the prosecutor must decide to prosecute and not to reduce to a lesser charge; the jury or judge must decide to convict; and the sentence must not be suspended or probation substituted.[13] Frequent offenders are in all likelihood aware that probability of arrest for driving while impaired is very low; and those who have been through the system a few times should know that the probability of conviction is small.

Aware of how the system works, officials of the U.S. National Highway Traffic Safety Administration attempted in the early 1970s to implement Alcohol Safety Action Projects (ASAP) in selected jurisdictions, mainly urban areas, based on a "systems approach." Through grants to local agencies and consultation on a variety of approaches, the federal agency tried to alter the probability of arrest and conviction, change the use of rehabilitation in some cases as an alternative to conviction, and implement public information and educational campaigns.[14] About $78 million in federal funds was expended in the initial thirty-five projects.

Independent of the agency, research that compared areas with ASAPs to otherwise similar areas without special programs, could not find any significant impact of the programs on motor vehicle fatalities.[15] According to the officials who ran the programs, some areas manifested increases in arrests, and roadside surveys indicated a slight decrease in drivers with illegal blood alcohol concentrations.[16] In contradiction to these results is the study, undertaken as part of an ASAP project, that found *increased* crashes when a rehabilitation program was substituted for license suspension, as mentioned in chapter 5. It appears that increased probability of arrest in some areas may have had a small favorable effect, but that was largely offset by other actions resulting in an adverse effect. The net result was no detectable overall effect of the projects.

Other than occasional increased perception of probability of arrest achieved during periods of publicized crackdowns, and separately the threat of loss of license, the legal measures directed at apprehending, convicting, and rehabilitating or punishing drunk drivers have failed to have a perceptible impact on the occurrence of crashes in which alcohol plays a role. How often a jurisdiction can announce a program of increased detection and arrests and create a temporary effect remains to be demonstrated. The tendency of the news media to consider anything that did not happen today as stale news suggests that gaining adequate and frequent attention to periodically renewed enforcement efforts would be difficult.

One policy that has a demonstrably consistent effect in a highly vulnerable age group is the legal minimum age for purchasing alcoholic beverages. Misnamed the legal minimum drinking age, which it obviously is not, the policy does have an effect on fatal crash involvement of teenage drivers. Comparison of areas that lowered the miniumum purchasing age from twenty-one to eighteen with similar areas that retained age twenty-one found about a 5 percent increase in fatal crashes of drivers less than twenty-one attributable to the change in law. The increments were larger in night and single-vehicle crashes, where alcohol is more often involved. The increase in fatalities was apparent, though smaller, among drivers younger than eighteen, giving evidence of a "trickle down" effect into age groups less than but near the legal purchasing age.[17]

Recent research has found the effects of increasing the minimum age parallel their movement in the opposite direction. States that have increased their minimum age for purchasing alcohol have experienced reduced fatalities involving underage drivers when compared to states that retained the reduced age during the same period.[18]

An important aspect of these laws is that they are directed at the seller of alcoholic beverages rather than at the purchaser. The law is enforced largely by proprietors of establishments that sell the beverages rather than the police, although the threat of enforcement to the seller is no doubt paramount. As shall be noted further in other contexts, those statutes that give key members of society a reason to influence the behavior of those at risk tend to be more effective than laws without this feature.

Attempts have been made to control alcohol use in other settings as well, but the research evidence on viable efforts is thin or nonexistent. Corporate programs for alcohol addiction, for example, vary in content and some include rules regarding use while on the job. Some of these programs claim success in rehabilitation of alcoholics,[19] but detailed analysis of problem identification, specification of program elements that did or did not have an effect, and adequate accounting of those who dropped out of programs or left companies has not been forthcoming. Several corporations have a policy of requiring a test for blood alcohol concentration from workers injured on the job. The author is unaware of any evidence generated on the effectiveness of such a policy in injury reduction or of instances in which a breath test is required before hazardous activity. Commercial pilots are not supposed to use alcohol for a specified period before a flight, but breath tests prior to flights are not routinely applied.

An air force base demonstrated the effective use of sanctions in the form of threatened discharge or psychiatric referral for lost time because of injury in a privately owned vehicle. Driving after use of alcohol was depicted as sick behavior in meetings, on bulletin boards, and in the newspaper. Comparison of the injury rate before and during the year of the imposition of the sanctions with the rate at a base without any program found a significantly reduced injury rate attributable to the effort.[20] While it is more difficult to initiate and administer such a program in organizations with less control of their members' behavior, these results do suggest that injuries can be reduced in organizations with administrative control over behavior through sanctions in combination with an effort to change the image of alcohol use. Organizations that wish to reduce their injury-related losses have the opportunity to test various approaches on an experimentally controlled basis in an effort to specify what elements or combinations of elements are the most successful.

Speeding Laws

Laws regarding more directly observable behaviors, such as driving above the speed limit, are more enforceable than laws against less easily identified behavior, such as driving with certain blood alcohol concentrations. Speeding is the most commonly cited moving violation, but the frequency of citations does not indicate the extent of deterrence as much as it does police effort. The effect of laws limiting speed of vehicles is a combination of general compliance and compliance resulting from intensity of enforcement.

The reduction of the maximum speed limit on high-speed highways to fifty-five miles per hour from as high as eighty miles per hour on some interstate highways resulted in a reduction of motor vehicle fatalities of about 10 percent in the mid-1970s. The speed limit reduction occurred at the same time as economic recession and reductions in travel, both in response to energy shortages. This combination has made a precise estimate of the effect of reduced speed limits more difficult. The total reduction in deaths was about 20 percent, with the speed limit accounting for about half of the decline.

Surveys of average speed on various highway systems found substantial declines in average speeds and a narrowing of the variation around the average. Vehicles were not only driven more slowly after the law changed but the flow of traffic was more uniform. The largest declines in deaths occurred on roads where the speeds declined the most.[21] Given the known exponential relationship between speed and crash severity (chapter 2) and the facts regarding the correlation of speed and fatality changes, the argument that the change in speed limit had no effect by those opposed to the 55-mile-per-hour limit is not credible.

Average speeds increased slightly in subsequent years but did not return to the averages prevailing before the change in law. Some state legislatures weakened penalties for speeding, and others have considered proposals to repeal the 55-mile-per-hour limit. The threat of loss of federal funds, along with the arousal of public opinion, has apparently restrained such efforts. National public opinion surveys repeatedly find that a substantial majority of drivers prefer the 55-mile-per-hour limit to higher limits, despite the fact that the average speed on most roads is somewhat above the limit. The near compliance of most drivers is perhaps as much or more a result of the increased comfort or reduced fear of traveling when vehicles are moving more uniformly at lower speeds than the result of enforcement.

The extent to which enforcement crackdowns affect speeding has been the subject of limited investigation. Most drivers exceeding a speed limit will slow down when they see a patrol car, but the limited number of police cars even during periods of intense enforcement must of necessity limit such immediate effects. Claims of substantial consequences of enforcement crackdowns usually exceed their demonstrable effects.

One of the difficulties in evaluating the effectiveness of selective enforcement efforts is that selection of areas for enforcement is not random. While it may seem reasonable to assign police to areas of high fatal-crash rates, from a research viewpoint any before-after comparison that claims a reduction in deaths due to the enforcement in such areas is highly suspect. Fatality rates fluctuate for a variety of reasons. Extremely high or low numbers away from the average in a given period are likely to be nearer the average in a subsequent period—a phenomenon long known to statisticians.[22,23] Indeed, if enforcement crackdowns were introduced in given areas following extremely low fatality rates, the subsequent rates would probably increase.

An example of false inference of effects based on poor choice of enforcement areas occurred in the National Highway Traffic Safety Administration's fatal crash reduction program. Five counties in Michigan and one in Texas were chosen for an increase in enforcement because of fatality rates much higher than average in those states. Federal funds were provided primarily for salaries and fringe benefits for police officers who worked overtime or on a reassignment basis in the areas with high incidence of fatal crashes. Before-after comparison of fatalities resulted in claims of more than 20 percent reduction in fatalities attributable to the effort.[24] In the following year, $10 million (1973 dollars) in federal funds were allocated to the fifty states to implement the program nationwide.

A reanalysis of the Michigan data compared to data from alternative counties in Michigan not chosen for the program and from the neighboring state of Indiana suggested that little, if any, of the change in fatalities could be attributed to the enforcement program. Alternate counties in Michigan and those in Indiana that had extremely high fatality rates during the same period used to select counties for enforcement in Michigan experienced a decline similar to that in the chosen counties. Thus, the change in fatalities is unlikely to have resulted from special enforcement.[25]

Claims of effectiveness of increased sanctions for drivers convicted of speeding in Connecticut also proved overstated when subjected to scientific analysis. The governor proclaimed that speeding convictions would result in a thirty-day license suspension for a first offense, sixty days for a second offense, and indefinite suspension with a hearing after ninety days upon a third conviction. In the subsequent months suspensions increased dramatically and deaths were fewer than in the previous year. Increased enforcement by unmarked police cars was announced at midyear; and by the end of the year,

Laws Directed at Individuals

deaths had declined by about 12 percent from the previous year. The governor attributed the reduction in deaths to the state's efforts.

Subsequent analysis of a longer time period—nine years—indicated that fatalities in the year before the crackdown had been much higher than average and that the decline during the crackdown was little different from other year-to-year changes, up and down, during the nine-year period. Furthermore, comparison with four adjacent states during the same nine years found an increase in fatality rates in three of them during the year before the Connecticut crackdown and a decline in all four during the year of the crackdown. Therefore it is likely that much, if not all, of the reductions attributed to the crackdown was actually a part of trends occurring in the region generally and affected by factors other than the state's speed-enforcement efforts.[26]

The response of drivers to speed limits—driving a few miles per hour above the limit, on average—appears to be an effect of the law to deter substantially higher speeds. A large marginal gain above that effect from special enforcement is apparently difficult to obtain.

Other Studies of Deterrence

Outstanding among research on deterrence is a controlled experiment on the effects of various types of police patrol and response to emergencies on a variety of crime rates and motor vehicle crashes. Fifteen police districts in Kansas City were divided into three groups of five each: one set had the usual preventive patrol activity of a patrol car per district, a second group had double to triple the usual preventive, and a third had no preventive patrol—the police responded only when called regarding a problem. The experiment continued for more than a year.

Comparisons of the areas in terms of crimes and motor vehicle crashes reported to the police and victimization surveys to assess unreported crime revealed that areas with regular or more concentrated preventive patrol were no different in assaults or motor vehicle crashes than areas where police only responded to calls. Only three of numerous comparisons were statistically significant—those for sex crimes other than rape, home burglaries, and community vandalism—and these did not consistently favor the more concentrated preventive patrol.[27]

This research suggests that doubling or tripling the number of police patrols above current practice would have little or no effect on motor vehicle or assaultive injuries, at least in the short run. There is probably a point of intensive patrol at which an effect would be realized: surely a patrol car in every block or perhaps, more appropriately, a police officer in every bar, would have some deterrent effect. The extent of patrol necessary to produce these results, however, and the public acceptability of the expense and appearance of a police state remain to be demonstrated.

As noted in the section on alcohol, incidence of reported crime has been found to decline on average as the arrest rates increase above 30 percent of reported incidence, with no apparent effect of arrest rates below that level.[28] The arrest and conviction rate for homicide is substantially higher than 30 percent in most jurisdictions, and homicide is less frequent per capita in areas where certainty of imprisonment and/or length of sentence is greater.[29]

A cautionary note regarding this conclusion has been sounded. Imprisonment rates tend to be more constant over time than crime rates. Depending on the assumptions one is willing to make in statistical analysis, one can infer that the negative association between imprisonment and crime rates is more a function of the adjustment of the criminal justice system to the crime rate than it is of a deterrent effect of imprisonment.[30]

Any effect of the death penalty as a deterrent to homicide is difficult to demonstrate. Comparison of homicide rates in states that abolished the death penalty with those of states that retained it during the same periods reveals no consistent pattern that would support use of the death penalty as a deterrent.[31] This lack of significant inhibiting effect, coupled with the finality of the punishment, suggests that institution of the death penalty would cause more innocent people, falsely convicted, to be executed than the number of people saved from assaultive homicide. Apparently prison sentences are not only more effective as a deterrent but they can also be commuted if the accused is subsequently found innocent.

In countries where ownership of handguns is severely limited, the homicide rate is substantially below that of the United States.[32] As the disproportionate role of guns in the incidence of homicide has become apparent, laws directed at control of handguns, in particular, have been enacted in a variety of U.S. jurisdictions. Gun laws in the United States are a hodgepodge of licensure requirements for dealers and/or buyers, registration requirements, restrictions on conditions under which guns can be conveyed, and penalties for violation of any of these or use in a crime. A local jurisdiction may have none or several such laws and may be adjacent to a jurisdiction with very different laws. Without uniform difficulty of purchase or sanctions for use across large areas, the effects of these laws are greatly diluted.

Gun ownership is dynamically related to crime rates, increasing somewhat in response to incidence of violent crime and, in turn, increasing the level of violence when available for use in robberies or moments of interpersonal or group conflict. Increases in new gun sales are particularly notable following civil disturbances.[33] Research comparing states with different types of laws finds lower rates of homicide, suicide, and unintentional death by handguns in states that have more laws restricting their sale and use. The study controlled statistically for other factors that might affect the rates, including income, education, sex, age, race, and population density. Laws regarding dealer licensure, record keeping, and licensure to purchase handguns were more effective than laws directed at conveyance and use by particular groups.

Based on the evidence, the authors concluded that some 4,200 to 6,400 fewer deaths from firearms would have occurred annually in the late 1960s if all states had adopted the laws of the state with the strictest laws at that time.[34]

As part of the concern for law and order in recent years, proposals have surfaced to remove the discretion of prosecutors and defense attorneys to negotiate pleas (plea bargaining) and of judges or juries to impose light sentences or probation. A few laws have been enacted specifying mandatory sentences upon conviction for certain offenses. When Michigan required an additional mandatory two-year sentence for persons convicted of a felony if a firearm were used, Wayne County's chief prosecutor prohibited his staff from plea bargaining the cases in an attempt to prevent that ploy from undermining the intent of the law. Although the prosecutor was successful in this goal, there was little change in the actual length of sentences imposed when firearms were used. Judges and juries reduced the sentences for the felony itself so that the additional required two years seldom resulted in a longer total sentence than previously imposed.[35]

Aside from the question of a possible general deterrent effect of announced mandatory sentences, which is difficult to establish, the potential effect of such sentences on violent crime because of the longer incarceration of recidivists has been investigated. Previous records of persons charged with violent felonies—murder, manslaughter, robbery, assault, and violent sex offenses—were examined to determine what proportion of such offenses in a year would not have occurred if the accused had received a mandatory sentence for the prior offense. In other words, the accused would not have been able to commit the offense while in prison, at least against members of the nonincarcerated public (prison assaults were ignored).

The researchers found that less than one in three of the charged offenders had any prior felony conviction and only 11 percent had a conviction for a violent felony. If a five-year mandatory sentence had been imposed for the most recent felony, violent or not, only 4 percent of the violent crimes currently charged would have been prevented by incapacitation of the prior sentence.[36]

Laws Requiring Protective Behavior

The purpose of laws requiring the use of protective equipment—motorcycle helmets, seat belts, child restraints—is to prevent injury or decrease its severity should an unexpected encounter with potentially damaging energy occur. The consequences of these laws in actual injury reduction have been mixed and, in the case of motorcycle helmet laws in the United States, difficult to keep on the books in the face of concentrated lobbying by a minority of motorcyclists.

In 1967-69, in order to qualify for safety program and highway funds, thirty-seven states enacted laws requiring motorcyclists to wear helmets in accordance with federal standard for state highway safety programs. The efficacy of helmets in reducing severe and fatal head injuries to motorcyclists had been known since World War II,[37] but only three states had laws requiring their use prior to the federal standard.

The law resulted in helmet use by more than 99 percent of motorcyclists in states where observed use was recorded at selected sites. In two states without the law, helmet use varied widely: 60 percent in California but only 25 percent in Illinois. The laws had a dramatic effect on motorcyclists' fatalities. A study of eight states that adopted the law, compared to eight contiguous states without the law during the same period, found that motorcyclist deaths declined an average 30 percent following enactment of the law but did not change appreciably in the other states.[38]

By 1975 all but three states had helmet-use laws that met the federal standard, but refusal by these states to comply did not result in loss of funds. Instead, Congress removed the government's authority to impose the financial penalty. Within three years, twenty-six states changed their laws to allow most motorcyclists to ride without helmets, the exception being those less than a certain age in some states. Comparison of helmet use and motorcyclist deaths before and after the repeal of the laws found use declined by more than half, on average, and deaths increased to rates that prevailed prior to the original enactment of the helmet-use laws.[39]

Aside from the philosophical and political issues involved in the imposition and repeal of these laws, to be discussed subsequently, their most interesting aspect is their remarkable effectiveness in gaining compliance. Unfortunately, data on enforcement activities are unavailable, so we do not know how much emphasis police gave helmet use. An obvious factor that probably contributed to the high compliance is the ease of observation of the behavior by police.

Somewhat less easily observable, but reliably so at carefully chosen points, is seat belt use by vehicle occupants. Laws requiring belt use were enacted in many countries, states, and provinces—though not in any U.S. state—during the 1970s following reports of a successful law in Australia. Based on reduced injuries to truck drivers required to wear belts on a large construction project, the state of Victoria, Australia in 1971 enacted a statute requiring most adult vehicle occupants to use belts when vehicles are in motion.

Belt use in vehicles fitted with belts increased to about 70 percent compliance[40] in the first year of the law and had increased to 80 percent by 1976.[41] The best study of the effect of the law on fatalities compared Victoria and other Australian states before and after the law in Victoria, but before the law was adopted in the other states. Controlling for economic and other factors, the law reduced occupant fatalities in urban areas by 20 percent and in rural areas by 10 percent.[42]

A later study that used an econometric model to compare projected and actual death and injury rates claimed that the belt-use laws in Australia

Laws Directed at Individuals

increased the hazard to other road users—pedestrians, bicyclists, and motorcyclists—because drivers allegedly increased risky driving as a result of their own increased protection.[43] Since econometric models frequently fail in their projections of the economy, there is no reason to believe their projections of motor vehicle fatalities. The earlier, better study comparing Victoria and other states found no change in fatalities of road users other than vehicle occupants that could be attributed to the law.[44] The econometrician did not cite the better study.

While a 10 to 20 percent reduction in occupant fatalities is a substantial achievement, it is not as much as would be expected from the known effectiveness of belts when worn at the reported usage rates. An explanation for the less-than-fully-realized effect is found in the use rates of different groups of the population. Young drivers, particularly teenagers, are less often in compliance with the law than older drivers.[45] Drivers involved in crashes with high blood alcohol concentration are less often found using belts than drivers in crashes without alcohol in blood.[46] To the extent that such drivers (or their passengers) who are more likely to be in severe crashes are less often in compliance with the law, the law's effect will be less than the potential effect. Also, among belt users, many belts were observed in a twisted or loose position, reducing their effectiveness in a crash.[47]

In Europe, a geographer argued that the apparent lack of change in death trends following passage of the belt-use law in Sweden and other countries was the result of more aggressive driving by those required to use belts. But a detailed analysis of the Swedish data indicated that nonuse of belts by those more likely to be in severe crashes accounted for the less-than-expected effect of the law.[48]

Factors in the extent of belt use following a law are exemptions, degree of enforcement, and penalties. An example of introducing exemptions after a law is in force occurred in Ontario, Canada. Belt use increased from 20 percent to 70 percent in the month before to the month after the law was put in force. Within two months, shoulder belt use in cars manufactured before 1974 was exempted because of complaints of the discomfort of those belts that did not have inertial reels. Six months after the law, belt use in nonexempt as well as exempt cars declined to 50 percent.[49]

Using the same observation methods in a variety of countries, belt use by drivers in countries with belt-use laws has been found to vary from a low of less than 1 percent on Japanese limited access highways (the only place that belt use is required in that country and with no penalties) to a high of 80 percent in Sydney, Australia.[50] Surveys in Canadian cities where belt use is required revealed 30 to 40 percent use at night compared to 40 to 60 percent use during daylight hours.[51] This pattern also contributes to reduced effectiveness because of the greater frequency of severe crashes at night.

Selective enforcement campaigns in Ontario have temporarily increased belt use to near the Australian use rate. In one area the rate increased to 80 percent during special enforcement but declined to 66 percent two years later. Publicity campaigns and signs reminding people of the law had little effect in the absence of increased police enforcement.[52]

Recent experience with child restraint-use legislation in the United States indicates less success than with belt use for adult occupants in other countries. No U.S. state has a belt-use law at this writing. Child restraint use was first required in Tennessee, with travel in an adult's arms exempted. Travel of small children in appropriately anchored child restraints or in seat belts increased from 8 percent before the law to 29 percent in the third year afterward. Comparison with the number of children restrained in vehicles while traveling in the contiguous state of Kentucky, without a law, supported the conclusion that the increased use in Tennessee resulted from the law.[53] At first travel in an adult's arms increased in one city in Tennessee, but later declined and that exemption was later removed from the law.[54]

The second state to enact a child restraint-use law, Rhode Island, required use in front seats only. Observations before and four months after the law indicated an increase in rear-seat travel as well as increased restraint of children in both front and rear seats. Nevertheless, about 60 percent of children traveling in front seats were unrestrained despite the law.[55] Apparently, the added inconvenience associated with use of the special seats, the protests of some children at being confined, and the extra cost involved combined to generate considerable resistance to compliance with the law.

Seventeen U.S. states had adopted some form of child restraint-use laws for automobiles by mid-1982.[56] Ironically, although seat belt use has been required of adult passengers in commercial airplanes during takeoff and landing for decades, infants have been exempted from any required restraint use in planes. A recent report of plane crashes during 1976-1979 found that infants were about six times more likely to die in such crashes per capita involved than non-infants. The researchers noted that infant restraints for use in cars could also be used in airplane seats with the type of seat belt that could be used to hold the infant restraint in place.[57]

A law's effect depends on public awareness. As noted in chapter 5, advertising campaigns in the absence of a law do not result in many changes in protective behavior. There is evidence that publicity about a law and the efficacy of compliance can increase the target behavior. In New South Wales, Australia, two years after a child restraint-use law went into force, a mass media campaign was launched to reinforce public information about the law and the hazards to children of nonuse of restraints. The use of restraints by children observed in cars increased from 40 percent at the beginning of the campaign to 55 percent a year later.[58]

Laws Directed at Individuals

A systematic survey of use of equipment in work settings where required by administrative rule has apparently not been done. The general impression of the author in touring metal-working plants and observing construction sites is that use of helmets, safety glasses, and protective shoes is very high. Research is needed on the extent to which this observation is valid and the conditions of enforcement, communication to workers, and other factors that result in high or low compliance with such rules.

Generalizations

Although there are important gaps in knowledge about the effects of laws and administrative rules directed at individual behavior, the evidence available suggests some emerging principles regarding what works and what does not. Table 6-1 presents a proposed set of factors that are related to compliance with such laws intended to reduce injuries. Since several are variable by degree rather than in the absolute (presence or absence), the importance of their effects relative to each other can vary from the order suggested.

The first is obvious and negates the need for formal rules—that is, the behavior would occur irrespective of law. The second factor probably contributes the most to conformity with laws and rules where the behavior would not otherwise occur. To the extent that there is compliance with essentially unenforceable laws such as those limiting blood alcohol concentration while driving, the propensity to conform with the law because it is the law, along with the moral overtones of failure to comply is a potent force for compliance. Efforts in detection and conviction vary widely and

Table 6-1
Some Suggested Factors That Contribute Differentially to Individual Compliance with Laws and Administrative Rules

1. Behavior would be a part of the individual's usual behavioral repertoire irrespective of laws or rules.
2. High individual propensity exists to conform to the law or rule on moral or other grounds.
3. There is a high probability of detection and conviction.
4. Compliance does not interfere with such needs as comfort, convenience, and pleasure.
5. Few, if any, exemptions from compliance are allowed in the law.
6. Enforcement can be augmented by persons other than police.
7. Observation of regulated behavior by authorities is obviously easy.
8. A perception of increased concentration of enforcement to detect nonconformity affects behavior.
9. Conviction occurs soon after detection.
10. Conviction results in a relatively severe punishment.

have no apparent effect below a certain percentage of incidence of the behavioral act. Perception of increased enforcement has some temporary effect; but if the actual enforcement is not increased to apprehend and convict more than 30 percent of the violators, the effect is temporary. Publicized drunk-driving crackdowns are illustrative of this result. Exemptions for easily detected acts reduce overall compliance.

Although the evidence suggests that behavior is as much or more the result of social learning, impulse, addictions, and habit as of hedonism, to which it is ascribed by many popular economic and psychological theories, there is in fact resistance to compliance with laws that result in discomfort, inconvenience, and costs. The low use of child restraints even where their use is required by law is a probable result of this phenomenon. The importance of the extent to which the law's enforcement is augmented by persons other than the police is emphasized by the effects of minimum purchasing age for alcohol use, mainly enforced by proprietors of bars and stores; licensure of dealers and purchasers of guns, mainly enforced by the dealers themselves (albeit out of fear of loss of legitimate business); and minimum driving age. Parents usually do not allow their youngsters below the minimum legal driving age to operate the family car. Recent research comparing states with and without laws specifying curfews on driving during certain night hours for drivers less than a certain age found dramatically lower crash rates during those hours among those to whom the laws applied. There were no apparent offsetting increases during other hours of the day.[59]

Also, a law may augment resistance to peer pressure. Although as yet unsubstantiated by research, it is conceivable that the presence of a law proscribing or requiring certain behaviors is helpful to persons who would otherwise bend to peer pressure. For example, the youngsters who do not use motorcycle helmets for fear of tarnishing their macho image among their friends apparently do use the helmet when there is a law: use is virtually 100 percent in states that have them.

To the extent that police enforcement is effective, the observability of the behavior is obviously important. The relative success of laws requiring motorcyclists to use helmets and vehicle occupants to use seat belts is likely due to the fact that noncompliance is easily observed. These laws are difficult to enact and keep on the books in the United States.

For the next to last item in the table, delay between detection and conviction, evidence of effect as separate from other factors, is difficult to find, but it may be of some importance. Apparently, least effective is increased severity of punishment for persons who do not comply with the law. An irony of our society is that much of the public debate and legislative energy concerned with law enforcement is directed at this least important factor in the injury-reducing consequences of laws directed at individuals.

References

1. H.L. Ross and M. Blumenthal, "Some Problems in Experimentation in a Legal Setting," *American Sociologist* 10(1975):150-55.
2. W. Haddon, Jr. and M. Blumenthal, "Foreword." In: H.L. Ross, *Deterring the Drinking Driver: Legal Policy and Social Control* (Lexington, MA: Lexington Books, 1982).
3. H.L. Ross, *Deterring the Drinking Driver*, pp. 83-85.
4. F. McDermott and P. Strang, "Compulsory Blood Alcohol Testing of Road Crash Casualties in Victoria: The First Three Years," *The Medical Journal of Australia* 2(1978):612-15.
5. J. Andenaes, *Punishment and Deterrence* (Ann Arbor, MI: University of Michigan Press, 1974).
6. G.A. Beitel, M.C. Sharp, and W.D. Glauz, "Probability of Arrest While Driving Under the Influence of Alcohol," *Journal of Studies on Alcohol* 36(1975):109-16.
7. C.R. Tittle and A.R. Rowe, "Certainty of Arrest and Crime Rates: A Further Test of the Deterrence Hypothesis," *Social Forces* 52(1974):455-62.
8. H.L. Ross, "Law, Science and Accidents: The British Road Safety Act of 1967," *The Journal of Legal Studies* 2(1973):1-78.
9. L.W. Chambers, R.S. Roberts, and C.A. Voelker, "The Epidemiology of Traffic Accidents and the Effect of the 1969 Breathalyser Amendment in Canada," *Accident Analysis and Prevention* 8(1976):201-6.
10. H.L. Ross, *Deterring the Drinking Driver*, pp. 71-85.
11. H.L. Ross, "The Scandinavian Myth: The Effectiveness of Drinking-and-Driving Legislation in Sweden and Norway," *The Journal of Legal Studies* 1(1975):285-310.
12. L.S. Robertson, R.F. Rich, and H.L. Ross, "Jail Sentences for Driving While Intoxicated in Chicago: A Judicial Policy That Failed," *Law and Society Review* 8(1973):55-67.
13. F. Zimring and G. Hawkins, *Deterrence: The Legal Threat in Crime Control* (Chicago: University of Chicago Press, 1973).
14. National Highway Traffic Safety Administration, *Alcohol and Highway Safety Projects: Evaluation of Operations* (Washington, DC: U.S. Department of Transportation, 1974).
15. P.L. Zador, "Statistical Evaluation of the Effectiveness of 'Alcohol Safety Action Projects,'" *Accident Analysis and Prevention* 8(1976):51-66.
16. National Highway Traffic Safety Administration, *Alcohol Safety Action Projects Evaluation of Operations: Data, Tables of Results and Formulation* (Washington, DC: U.S. Department of Transportation, 1979).
17. A.F. Williams, et al., "The Legal Minimum Drinking Age and Fatal Motor Vehicle Crashes," *The Journal of Legal Studies* 4(1975):219-39.

18. A.F. Williams, et al., "The Effect of Raising the Legal Minimum Drinking Age on Fatal Crash Involvement," *The Journal of Legal Studies*, in press.

19. R.L. Williams and G.H. Moffat, *Occupational Alcoholism Programs* (Springfield, IL: Charles C. Thomas, 1975).

20. J.B. Barmack and D.E. Payne, "The Lackland Accident Countermeasure Experiment." In: W. Haddon, Jr., E.A. Suchman, and D. Klein, eds., *Accident Research: Methods and Approaches* (New York: Harper and Row, 1964).

21. W.J. Kemper and S.R. Byington, "Safety Aspects of the 55 MPH Speed Limit," *Public Roads* 41(1977):58-67.

22. E.J. Gumbel, *Statistics of Extremes* (New York: Columbia University Press, 1958).

23. H.M. Walker, *Studies in the History of Statistical Methods* (Baltimore, MD: Williams and Wilkins, 1929).

24. National Highway Traffic Safety Administration, *Fatal Crash Reduction Program: A Demonstration Project* (Wahsington, DC: U.S. Department of Transportation, 1973).

25. A.F. Williams and L.S. Robertson, "The Fatal Crash Reduction Program: A Reevaluation," *Accident Analysis and Prevention* 7(1975): 37-44.

26. D.T. Campbell and H.L. Ross, "The Connecticut Crackdown on Speeding: Time-Series Data in Quasi-Experimental Analysis," *Law and Society Review* 3(1968):33-53.

27. G.L. Kelling, et al., *The Kansas City Preventive Patrol Experiment* (Washington, DC: The Police Foundation, 1974).

28. C.R. Tittle and A.R. Rowe, "Certainty of Arrest and Crime Rates," pp. 458-459.

29. J.P. Biggs, "Crime, Punishment and Deterrence," *Southwestern Social Science Quarterly* 48(1968):515-30.

30. D. Nagin, "Crime Rates, Sanction Levels, and Constraints on Prison Population," *Law and Society Review* 12(1978):341-63.

31. W.J. Bowers, *Executions in America* (Lexington, MA: Lexington Books, 1974).

32. G.D. Newton and F.E. Zimring, *Firearms and Violence in American Life: A Staff Report to the National Committee on the Causes and Prevention of Violence* (Washington, DC: U.S. Government Printing Office, no date).

33. C.T. Clotfelter, "Crimes, Disorders, and the Demand for Handguns: An Empirical Analysis," *Law and Policy Quarterly* 3(1981):425-41.

34. M.S. Geisel, R. Roll, and R.S. Wettick, Jr., "The Effectiveness of State and Local Regulation of Handguns: A Statistical Analysis," *Duke Law Journal* 1969(1969):647-76.

35. M. Heumann and C. Loftin, "Mandatory Sentencing and the Abolition of Plea Bargaining: The Michigan Felony Firearm Statute," *Law and Society Review* 13(1979):393-430.

36. S. VanDine, S. Dinitz, and J. Conrad, "The Incapacitation of the Dangerous Offender: A Statistical Experiment," *Journal of Research in Crime and Delinquency* 14(1977):22-34.

37. H. Cairns and H. Holburn, "Head Injuries in Motorcyclists with Special Reference to Crash Helmets," *British Medical Journal* 1(1943):591.

38. L.S. Robertson, "An Instance of Effective Legal Regulation: Motorcyclist Helmet and Daytime Headlamp Laws," *Law and Society Review* 10(1976):456-77.

39. G.F. Watson, P.L. Zador, and A. Wilks, "The Repeal of Helmet Use Laws and Increased Motorcyclist Mortality in the United States, 1975-1978," *American Journal of Public Health* 70(1980):579-92.

40. D.C. Andressand, "Victoria and the Seat Belt Law," *Human Factors* 18(1976):593-600.

41. L.S. Robertson, "Automobile Seat Belt Use in Selected Countries, States and Provinces With and Without Laws Requiring Belt Use," *Accident Analysis and Prevention* 10(1978):5-10.

42. L.A. Foldvary and J.C. Lane, "The Effectiveness of Compulsory Wearing of Seat-belts in Casualty Reduction," *Accident Analysis and Prevention* 6(1974):59-81.

43. J.A.C. Conybeare, "Evaluation of Automobile Safety Regulations: The Case of Compulsory Seat Belt Legislation in Australia," *Policy Sciences* 12(1980):27-39.

44. L.S. Foldvary and J.C. Lane, "The Effectiveness of Compulsory Wearing of Seat-belts in Casualty Reduction," pp. 59-81.

45. L.S. Robertson, "Automobile Seat Belt Use in Selected Countries, States and Provinces," pp. 5-10.

46. J.B. Dalgaard, "Experiences with the New Seat Belt Law on Fatal Lesions of Car Occupants in Denmark," in *Proceedings of the Sixth International Association for Accident and Traffic Medicine* (Melbourne, Australia: Royal Australasian College of Surgeons, 1977).

47. P. Vulcan, "Australia's Safety Belt Use Laws: The Results of the Law," *Proceedings of the National Safety Belt Usage Conference* (Washington, DC: National Highway Traffic Administration, 1973).

48. C. Tingvall, "Is Adams right?—Some Aspects of a Theory Concerning Effects of Seat-Belt Legislation," *Journal of Traffic Medicine* 10 (1982):41.

49. L.S. Robertson, "The Seat Belt Use Law in Ontario: Effects on Actual Use," *Canadian Journal of Public Health* 69(1978):154-57.

50. L.S. Robertson, "Automobile Seat Belt Use in Selected Countries, States and Provinces," pp. 5-10.

51. A.F. Williams and B. O'Neill, "Seat Belt Laws: Implications for Occupant Protection," Presented at the Passenger Car Meeting of the Society of Automotive Engineers (Washington, DC: Insurance Institute for Highway Safety, 1979).

52. B.A. Jonah, et al. "Promoting Seat Belt Use: A Comparison of Three Approaches," *Twenty-sixth Annual Proceedings of the American Association for Automotive Medicine* (Morton Grove, IL: American Association for Automotive Medicine, 1982).

53. A.F. Williams and J.A.K. Wells, "The Tennessee Child Restraint Law in Its Third Year," *American Journal of Public Health* 71(1981):163.

54. R.S. Sanders, "Legislative Approach to Auto Safety: The Tennessee Experience." In: A.B. Bergman, ed., *Preventing Childhood Injuries* (Columbus, OH: Ross Laboratories, 1982).

55. A.F. Williams and J.A.K. Wells, "Evaluation of the Rhode Island Child Restraint Law," *American Journal of Public Health* 71(1981):742-43.

56. Insurance Institute for Highway Safety, "Four More States Enact Child Restraint Laws," Status Report 17(1982):4-5 (September 2 ed.).

57. D. Fife, B. Rosner, and W. McKibben, "Relative Mortality of Unbelted Infant Passengers and Belted Non-infant Passengers in Air Accidents With Survivors," *American Journal of Public Health* 71(1981):1242-46.

58. K. Freedman and J. Lukin, "Increasing Child Restraint Use in N.S.W. Australia: The Development of an Effective Mass Media Campaign." In: *Proceedings of the 25th Annual Conference* (Morton Grove, IL: American Association for Automotive Medicine, 1981).

59. D.F. Preusser, et al., "The Effect of Curfew Laws on Motor Vehicle Crashes," mimeo (Washington, DC: Insurance Institute for Highway Safety, 1982).

7
Control Strategies: Policies Directed at Agents and Vehicles of Injury

Occasionally people are injured by exchanges with energy in the environment that has not been altered by human use, such as that from lightning, a meteorite, or a flow of lava from a volcano. The vast majority of injurious human contact with energy, however, is the result of human use and alteration of that energy, usually in ways that increase its concentration at points where it is likely to do harm in contact with human beings. The vehicles that convey or contain this energy range through the products of modern industry in everyday or frequent use: among them, motor vehicles, industrial machines, guns, bicycles, multistoried buildings, furniture, matches, cigarettes, clothing, swimming pools, water craft. The failure of those who manufacture, process, and distribute these vehicles of energy to reduce their potential for injury has prompted governments to enact laws and regulations that specify procedures and design or performance criteria to achieve injury reduction.

The effectiveness of regulation is dependent on the technological feasibility and adequacy of a given rule in reducing injury, as well as on the extent of compliance with the rule by those who are directed to change a product or process. Some economists argue that optimal trade-offs between usefulness of products and their hazards will be determined by the choices of consumers in the marketplace and that government interference merely introduces inefficiencies. Such economic theories usually ignore the difficulty of inexpert consumers learning about the hazards of a plethora of products that undergo frequent changes by their producers, who may themselves be equally inexpert in the hazards of their products. For regulation to be effective, rule makers must have expertise in the nature of the hazard and alternative means of amelioration. Those to whom the rules apply must either have such expertise or the rules must be so specific that expertise is not required for compliance.[1]

Because legislators themselves seldom have the technical expertise or the time required to enact detailed rules or to keep them up to date, they usually authorize or direct a specific agency to develop the expertise and impose the rules. The authorization may provide a rather broad general mandate to develop ameliorative regulations or it may narrow the focus by declaring certain types of rules or products and processes off limits for the regulatory agency. Also, an agency can interpret the language of legislation in ways that broaden or narrow its focus. Finally, an agency can be authorized to develop new technology itself or force its development and use by rule making; but oversight by legislators as to the extent that such activity is being pursued within the technological state of the art requires expertise that the legislators or their staffs may not have developed.

In this chapter, some major agencies and their rules and evaluations of their consequences are described. The broader issues of the economics, philosophy, and politics of injury-control efforts are reserved for the subsequent two chapters.

Motor Vehicles

Other than the setting up of periodic vehicle inspection in certain states and the adoption of a few consensus standards, such as for headlamps, legislators did not seriously consider regulation of injury-producing characteristics of motor vehicles until the sixth decade of their use. Congressional hearings were held in the 1950s but no legislation was enacted. A few state governments required the installation of lap belts in the front outboard seats of new cars sold in their states in the early 1960s. By 1964, fourteen states required lap belts and manufacturers began installing them in all cars as standard equipment.[2] Also in 1964, Congress authorized the General Services Administration (GSA), the federal government's management and purchasing agency, to specify safety standards for vehicles sold to the federal government. Requirements for equipment such as energy-absorbing steering assemblies to reduce penetration or crushing of chests in frontal crashes and high penetration-resistant windshields to reduce ejections and severe lacerations were adopted, applicable to 1966 and subsequent model years. The manufacturers responded by providing the equipment somewhat earlier in some cases and as standard equipment in high-volume models sold to the public as well as to the government.

In 1966, Congress enacted and President Lyndon B. Johnson signed the National Traffic and Motor Vehicle Safety Act[3] along with the separate Highway Safety Act,[4] the latter to establish standards for state programs and assistance in their implementation. The Motor Vehicle Safety Act directed the establishment of a National Traffic Safety Agency in the Commerce Department, which later evolved into the National Highway Traffic Safety Administration (NHTSA) in a newly created Department of Transportation. The act specified that "initial standards" for manufacture of new cars be in effect, based on existing safety standards available at the time, on a prompt schedule—by January, 1968. Also, research and development were to begin toward the initiation of subsequent standards. Provision for required notice to owners by manufacturers regarding vehicle defects was also included in the act and subsequently resulted in recall of tens of millions of cars.

Policies Directed at Agents and Vehicles

The act and the history of legislative intent in its formation specified that the standards for new cars would not indicate details of design of equipment but instead would contain performance criteria. In illustration, a standard for brakes would be specific as to maximum distance allowed in stopping the vehicle during a braking maneuver under specified test conditions but could not require a particular kind of brake design to achieve that performance. The rationale for this provision was to prevent stagnation in the development of new technology and to allow manufacturers the leeway to achieve greater efficiencies in meeting the standards.[5]

Among the initial standards issued by the agency were crash avoidance standards, including reduced glare in drivers' eyes, redundant braking systems, side marker lights, and tire performance and loading. Standards to reduce the severity of injury during a crash specified performance of energy-absorbing steering assemblies, seat belts, windshields, head restraints, and other interior structures as well as performance of door locks and doors to reduce injection or penetration. Postcrash, the reduction of fire was the primary focus.[6,7]

Evaluation of the effectiveness of these standards has produced some contradictory conclusions, but the overwhelming evidence suggests about 40 percent fewer occupant deaths in cars meeting the standards (trucks were exempted from many) and some reductions in injuries to persons struck by regulated vehicles. The initial investigations of effectiveness focused on the reductions attributable to specific standards, mainly those concerned with severity during the crash. Comparison of injuries to occupants of vehicles with and without penetration-resistant windshilds and energy-absorbing steering assemblies found substantially reduced head and chest injuries to persons in vehicles that met the safety standards.[8,9] The rate of death in crashes among those wearing seat belts was reduced to 40 to 50 percent of the rate of those who neglected this precaution.[10]

Controversy regarding the effects of the standards was generated by an economist who claimed that drivers whose protection in a crash was increased would drive more "intensively" and pose a greater hazard to pedestrians and other road users. He assumed that individuals have a "demand for risk" or a constant rate of risk that they are willing to accept and that they adjust their behavior when the risk is reduced, as it was by the occupant-protection standards.[11]

The fact that a few drivers occasionally adjust their behavior by driving more slowly or using their seat belts when roads are wet gives some credence to the notion of adjustment of behavior to fit changing conditions. Not taken into account, however, are the human limitations in ability to adapt—such as the large-scale misperception of speeds, distances, and motorcycles noted in chapter 3. Even if individuals have a constantly ranked set of goals in their heads and a gyroscope to guide them toward maximization of goals, as utility theorists would have us believe, scientific research has found their ability to perceive risks and adjust their behaviors accordingly as severely limited. And, even without such human limitations, the information needed to balance risks against goals is formidable. How many of us have any precise notion of the probability of a collision on sections of roads that we use frequently, such as that between home and work? And how many of us know the precise reduction of risk of injury that safety standards have provided?

The ultimate test of a theory is its ability to predict empirical evidence. The proponent of the risk-adjustment theory attempted to prove the theory using data on yearly fatalities and other factors. On the basis of correlations of fatality rates with consumption of alcohol per capita, average speeds on rural roads, ratio of younger to older drivers, income, and cost of crashes from 1947 to 1965, he projected the number of fatalities to vehicle occupants and other road users that would be expected in the years 1966 to 1972. When actual occupant deaths were less than projected but were offset by greater-than-projected nonoccupant deaths, he pronounced the theory as confirmed.[11]

A re-analysis of the data turned up numerous reasons why the empirical test was inadequate. The correlations among the predictor variables were changing over time, resulting in a failure to accurately project death rates prior to regulation. For example, the 1947-1959 data did not accurately project the 1960-1965 preregulation death rates. Therefore, projections from the data could not be used to determine accurately the expected effect of no regulation. Motorcycle fatalities were counted by the economist as pedestrians, with no attempt to control for the fact that motorcycle registrations were doubling every five years during the 1960s.

The regulated vehicles were also not properly disaggregated. Occupant deaths in largely unregulated trucks and other vehicles were included with those of car occupants.[12] The "intensive driving" variable that supposedly intervened between risk perception and death rates was not operationally defined, but the discussion of optimizing time to pursue other goals suggested that speed would be a primary component. Yet, in the analysis, speed was curiously used as a predictor variable rather than an outcome variable.

Contrary to the theory, other possible components of intensive driving, such as running through red lights and close following distance behind other vehicles in traffic, have been found to be more frequent among persons not using seat belts. Belts were in use by only 1 percent of drivers who drove through an intersection while a stoplight was red, compared to 9 percent belt use among drivers who were the first to stop when the light changed to red.[13] If drivers run red lights more often while wearing seat belts, the alleged effect cannot be large with only 1 percent belt use among the light runners.

Policies Directed at Agents and Vehicles

In areas where belt use is voluntary, users allow greater distance between themselves and a vehicle they are following than do nonusers. Furthermore, the distribution of following distances for users and nonusers is similar in Windsor, Ontario, where belt use is required by law, and across the river in Detroit, Michigan, where belt use is less than a third of that in Windsor.[14] Belt use increased by law does not result in reduced gaps in following, again in contradiction of the theory. Proponents of risk-adjustment theories cite a study that found slightly higher speeds on curves by drivers whose vehicles were equipped with studded tires compared to those without such equipment.[15] The tire-gripping capability of the studded tires more than compensated for the higher speeds, however, and the possibility that those who drive faster more often buy studded tires is at least as reasonable an interpretation of the finding as an attempted adjustment of driving speed to the equipment once purchased.

The issue of whether or not regulated vehicles increase hazards to other road users is resolved by comparing the involvement in severe crashes per miles driven of specific vehicles meeting safety standards to those that do not. To accomplish this comparison, all fatal crashes in the United States during 1975-1978 were classified as to the type of regulations that applied to the vehicles involved and the persons fatally injured—occupants, pedestrians, motorcyclists, and bicyclists. Using data available on the annual miles driven by vehicle age and in each calendar year, the fatalities per miles driven for each set of vehicles were calculated for each calendar year and the average involvement of vehicles by type of regulation was compared.

The results can be seen in figure 7-1. Occupant deaths per mile in cars that had lap seat belts as the result of state laws, some of which had occupant-protection improvements to meet standards for government purchase (1964-1967 models), were lower than in unregulated cars. These occupant-protection standards had no effect on other road users. Cars that met the full array of federal safety standards (1968 and subsequent models) not only had much lower occupant death rates but also struck pedestrians, motorcyclists, and bicyclists less often than vehicles that were unregulated or only complied with occupant-protection standards. The crash-avoidance standards, ignored by the risk-adjustment theorists, apparently had a substantial effect on risk to nonoccupants as well as occupants of regulated vehicles. Trucks, which had fewer regulations, showed less variation. Statistical controls for ages and types of vehicles found that the regulations accounted for a major part of the variations among the vehicles.[16]

During the 1975-1978 period, more than 9,000 persons per year avoided death as a result of the federal motor vehicle standards. This study period was situated after the decline in death associated with the oil embargo of 1974 but before the Iranian revolution of 1979 that also interrupted oil supplies. Therefore, the effect of the regulations is in addition to the reductions

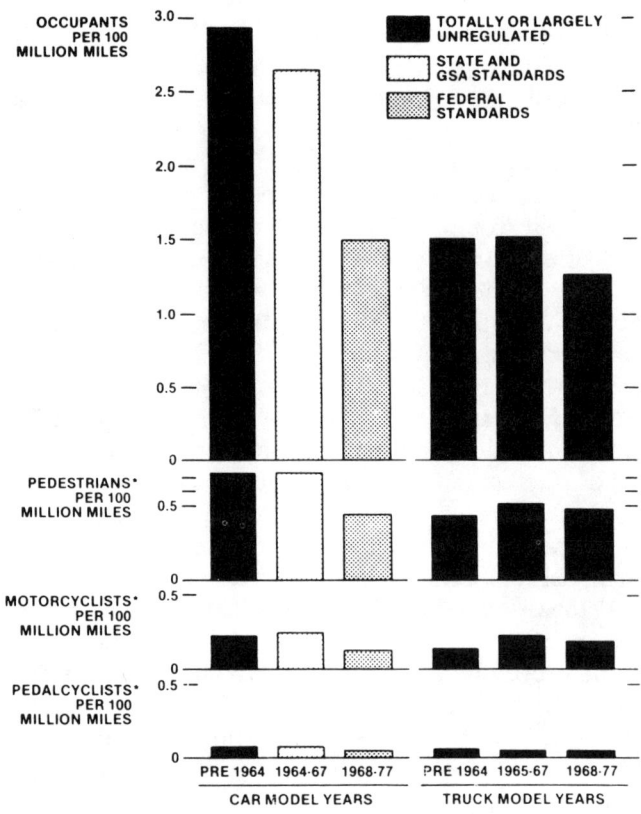

Source: Reprinted with permission from L.S. Robertson, "Automobile Safety Regulations and Death Reductions in the United States," *American Journal of Public Health* 71 (American Public Health Association, 1981):819.

Figure 7-1. Average Annual Fatal Crashes per 100 Million Miles, United States, 1975-1978

attributable to reduced speed limits and travel associated with the oil shortages. Because the effect of the regulations occurred gradually as the old, unregulated cars were replaced by regulated vehicles over the decade following 1967, it did not appear as dramatically as that of the 55-mph speed limit. It is nevertheless real and, in the long run, more sustainable than decreases through legal speed limits.

Research on occupant-protection standards in Sweden also found no support for the notion of risk adjustment in response to safety standards. Speed limits were first adopted in 1966 and occupant crash-protection standards were adopted for 1969 and subsequent models. Occupant deaths were about 20 percent less than predicted by an econometric model by 1973 and nonoccupant deaths were a few percent less than predicted.[17]

Rail Transport

The development of rail transit in the nineteenth century introduced a new hazard to travelers, workers, and persons along the rights of way. While the speed of the early trains could be equaled by a good horse, the mass of the trains along with the poor braking and coupling systems presented grave gaps between their stopping distances and those needed in emergencies. As the use of the rails increased, head-on and rear-end collisions were not uncommon. Flimsy wooden passenger cars were easily shattered and wood and coal burning stoves were tipped over, resulting in conflagrations. The coupling of cars joined by chains that could gain or lose slack while being handled was a hazardous occupation. Persons crossing or walking on the tracks as well as those in horse-drawn buggies crossing tracks were often struck. Bridge collapses and derailments were other sources of disasters.

Until the end of the century, concern for injuries was left mainly to the conscience of the railway operators and coroner's juries that ordered compensation to the injured when the railroad was considered negligent. Widespread adoption of innovations such as the Westinghouse automatic brake, automatic couplers, and automatic spacing and signal systems was delayed for decades while their merits were argued.

Present-day psychologists and economists who claim to have originated the theory that automatically decreased hazards are offset by increased hazardous behavior must acknowledge the nineteen-century railroad owners who made the same argument to resist adoption of automatic signal systems. A scion of the family of two early U.S. presidents wrote that the argument against electrical signal systems by "those who prefer to exercise their ingenuity in finding objections rather than in overcoming difficulties, is that they breed dependence and carelessness in employees." He went on to quote an 1873 report to the British Board of Trade in which just the opposite argument was made: "The more they [railway employees] are accustomed to incur risk in order to perform their duties, the less they think of it, and the more difficult it is to enforce discipline and obedience to regulations."[18] A footnote to this argument: those railroad employees who thought their actions or lack thereof contributed to fatalities were not without remorse. Several cases of suicide resulting from despondency over self-attributed fault for fatal railway crashes were documented.[19]

The Westinghouse automatic brake was patented in 1869 and was adopted by the Pullman Car Company but not by many of the locomotive manufacturers. The latter claimed that the system was too complicated to be reliable or understood by mechanics, despite the fact that it was far less complicated than several other components of their locomotives. In England, an experiment to demonstrate stopping distance at various speeds was held to illustrate that, with the brake, a train could be stopped in about one quarter of the distance as one with a brakeman operating a hand brake on each car. In 1876, a train crash occurred in which the front part of the train, which lacked the brake, was demolished while the Pullman cars with the brake were stopped without loss of life. Five people died in a comparable crash in 1877 when a train without automatic brakes on any of its cars experienced the mutual crushing of passenger cars that was common when they were not uniformly braked.[20]

The U.S. Congress did not get around to action on the hazards of rail travel until 1893. The Safety Appliance Act in that year specified the use of power-driven brakes by 1898 and control of speed by the locomotive engineer without hand brake use by brakemen. Automatic couplers and handholds for workers near the connection between cars were also required. Apparently, there was more than a little lack of compliance with the law. In 1903, the act was amended to require that by 1910, 85 percent of cars on a train would have their brakes under control of the locomotive engineer.[21]

At present the regulation of railroad vehicle standards is the responsibility of the Federal Railroad Administration in the U.S. Department of Transportation, where it was placed in 1967 when the department was created. Passenger travel by rail has declined, partly in response to preference for freight hauling and accompanying neglect of passenger services by the railroads and partly because of the greater flexibility of use of automobiles and speed of airplanes. The decline is surely not for lack of safety. By 1940, the railroads had fewer than 100 deaths to passengers annually, less than three per billion passenger miles, and that number was exceeded in only four years in subsequent decades.[22]

To document with any precision the effect of regulation on reductions in injury to rail travelers would probably be impossible. While data on numbers of fatalities were kept with probable reliability after the Interstate Commerce Commission was authorized to obtain the information from the railroads in 1903, the details of the types of equipment on trains in which people were killed compared to the extent of such equipment in the rolling stock at the time is not likely to be found.

Air Travel

Regulation of the safety of civilian aircraft is the responsibility of the Federal Aviation Administration (FAA), which was formed from several agencies and placed in the then new Department of Transportation in 1967.

Policies Directed at Agents and Vehicles

The authority to certify airworthiness of aircraft and components was first located in the Department of Commerce by the Air Commerce Act of 1926. Rules for air traffic control, pilot licensure, and crash investigation were also made federal responsibility at that time, in contrast to the states' role in these functions for motor vehicle use. A chronological history of regulatory activities in these areas is available.[23] The addition and revision of rules was frequent as air traffic increased and the technology available for aircraft design and construction as well as monitoring or control of traffic was developed.

In recent years, injuries to passengers on regularly scheduled, U.S. domestic airlines have been relatively rare. During the 1970s, fatalities ranged from only 1 in the year 1976 to 262 in 1979. In four of the five years from 1976 through 1980, there were fewer than 100, compared to between 113 and 174 per year in the previous five years. The passenger miles doubled during the decade.[24]

The largest reductions in risk of commercial air travel occurred in the 1940s and 1950s when fatalities per miles traveled were reduced by more than 80 percent.[25] During this period, the technology changed drastically as jets increasingly replaced propeller-driven engines. Radar and other technologies greatly improved traffic control. Training of pilots in the military provided a ready supply of pilots who had survived the rigors of training as well as, for many, combat in World War II and Korea. Still, no one has researched the relative effects of these factors along with the regulatory provisions on the decline in death rates.

So-called general aviation, involving non-military, non-commercial aircraft not scheduled for commercial passenger business, remains a greater problem. Many more people, some 1,300 to 1,400 people per year, died in crashes of these craft than in commercial craft during the 1970s. The deaths per 100,000 aircraft hours flown in general aviation declined from 2.6 in 1971 to 1.6 in 1980[26] following a less sharp decline of 3.1 to 2.6 in the previous decade.[27]

It is interesting that the decline in death rates accelerated after a scandal regarding an internal report that was suppressed by FAA according to the report's author. In 1970, he claimed he was forced to resign by persons within the agency who, the report had implied, had been negligent in performing their duties regarding general aviation. His charges were carried in newspapers and magazines. The crash in the Rocky Mountains of a leased plane carrying part of a football team from Wichita State University six months after the report was submitted to senior FAA executives would have been prevented, said the author, had the report's recommendations been adopted.[28] The extent to which the accelerated reduction in the death rate in the 1970s can be attributed to regulated changes in pilot qualifications, aircraft construction, or control of traffic, as opposed to evolution in the designs and uses of planes, would be a worthwhile topic for research.

Boats

Federal regulation of water transportation is the responsibility of the U.S. Coast Guard. Some states and local police have authority for licensure of vehicles and their operation; but the standards for watercraft, offshore platforms, personal flotation devices, and hazardous cargoes are established by the Coast Guard. The Boat Safety Act of 1971 resulted in improved criteria for flotation of boats of all sizes and types to reduce injuries associated with capsized or damaged craft. A personal flotation device meeting federal standards was required for each passenger in a boat. Specifications of limits on passenger-weight capacity and on power for the type and size of boat were included, along with criteria for electrical components, fuel systems, lights for night use, and the like.[29]

No studies comparing injuries associated with vessels that met particular standards were found in the research literature. From 1961 to the 1971 changes in regulation, there was little variation in fatalities per estimated number of boats: they ranged from 19.0 to 21.4 per 100,000 boats with no apparent year-to-year trend. In 1972, the rate dropped to 16.9 from 20.2 the year before, and by 1979 it had decreased to 9.7 per 100,000 boats.[30] Boat use doubled during the period and, without data on use and users by type of boat, the extent to which the 1971 regulations resulted in halving the death rate cannot be separately assessed. The data raise the suspicion that the regulations account for at least a portion of the declining death rate.

Occupational Injuries

The regulation of most work places to reduce the hazards contributing to worker injuries was left to state governments until 1971. Examinations by federal inspectors of mines, docks, and work done under federal contracts began earlier, but high-injury industries such as private construction and manufacturing were not subject to uniform standards. Many states relied on voluntary compliance by the industries within their borders.[31] The Occupational Safety and Health Act of 1970 established an Ocupational Safety and Health Administration (OSHA) in the Department of Labor to adopt and enforce federal safety and health standards in work places of industries involved in interstate commerce. It also provided for a research institute in the Department of Health and Human Services called the National Institute for Occupational Safety and Health. Mine safety remained the responsibility of a separate agency.

OSHA was specifically directed by the act[32] to adopt all national consensus standards recommended by private, voluntary standard-development groups and any federal standards in use for federal contractors, unless such rules could be shown to be ineffective. Since little evidence regarding efficacy existed, some 4,000 rules were adopted by early 1971, with little regard for their relative importance or the impossibility of enforcing such a large number.

Also, the potential effectiveness of the act is limited by its covering some 4 million business establishments. To the extent that there is compliance without inspections, some positive change could occur anyway; but if the effect of the act is limited to corrections of hazards or change in work practices through specific citations, the number of inspectors necessary to enforce the regulations would be very large. In 1977 OSHA employed approximately 1,250 inspectors and state programs approved to enforce OSHA standards employed an additional 900 or so.[33] At the 1977 rate of 200,000 inspections per year, a business could expect to be inspected once in twenty years if the inspections were done at random. OSHA adopted a somewhat more rational approach with inspections targeted at larger industries with higher injury rates, but inspections were nevertheless infrequent even for businesses with high injury rates.

Another impediment to OSHA's influence on the rate of severe, particularly fatal, injuries is that its rules do not apply to two major contributors to worker death: motor vehicles and guns. In a study of one state's worker deaths from injury while on the job in 1978, 41 percent of the deaths were associated with transportation vehicles, 25 percent in road use and 16 percent off-road use, and 11 percent involved guns, usually handguns.[34] As noted earlier, trucks are less regulated by the National Highway Traffic Safety Administration than are cars. There are no federal regulations of guns other than prohibition of interstate movement of certain types, such as machine guns; and states have passed a haphazard variety of laws regarding ownership, possession, and use (see chapter 6).

Most of the research attempting to assess the effects of OSHA on worker injuries has used data aggregated by years or industries and correlated the change in injuries per numbers of workers to OSHA inspection activities. Studies of changes in time are complicated by the fact that the criteria for reporting injuries were changed in 1971 at the same time that OSHA standards were adopted. The use of aggregated data also increases the danger that uncontrolled variables at individual or other levels will result in invalid conclusions similar to those noted previously for motor vehicles.

This type of research turned up little evidence that OSHA had reduced injuries during its first few years. During 1972-1973, comparison of injury rates in industries targeted for frequent inspections to those in other industries, controlling for prior injury rates and changes in employment, found no significant effect of OSHA efforts.[35] Projected trends in the types of injuries that OSHA would likely have reduced were only a few percent above actual trends in California through 1974.[36]

One economist derived an elaborate model of worker and firm behavior in which the notion of risk adjustment by workers to reduced hazards was hypothesized as probably offsetting any effect of reduced hazards. At the low rate of enforcement, the model predicted little investment by industry in hazard reduction for economic reasons. The fines being imposed, so went the theory, were not large enough to result in investment to offset them. No effect of OSHA on injury rates or investment in injury control was found based on data aggregated by industry during the years 1972 through 1975.[37] However, based on plant level data in 1973 through 1974, one researcher found a 16 percent reduction in injuries associated with OSHA inspections in 1973 and a 5 percent reduction in 1974, the latter not statistically significant.[38]

More recent research at the plant level found not only a greater effect of OSHA citations but also an explanation for the failure to find an effect in the research using aggregated data. Despite the economic orientation of the prior research, the potential effect of state programs to compensate workers for work time lost due to injury and illness had not been accounted for adequately. If, as some economists hypothesize,[39] workers would respond to increased compensation with more claims or even less caution in their behavior, then increases in worker's compensation at greater than the inflation rate could potentially offset injury reductions attributable to OSHA.

Data on individual injuries in three plants in separate states during 1973 through 1980 were examined and annual expected rates were generated from the contribution of differential exposure to hazard in different departments and individual attributes that were correlated with individual incidence, such as age, formal education, number of previous jobs before joining the company, and length of experience in the relevant departments. Annual variation from these expected rates was strongly related to OSHA citations and increments in worker's compensation above the inflation rate.

Injury claims increased in relation to increases in worker's compensation above the inflation rate, but these increases were confined to nonverifiable injuries such as back strain and pain. Worker's compensation had no effect on the incidence of verifiable injuries such as fractures, lacerations, and contusions—contrary to the notion that workers are less careful when compensation for injury is increased—but day-loss injuries for both verifiable and nonverifiable injuries increased in association with worker's compensation. When worker's compensation was controlled, the OSHA inspections had a substantial reducing effect on objectively verifiable injuries in a given plant during the year following a given citation. Such injuries were about 40 percent less in the year of the citation but the effect did not last into subsequent years.

Apparently, management pays attention to the problem of injuries for a time after a citation, particularly with respect to transient hazards and behavior; but the citations are confined to one or a few specific hazards and

Policies Directed at Agents and Vehicles 151

little general, permanent modification of the hazards in the work environment has resulted from OSHA citations. Nevertheless, the regulation did result in substantial injury reduction—a reduction that was masked in aggregate trend data by the increase in nonverifiable claims related to increasing worker's compensation during the 1970s.

An analysis of lost workdays due to injury in all manufacturing industries with 5,000 or more workers in twenty states during 1975-1976 produced similar results. Days lost increased from 1975 to 1976 in association with increases in worker's compensation and declined in association with increased OSHA inspections.[40] This suggests that the results of the three-plant study are generalizable. Apparently, the large increases in worker's compensation in the 1970s more than offset the injury-reducing effects of OSHA.

Mining as a Special Case

Historically, underground mining has been among the most hazardous of occupations. This characterization is particularly true of coal mines, which share the danger of cave-in and moving machinery in close quarters with other mines but in addition are prone to the accumulation of gases that can explode or asphyxiate if not removed. The federal government established a Bureau of Mines in 1910 to provide research and advisory inspections and investigations. Since the inspectors had no enforcement powers, this effort was not in itself regulation. A 1941 law empowered federal investigators to enter mines uninvited but no enforcement powers were included. The first code of regulations, again only advisory without provision for enforcement, was enacted in 1947.

The first authority for federal inspectors to issue notices of violations and to order withdrawal of workers from areas deemed particularly hazardous was enacted in a 1952 law. Mines with fewer than fifteen employees, which were frequently very hazardous, and surface mines were exempted. The exemption based on number of employees was removed in 1966 and enforcement powers were extended in 1969. The regulatory agency, which had been in the Department of the Interior, was placed in the Department of Labor and renamed the Mine Safety and Health Administration in 1977. Surface mines were included and a minimum of two inspections per mine per year was specified in the legislation.

Recent enforcement activity is remarkably more intense than that of OSHA for other industries. In 1978, there were 34,641 inspections in the 2,131 active underground coal mines. Some 76,000 citations and notations of violations were issued and 2,057 orders to withdraw workers from hazardous areas were enforced, an average of almost 1 per mine. Other mining operations had about 2 inspections and 5 citations per mine with almost one in three receiving an order of withdrawal from a hazardous area.[41]

An adequate evaluation of the effects of mine safety regulation has not been done. The death rate per hours worked declined by 70 percent from 1940 to the mid-1970s in underground coal mines. Based on crude trend analyses, economists have attributed the total of this decline to changing technology and size of mining operations.[42,43] These analyses did not include detailed enforcement data and information on changes in the working population. The presence or absence of the various laws stood as proxies for the extent of regulation; and factors such as the postwar baby boom that resulted in a large increase of younger workers in the late 1960s and 1970s were ignored. The authors of one of the studies candidly admitted that the statistical models were of questionable value and that there were several anomalies in the data, such as shifting correlations of variables from one time period to the next.[44]

To the extent that data are available, a study of the detailed characteristics of specific mining operations and their workers, along with citation and withdrawal rates in relation to injuries, could be useful in specifying not only the extent of the effect of specific enforcement but also the specification of optimal enforcement activity. With the intensity of enforcement in this industry, there should be sufficient variation in inspections and citations to be able to indicate a point beyond which enforcement activity yields little extra benefit. It is also conceivable that an effect analogous to that noted with respect to laws directed at individuals (chapter 6) would be found—that is, no effect if enforcement is below a certain level, but reduced injury rates in correlation with enforcement above that level.

Consumer Products

In 1973, the Consumer Product Safety Act designated the establishment of a Consumer Product Safety Commission consisting of five members, each to be appointed by the president for seven-year terms. The commissioners and staff are "independent" in that they are not located within a governmental cabinet department but, instead, report directly to the Congress and the president. They are charged with the administration of several prior congressional acts such as the Refrigerator Safety Act of 1956 and the Poison Prevention Packaging Act of 1970, as well as with the research and formation of standards for a wide array of consumer products.

The commission has concentrated most of its regulatory efforts on products that injure children less than ten years of age and has established a sample of hospital emergency rooms that report injuries related to specific consumer products.[45] Because motor vehicles and guns were not included in the Commission's jurisdiction, they are not regulated by the commission; and for years injuries associated with their use were not included in the reporting system.

Policies Directed at Agents and Vehicles

On the basis of investigations of involvement in childhood deaths and injuries, the commission has banned the manufacture of unstable refuse bins and flammable contact adhesives as well as other health hazards such as certain lead paints and materials that contain free-form asbestos. Standards to reduce hazards have been applied to architectural glazing (such as window and door glass), matchbooks, power mowers, swimming pool slides, bicycles, and the flammability of children's sleepwear as well as carpets, rugs, and mattresses.

Investigations have also resulted in the voluntary recall of several hundred products that did not meet standards or were otherwise found to be hazardous. Legal action has been undertaken in a few cases, such as those concerning aluminum wiring that allegedly causes a substantial increase in the probability of fire in the 1.5 million homes in which it was used during 1965 through 1973.

The agency is too young for a comprehensive evaluation of its effectiveness in reducing hazards. Many of the mentioned standards were not adopted until the late 1970s and their effects will only become known as old products are discarded and new ones meeting the standards replace them. A few of the older standards, however, have already had an apparent effect. Child-resistant packaging and reductions in amount per container were voluntarily applied to children's aspirin containers in the late 1960s. Deaths from aspirin ingestion among children less than five years old declined more than 80 percent from 1964-1965 to 1975.[46]

During 1973-1974, regulations requiring child-resistant packaging were adopted for a variety of drugs and household products containing chemicals potentially hazardous to children. Using the data on emergency-room visits from the surveillance system from 1973 to 1975, changes in visits associated with the regulated products and a set of products that were unregulated during the period were compared. Reported ingestions of the regulated products declined by more than a third, while ingestions associated with unregulated products increased by 20 percent.[47]

Since the population base for these emergency rooms is difficult to establish, possible increases or decreases in the age group at risk are unknown. Also, the completeness of reporting increased as the system developed, so one must be cautious in interpreting these results. At worst, some children could have substituted an unregulated product for a regulated one when they could not open the child-resistant package. If this happened, there was nevertheless a net decline in ingestions and the substances ingested were more often benign. At best, there was an increase in the population at risk resulting in greater numbers of attempted ingestions reflected in the ingestions of unregulated products and an effective reduction of ingestions by regulated packaging of substantially more than a third.

Crib-related injuries reported to emergency rooms declined 44 percent and deaths per number of infants declined 34 percent in association with warnings issued by the agency regarding falls from cribs and heads being caught between slats, as well as regulations to reduce such incidents.[48] Again, this research does not contain adequate controls for other factors that could have contributed to the change, but it is likely that at least some of the decrease resulted from the commissioners' actions.

The effects of the flammability standard for sleepwear for children aged seven to fourteen have been studied. Since such sleepwear seldom lasts more than a year or so, the replacement is rapid relative to some of the other products. Using data from the National Center for Health Statistics on fire and flame burn deaths along with data for changes in the population at risk, a reduction of eight to thiry-four deaths in 1975 as estimated. Data on hospitalized burn injuries in combination with estimates of the involvement of sleepwear in such injuries were used to calculate the expected number. Some 1,600 fewer children in the age group were hospitalized for burn injuries than would have been expected in 1975.[49]

An attempt to estimate the effect of the mattress flammability standard failed to find a statistically significant effect in cases reported to the National Institute for Burn Medicine.[50] The researcher used a rather crude trend anlaysis similar to those that were discredited in the cases of motor vehicle safety regulations and occupational safety regulations. Although the alteration in trend from 1965 to 1973 before the standard to the 1974 to 1977 period afterward was not statistically significant, the estimated reduction was larger each year, consistent with a possible effect given enough time for turnover in the mattress stock. Also, since 80 percent of the mattresses in use met the standard prior to its promulgation, a large effect during the period studied would not be expected.

Standard Development for Industry and Government Use

The federal agency charged with development and maintenance of standards for commonly needed weights, measures, and related instrumentation has also initiated standard development or been called upon from time to time as a source of investigations and standards relevant to injury control. Now located in the Department of Commerce, the National Bureau of Standards was authorized by law in 1900. A fire near the agency's housing in 1904 led to the discovery that hoses in separate buildings did not have compatible coupling. The agency undertook a study of the problem that contributed to a commonly adopted standard, but the adoption process among separate localities was slow. As late as 1964, fire companies called to districts other than their own might find hoses incompatible with theirs.[51]

A report of 42,000 train derailments in 1912 due to broken rails, wheels, flanges, and axles led the Secretary of Commerce to urge the agency to study the matter. The subsequent investigations of metallurgy probably contributed to the improved technology that resulted in reductions in a variety of failures of metal components of machinery and other structures. Similar investigations of building codes regarding the flammability of a variety of materials found "absurd data regulating the property of materials."[52] The bureau has been engaged in testing materials for flammability ever since and was the source, in collaboration with private standard-development groups, for many local building codes. These changes undoubtedly resulted in the greatly reduced numbers of urban conflagrations that were ten times as frequent as in European cities around the turn of the century.

In the 1920s studies of natural gas appliances revealed substantial problems of leakage. The bureau investigations, in cooperation with the Baltimore Gas and Electric Company and the city's public health department, resulted in the adoption of stringent standards by the industry for inspection and repair. Gas-related deaths in Baltimore declined from forty-two to none in the subsequent three-year period.[53]

The bureau has also been involved in investigations of motor vehicles, tires, aircraft and many other of the products involved in injury. The extent of the injury-reducing result of these efforts is undocumented, but it is unlikely to be trivial.

Private Professional and Industrial Standards:
Development and Application

The technical director of the Association of Home Appliance Manufacturers has been quoted as saying, "The only way to avoid government regulation is to move faster than the government. The alternative to government regulation is judicious self-regulation."[54] Some industries undoubtedly have low injury rates to their workers and/or to customers using their products because they have, as individual companies or in collaboration through trade associations and other arrangements, adopted standards that reduce injuries. Besides acting out of humanitarian reasons, some of the more enlightened business executives have seen the advantage of reducing the losses in liability suits and maintaining a good reputation for quality of products unsullied by association with injury causation.

Self-regulation in the form of industry-wide standards can be complicated by economic issues if the standards tend to bar entry into the market by new producers or to drive out small companies who find the standards too expensive to maintain. Such problems can also result from government standards, but it is the appearance of collaboration for economic gain that raises such antitrust issues in private collaborations. One of the economic advantages of uniform federal or industry standards is the avoidance of the widely differing standards for the same product or manufacturing process commonly imposed by the separate states.

Manufacturers, insurers and government officials have cooperated in some efforts such as the National Fire Protection Association in which representatives from each group have long been included on the board of directors.[55] The standards developed in these collaborative efforts have been adopted voluntarily by some industries, have been required of others for liability insurance coverage, and have been adopted at various levels of government.

Other important sources of standards in the private sector are the technical societies made up mainly of engineers and other professionals from industry. The Society of Automotive Engineers, for example, develops recommended practices for vehicle engineering but their use by the industry is, of course, voluntary. Nevertheless, the professional pride involved in such work can be an important factor in the voluntary reduction of hazards.[56]

Few formal studies of the effects of voluntary standard adoption have been published in the scientific literature, though there is evidence of enormous reductions in losses in a few instances. The nineteenth-century mill owners of New England reduced their fire insurance premiums by 98 percent when they developed standards for flame-retardant materials, sprinklers, and fire doors. When some of their fellow manufacturers did not conform, they approached governments and had the standards enforced by law.[57]

Effectiveness of standards in this chapter has been discussed somewhat loosely, as a mixture of the effect of a standard when used and the effect it would have if everyone used it. Industrial, professional, and other voluntary organizations have often done excellent work in developing standards, but they usually have no authority to enforce use and uniform adoption is long in coming. Also, there have been charges in recent years that private standard-development and testing organizations have been slow to change because they derive income from the testing or use of equipment specified in extant standards.[58]

Studies of Local Regulations

An excellent example of scientific specification of the circumstances of a set of injuries and successful regulatory follow-up is the New York City Health Department's work on fatal falls of children from heights. Using 1965-1969 data, the researchers found that the vast majority of such falls occurred from windows of multistoried buildings.[59] The department began a program of informing public officials and the public of the problem that included outreach workers who went door to door in high-incidence area. Some 16,000 free barrier devices that prevent children from crawling out of windows were distributed. Follow-up study indicated that no falls occured in households with the devices.[60]

In 1976, the New York Board of Health, which has regulatory powers, held public hearings and issued a rule that any window of an apartment that housed a child less than ten years of age, excepting those leading to fire escapes, would be required to have the preventive device. Within four years, the number of reported falls of children from windows in multistoried buildings had declined by 80 percent and the number of fatal falls was down also by 80 percent.[61]

A comparison of swimming pool drownings in Honolulu, Hawaii, and Brisbane, Australia, suggests that Honolulu's laws requiring fences around pools have an effect on the drowning rates. The annual pool-fatality rate in Honolulu was found to be 0.9 per 100,000 population compared to 2.6 per 100,000 in Brisbane with no rules regarding protective fencing. The two cities are similar in size and climate and have similar pool-to-household ratios.[62]

Both the local nature of certain types of hazards and the fact that particular types of regulation are left to local areas mean that local health departments and other agencies must undertake the effort to find those hazards and their result in damaged people. Injuries are just as deserving of attention as contaminated water or food, traditionally of concern to health departments. Using the options analysis in chapter 4, the possible means of ameliorating the problem can be identified and the appropriate authorities pushed to adopt the necessary measures. Follow-up study of the effects of such efforts and their reporting are important to alert others in similar areas of the hazards and probable success of particular efforts. It is also important to build a body of knowledge regarding the successes and failures of various types of public and private regulatory efforts.

Conclusion

The author has attended numerous conferences and seminars, as well as read accounts in the literature, in which economists and political scientists wring their hands or chortle, depending on their ideologic bent, because of so-called regulatory failure. In this chapter, the success in substantial reduction of injuries and fatalities by regulation of hazardous agents and vehicles has been noted in several cases in which the effects are well researched. In other cases, declines in fatalities are associated with such regulation, but the data are inadequate for a strong inference of regulatory effect. In still other instances the failure is not in the regulations but in the research methods of those who claim regulatory failure. Evaluation of public policy regarding injury and death is too important to be left to those who fail to find and analyze data other than that which can be copied from aggregated statistics in a library or agency file, or who are too ethnocentric to read the literature outside economics, political science or any other discipline that fails in use of relevant knowledge and research methods.

The evidence suggests that regulation is substantially successful when the nature of the hazards has been first clearly identified by experts in or out of a regulatory agency and the regulations are then directed at a relatively few changes that are likely to make a large and permanent difference in results. This sequence was followed with motor vehicle safety standards and, although less well documented, has probably been followed with other vehicles of transportation and specific consumer products. The regulation of consumer products and job hazards is a far more formidable task because of the number of business establishments and the variety of hazards involved. Occupational safety efforts in particular have been burdened with a large number of irrelevant standards. Nevertheless, there is evidence of reductions in injury attributable to some of the methods that have been used.

If lack of total success is interpreted as failure, then few regulatory agencies will survive the test. If the criterion of success is a substantially healthier population, in many cases regulation has made a contribution. This is not to say that laws creating regulatory processes have always chosen the most efficient or efficacious course nor that agencies have always done so within the bounds of the laws giving them authority. Regulation and other injury-control efforts sometimes impose costs as well as benefits. They operate in volatile social and political environments. And regulators and others involved often have agendas that result in diversion of effort from the primary course. The extent to which these limitations can be anticipated and considered in the choices of action is the subject of the next two chapters.

References

1. E.C. Wigglesworth, "Legislation and Injury Control," *Medicine, Science and the Law* 18(1978):191-99.
2. U.S. Department of Transportation, "Laws Requiring Seat Belts," *Traffic Laws Commentary* 1(1972):1.
3. Public Law 89-563, 89th Congress, S.3005.
4. Public Law 89-564, 89th Congress, S.3052.

5. W. Haddon, Jr., "Road Safety Problems and Action Programs—The U.S. Approach." In: *Proceedings of the National Road Safety Symposium* (Canberra, Australia: Australian Government Publishing Service, 1972).

6. *Code of Federal Regulations, 49 Transportation Part 51* (Washington, DC: U.S. Government Printing Office, 1974).

7. National Traffic Safety Agency, *Report on the Development of the Initial Motor Vehicle Safety Standards* (Washington, DC: U.S. Department of Commerce, 1967).

8. W. Haddon, Jr. "What We're Talking About." In: C.W. Wixom, ed., *Key Issues in Highway Loss Reduction* (Washington, DC: Insurance Institute for Highway Safety, 1970).

9. D.N. Levine and B.J. Campbell, *Effectiveness of Lap Seat Belts and the Energy Absorbing Steering System in the Reduction of Injuries* (Chapel Hill, NC: University of North Carolina Safety Research Center, 1971).

10. L.S. Robertson, "Estimates of Motor Vehicle Seat Belt Effectiveness and Use: Implications for Occupant Crash Protection," *American Journal of Public Health* 66(1976):859.

11. S. Peltzman, "The Effects of Automobile Safety Regulation," *Journal of Political Economy* 83(1975):677.

12. L.S. Robertson, "A Critical Analysis of Peltzman's 'The Effects of Automobile Safety Regulation,'" *Journal of Economic Issues* 11(1977):587.

13. D. Deutsch, S. Sameth, and J. Akinyemi, "Seat Belt Use and Risktaking Behavior at Two Major Traffic Intersections," *Proceedings of the Annual Meeting of the American Association for Automotive Medicine*, Morton Grove, IL, 1980.

14. L. Evans, P. Wasielewski, and C.R. von Buseck, "Compulsory Seat Belt Usage and Driver Risk Taking Behavior," *Human Factors* 24 (1982):41-8.

15. K. Rumar, et al., "Driver Reaction to a Technical Safety Measure—Studded Tires," *Human Factors* 18(1976):443-54.

16. L.S. Robertson, "Automobile Safety Regulations and Death Reductions in the United States," *American Journal of Public Health* 71 (1981):818-22.

17. B. Lindgren and C. Stuart, "The Effects of Traffic Safety Regulation in Sweden," *Journal of Political Economy* 88(1980):412.

18. C.F. Adams, *Notes on Railroad Accidents* (New York: G.P. Putnam's Sons, 1879).

19. R.B. Shaw, *Down Brakes: A History of Railroad Accidents, Safety Precautions and Safety Practices in the United States of America* (London: MacMillan, 1961).

20. C.F. Adams, *Notes on Railroad Accidents*, pp. 199-205.

21. *49 Code of Federal Regulation*, 200-268, 1981.
22. Shaw, *Down Brakes*, p. 463.
23. Federal Aviation Administration, *FAA Historical Fact Book* (Washington, DC: U.S. Department of Transportation, 1974).
24. Federal Aviation Administration, *FAA Statistical Handbook of Aviation* (Washington, DC: U.S. Department of Transportation, 1980).
25. Shaw, *Down Brakes*, p. 464.
26. Federal Aviation Administration, *FAA Statistical Handbook of Aviation*, p. 160.
27. Federal Aviation Administration, *General Aviation Statistics* (Washington, DC: U.S. Department of Transportation, 1969).
28. P.I. Ryther, *Who's Watching the Airways?* (New York: Doubleday, 1972).
29. *33 Code of Federal Regulations*, Parts 1-199, 1981.
30. U.S. Coast Guard, *Boating Statistics, 1979* (Washington, DC: U.S. Department of Transportation, 1980).
31. J. Mendeloff, *Regulating Safety: An Economic and Political Analysis of Occupational Safety and Health Policy* (Cambridge, MA: MIT Press, 1979).
32. Public Law 91-596, 91st Congress, S.2193.
33. Mendeloff, *Regulating Safety*, p. 2.
34. S.P. Baker, et al., "Fatal Occupational Injuries," *Journal of the American Medical Association* 248(1982):692.
35. R.S. Smith, *The Occupational Safety and Health Act: Its Goals and Its Achievements* (Washington, DC: American Enterprise Institute for Public Policy Research, 1976).
36. J. Mendeloff, *Regulating Safety,* pp. 171-177.
37. W.K. Viscusi, "The Impact of Occupational Safety and Health Regulation," *Bell Journal of Economics* 10(1979):117.
38. R.S. Smith, "The Impact of OSHA Inspections on Manufacturing Injury Rates," *The Journal of Human Resources* 14(1979):145.
39. J.R. Chelius, *Workplace Safety and Health: The Role of Worker's Compensation* (Washington, DC: American Enterprise Institute, 1977).
40. L.S. Robertson and J.P. Keeve, "Worker Injuries: The Effects of Worker's Compensation and OSHA Citations," mimeo (New Haven: Center for Health Studies, Yale University, 1983).
41. Mine Safety and Health Administration, *Annual Report and Achievements: Fiscal Year 1978* (Washington, DC: U.S. Department of Labor, 1979).
42. W.H. Andrews and C.L. Christenson, "Some Economic Factors Affecting Safety in Underground Bituminous Coal Mines," *Southern Economics Journal* 41(1974):364.

43. T.S. Witt, C.A. Palomba, and N.A. Palomba, "Some Economic Factors Affecting Safety in Underground Bituminous Coal Mines," *Southern Economics Journal* 44(1975):306.

44. Andrews and Christenson, "Some Economic Factors Affecting Safety in Underground Bituminous Coal Mines," *Southern Economics Journal* 41(1975):309.

45. *1979 Annual Report* (Washington, DC: U.S. Consumer Product Safety Commission, 1979).

46. A.K. Done, "Aspirin Overdosage: Incidence, Diagnosis and Management," *Pediatrics* (Supplement) 59(1978):890.

47. D.R. Howes, *An Evaluation of the Effectiveness of Child-Resistant Packaging* (Washington, DC: Consumer Product Safety Commission, 1978).

48. Office of Strategic Planning, *Impact of Crib Safety Activities on Injuries and Deaths Associated With Cribs* (Washington, DC: Consumer Product Safety Commission, 1979).

49. R. Dardis, S. Aaronson, and Y. Lin, "Cost-Benefit Analysis of Flammability Standards," *American Journal of Agricultural Economics* 60(1978):695.

50. P. Linneman, "The Effects of Consumer Safety Standards: The 1973 Mattress Flammability Standard," *Journal of Law and Economics* 23 (1980):461.

51. R.C. Cochrane, *Measures for Progress: A History of the National Bureau of Standards* (Washington, DC: U.S. Department of Commerce, 1966).

52. Cochrane, *Measures for Progress*, p. 130.

53. Cochrane, *Measures for Progress*, pp. 263-65.

54. M.S. Hunt, "Trade Associations and Self-Regulation: Major Home Appliances." In: R.E. Caves and M.J. Roberts, *Regulating the Product: Quality and Variety* (Cambridge, MA: Ballinger, 1975).

55. *The Story of the National Fire Protection Association* (Boston, MA: National Fire Protection Association, 1938).

56. *Industrial Standardization* (New York: National Industry Conference Board, 1929).

57. P.J. McKeon, *Fire Prevention, A Treatise and Textbook on Making Life and Property Safe Against Fire* (New York: The Chief Publishing Co., 1912)

58. "Why America Burns" (film), *Nova* (Public Broadcasting System, October 4, 1981).

59. L. Bergner, S. Mayer, and D. Harris, "Falls from Heights: A Childhood Epidemic in an Urban Area," *American Journal of Public Health* 61 (1971):90.

60. C.N. Spiegel and F.C. Lindaman, "Children Can't Fly: A Program to Prevent Childhood Morbidity and Mortality from Window Falls," *American Journal of Public Health* 67(1977):1143.

61. L. Bergner, "Environmental Factors in Injury Control: Preventing Falls from Heights." In: A.B. Bergman, ed., *Preventing Childhood Injuries* (Columbus, OH: Ross Laboratories, 1982).

62. J.H. Pearn, et al., "Drowning and Near-Drowning Involving Children: A Five-year Total Population Study from the City and County of Honolulu," *American Journal of Public Health* 69(1979):450.

8 The Economics of Injury Control

The historical accounts of injury-control efforts in important areas of the economy such as railroads, airplanes, and home construction seldom mention cost as an issue. The merits of particular changes, at least as portrayed by the historians, were argued on the basis of humane necessity and effectiveness. Resistance to automatic brakes, signaling systems, and couplers by the railroads, for example, may have been motivated primarily by the costs involved, but the explicit reasons given were not complaints about profit losses.[1]

In recent years, debates regarding government programs and regulation, particularly those directed at motor vehicles and other consumer products, have included economics as a primary component. One of the more dramatic moments in the 1965 Senate hearings on motor vehicle safety occurred when Senator Robert F. Kennedy asked the chairman of the board of the General Motors Corporation (GM) the amount of profits the company had made in the prior year and the amount that the company had expended for research on improving the crashworthiness of its cars. The answer, after some resistance based on the relevance of the information, was $1,700 million in profits and $1¼ million for crashworthiness research.[2] The senator was not alone in his expression of shock at the contrast.

None of the legislation that establishes regulatory agencies to control injuries specifies the precise extent to which costs of regulation are to be considered in decisions to impose particular standards. Words such as reasonable, feasible, and practicable are used in the laws as an indication that costs and effectiveness are not to be ignored, but judgment as to the specific criteria to be applied is left to the regulatory agencies. With increasing frequency, the use of cost-benefit analysis in making policy has been advocated by the regulated industries along with some academic and government economists. The President's Council of Economic Advisors, the Office of Management and Budget, and the former Council on Wage and Price Stability in the federal government have persuaded recent presidents to issue executive orders calling for such studies.

The fundamental premise of cost-benefit analysis is that the benefits of public policy should equal or exceed the costs. According to the theory, a misallocation of resources occurs when government action results in expenditures that exceed social benefits. A government action is efficient in increasing the welfare of society, according to one textbook, "if that activity results in a net increase in the value of goods and services produced throughout the economy."[3] The concept is static in that it accepts the prevalent distribution of income as given. Since the economic value of goods and services is what people are willing to pay for them given their incomes, the value would change if the distribution of incomes were different. Willingness to pay with the money one has is obviously different from willingness to pay if one had the money.

The distribution of benefits from regulatory action may be inequitable in practice—some people receiving more and others less or none—but many economists consider that outcome acceptable as long as, theoretically, the persons receiving fewer benefits or losses can be compensated in some way by the beneficiaries.[4] Here we have one of several slippery concepts because, in practice, losers are often not compensated.[5]

These notions raise all sorts of thorny issues. The maximization of output of goods and services that results in the rapid depletion of resources essential to the society's eventual survival is a curious notion of increased welfare. Even when the costs and benefits are goods and services on which monetary values can be placed by fairly reasonable assumptions regarding general supply and demand, severe difficulties arise when, for example, property that has priceless sentimental value to the owner is taken by eminent domain. When life must be sacrificed because it is not considered cost-beneficial to act to prevent the deaths, those who object to equating life with goods and services are upset. And egalitarians are unhappy with the assumption that present distributions of income are accepted without question.

The broader philosophies of government relevant to resource allocation are discussed in the next chapter. Here cost-benefit analysis, as applied to decisions regarding injury control, is examined on a more technical basis. In particular, what are considered as costs and how are they measured? Can all costs be anticipated? Similarly, how are benefits measured and equated to dollar values used in estimating costs? And, in practice, how has cost-benefit analysis been used in injury-control efforts?

The Estimation of Costs

The cost of a pork barrel project, such as a road or dam, can be anticipated by contractor bids if the government does not allow the contractor to exceed the budget. Similarly, the cost of government programs that are financed by government expenditure aimed at injury control, such as high-school driver education programs and television advertising, can be rather easily calculated. Police and fire departmental costs can be segmented into injury-control efforts and other functions by careful accounting.[6]

Compliance with the law may involve incremental costs to the citizenry that are not so easily assessed. What is the worth in dollars of the extra time for travel when a legal speed limit is lowered? For the traveling salesman or the truck driver at work, the answer may be calculable, although data on travel by purpose is limited; but the same amounts would not be applicable even to the same persons during a Sunday afternoon drive to view the scenery. Here the time spent at lower speeds is inherently valuable and the lack of pressure from following vehicles to move faster is a benefit rather than a cost. Also, for some who drive as part of a job, the driving may be inherently pleasurable and not simply a means to acquire income, just as work in general may be so.[7] Since it is customary to pay for work done rather than have persons pay for the privilege of working, there is no market that suggests the monetary value of the pleasure of work. Clearly, the greater the number of intangibles involved, the greater the potential for arbitrariness in divining costs and for sophistry in arguing their merits.

The costs of regulation are given more attention, not because they are any more important than those for government programs and laws directed at individual behavior, but because those affected—mainly regulated businesses—have greater means to bring them to the attention of the government and the public. In a few cases, these presentations are blatantly false and, in others, the assessment of true cost is less easy than might seem apparent.

Recent claims of the cost of motor vehicle safety regulations by automakers and the National Highway Traffic Safety Administration average around $400 per car.[8] Since these claims are based on information supplied by the regulated industry, which has consistently resisted the imposition of regulation, the amount is suspect. One of the issues in such an estimate is whether or not the companies in the industry have made every effort or even a reasonable effort to minimize costs. The evidence suggests that they have not.

The federal safety standards are performance, not design, standards (chapter 7) and add to costs of cars only if the manufacturer chooses designs that are more costly.[9] In one documented case, the manufacturers have not only used the more expensive design but they have also used, and continue to use in a majority of models, the less effective design.

Among the standards is one that requires an energy-absorbing structure behind the head to reduce the incidence and severity of so-called whiplash injuries. These structures are misnamed headrests in some owner's manuals, but they are more appropriately called head restraints. In some models, the manufacturers have installed seats that are taller than in preregulation models and extend up to the maximum level specified by the standard. This design, the automatic approach, requires no adjustment by driver or passenger. In other models, the restraints are adjustable.

In 1971, a comparison of neck injury claims in insurance company files by model of vehicle revealed that cars with head restraints had significantly fewer incidents of neck injury from rear-end collisions than cars not equipped with head restraints. Thus the regulation has had an effect but further evidence suggests that a much greater effect could be realized. Observations of vehicles in traffic indicated that more than three-fourths of drivers in cars with adjutable head restraints were traveling with the restraint in its lowest adjustable position, which, except for every short people, was not behind the head.[10]

This information certainly is well known to the auto manufacturers, having been made available in the regulatory agency's rule-making dockets. One would have thought that the continued use of adjustable restraints—rather than of seats with somewhat higher backs—occurred for reason of less cost. A recent report concluded that such was not the case. The adjustable head restraints cost more than the higher, integral seat back—an average $40 per car compared to an average $12 per car, a difference of $28 per car. The report also noted that integral restraints are 70 percent more effective but that 72 percent of vehicles manufactured from 1969 through 1981 had adjustable head restraints, thus adding substantially to the overall cost of the vehicles and causing a large reduction of realizable benefits.[11] While one might consider the automaker's behavior rational in terms of using the standard to increase profits in a time when car sales were good, their continuation of the practice in recent years, when inflation and interest rates have depleted sales and profits, as the public became more sensitive to price, seems nothing short of irrational.

Those standards that cannot be met without additional materials, such as the mentioned head restraints, obviously add cost to cars even if the manufacturers minimize costs. Many of the standards require only attention to injury-reducing performance of already extant parts, however; and, aside from costs of redesign that occur periodically irrespective of regulation, there may be no additional costs. Cost savings are even not out of the question. In the process of changing from rigid steel steering columns that speared drivers in the chest to energy-absorbing assemblies, cheaper materials could be used to decrease manufacturing costs and lighter materials to decrease fuel costs in operation.

One article characterized increased safety in cars as incompatible with increased fuel economy because of the increased weight of added materials that result in added fuel use as well as the inverse relationship between gross vehicle weight and crashworthiness. Its author argued that safety standards and fuel economy standards are conflicting objectives that result in excessive costs of vehicles.[12] That position is illustrative of common ignorance of physics and naive acceptance of manufacturer claims of costs and ways of doing business.

The Economics of Injury Control

As noted in chapter 2, weight is hostile to occupants of other vehicles and size, distributed properly, is protective of occupants in crashes. It is also, primarily, decreased weight rather than decreased size that improves fuel economy. Had the car manufacturers followed a socially responsible course, they would have maintained as much size of vehicles as necessary for crash protection while using lighter materials to achieve increased fuel economy. Instead, they spent huge amounts of capital "downsizing" for fuel economy but, in the process, reduced protective space needed in crashes without adding sufficiently compensating energy-absorbing materials.

The article went on to give a cost per life saved from the 1968 federal standards that could not be calculated from the estimates of costs of regulation and lives saved. The relationship of costs of emissions removal to proportion of emissions removed was stated in reverse of the actual relationship and two different amounts in the space of two paragraphs, differing by $80, were given for costs of automatically inflatable cushions that would meet a proposed federal standard.

Another inaccuracy was the 7,800 lives said to be saved in 1977 (see chapter 7 for evidence of more than 9,000 lives per year saved) at an estimate cost of $300 per car—totalling $889,000 expended for motor vehicle safety standards per life saved. Those numbers do not jibe. Cars were being junked after about ten years' use in the mid-1970s and replaced at about 10 percent of the fleet per year. Thus, a standard that would save 9,000 lives per year when fully implemented in the fleet would cost 9,000 lives for each year delayed because the vehicles would be in use about ten years. If about 10 percent of the fleet that was new each year at that time—some 11.7 million cars—had been equipped with items saving 7,900 lives and costing an extra $300, as the article claimed, the maximum cost per life saved for a model year cohort of vehicles would have been (11.7 million × 300) ÷ 7900, which is $444,300 per life saved exclusive of nonfatal injuries reduced in severity or prevented—less than half that claimed in the article.

As noted in the head restraint case, the extent of uncertainty in knowledge of actual incremental costs makes such estimates extremely tenuous. The author of the noted article correctly stated that "there is vast uncertainty in estimating the cost of each safety feature and the deaths, injuries, and property damage prevented by it,"[13] yet he estimated such costs to the penny in calculating benefit-cost ratios for each standard and miscalculated his overall conclusion.

If the 1968 motor vehicle safety standards cost $300 in 1977 and $400 in 1981, as has been claimed, those costs were not reflected in increased car prices when the regulations were introduced. The Bureau of Labor Statistics Producer Price Index for motor vehicles increased substantially less than other durable goods from 1964 before the regulations to 1973 when most were in place (table 8-1). In 1968 and 1969—the years of most of the equipment

Table 8-1
Motor Vehicle Price Index and Sales, 1964-1973

Year	Producer Price Index[a]			Passenger Car Sales[b] (U.S. plants) in Millions
	Motor Vehicles	All Durables	All Commodities	
1964	100.0	94.7	94.7	7.7
1965	99.6	95.9	96.6	9.3
1966	99.0	98.1	99.8	8.6
1967	100.0	100.0	100.0	7.4
1968	102.2	103.4	102.5	8.8
1969	103.7	107.8	106.5	8.2
1970	107.3	112.4	110.5	6.5
1971	113.2	116.9	114.0	8.6
1972	116.0	121.1	119.1	8.8
1973	116.7	127.9	134.7	9.7

Source: Motor vehicle sales reprinted with permission from *Motor Vehicle Facts and Figures '78* (Detroit: Motor Vehicle Manufacturers Association, 1978).
[a]Bureau of Labor Statistics, *Handbook of Labor Statistics* (Washington, DC: U.S. Department of Labor, 1980).
[b]*Motor Vehicle Facts and Figures* (Detroit: Motor Vehicle Manufacturers Association, 1976).

changes to comply with the regulations—the increase of car prices was about half that of other durable goods. During the decade from 1964 to 1973, producer prices for all durable goods rose 35 percent and producer prices for all commodities rose 42 percent—substantially more than the 17 percent increase in the price of cars. Passenger car sales by U.S. producers fluctuated during the period with the only major dips occurring in the 1967 and 1970 recessions. Sales reached their highest level in history in 1973, the year that the manufacturers chose to install the unpopular buzzer-light system rather than increase automatic crash protection.

It can be argued that car prices could have increased even less if there had been no regulations. This is true, but the attempt to specify the costs of regulation exactly enough to balance them against the reductions in injuries is a dubious exercise. Attempts to adjust changes in prices for changes in quality unrelated to injuries is a difficult exercise in itself.[14] People buy cars for all sorts of reasons besides transportation, including the use of price as a display of wealth.

A perhaps more realistic view of the cost of safety regulations was revealed in a survey of the manufacturers in which they were asked how much they would reduce car prices if safety standards were eliminated. The sales-weighted amount was $80 for 1978 models,[15] in contrast to the claimed $300 to $400 cost per car in the estimates quoted earlier.

Shareholders in the domestic auto companies during the period that the major safety regulations were adopted did well in some cases and less so in others. From 1964 to 1973, per share earnings increased 20 percent for

American Motors, 100 percent for Ford Motor Company, and 38 percent for General Motors, declining only at the ill-managed Chrysler Corporation by 12 percent.[16] The domestic industry generally has not fared as well in subsequent years due to the enormous increases in fuel costs and foreign competition, but safety regulation cannot be blamed for these problems. The foreign manufacturers have to meet exactly the same standards for cars they sell in the United States. There is good reason to believe that loss of market share to foreign manufacturers would have been even greater without the stimulus of fuel economy standards that forced the domestic manufacturers to improve fuel economy earlier than they would have done otherwise.

Both prices and profits are strongly influenced by management's ability to anticipate changes in markets and work forces. Those who organize their materials flow and workers to produce efficiently when demand is high and anticipate reduced demand to keep inventories from piling up will be able to keep prices lower and earn greater profits. Economies of scale reduce costs as volume increases.[17]

At least some of the differences in estimates of costs when new regulations are being debated can be attributed to differing assumptions about the mix of technologies to be employed and their resultant numbers. Estimates of the cost of automatic restraints—air bags that deploy in severe frontal crashes and automatic seat belts—have varied from less than $100 to more than $1,000 per car. While some of the higher price quotes are likely due to strategic pricing to scare politicians and the public, variation among manufactuers is a normal function of volume of different models. In 1981 dollars, air bags would cost about $185 per car if 2 million were produced but would increase in price as that number declined.[18] The manufacturer who intends to place them in 100,000 cars would charge substantially more because the unit price would be higher at the lower volume. If several small-volume models were designed to accommodate the same air bag components, however, the reduced costs that accompany economies of scale could be realized.

In public hearings regarding the standard to increase automatic protection, the manufacturers were found to be using an accounting variance that overstated the anticipated costs of compliance with the proposed standard. One secretary of transportation had the automakers' estimates audited and discovered that, in one case, research and development as well as tooling costs were being entirely included in the first-year estimated cost of the equipment to the customer, rather than spread over the life of the equipment and tools, as the industry does for other components. Other manufacturers had instead added unnecessary redesign costs that would make the standard more costly than it need be.[19]

In sum, costs of existent performance regulations are unknown and a prospective estimation of the cost of a regulatory standard cannot be precise.

If the government were to impose uniform and detailed design standards across entire industries, a relatively precise estimate based on design and materials costs at that economy of scale could be calculated. The government has usually chosen not to regulate in that fashion, however, to avoid freezing technology and efficiencies at prevalent levels. Most people who have given thought to the matter would prefer the uncertainty of eventual cost of a performance standard to the stifling of innovation that is likely to occur with detailed design standards. On the other hand, at least partly because of the uncertainty of estimated costs, the imposition of a standard can be, and in the case of increased automatic protection in cars has been, delayed for years as the debate over costs and benefits rages.

Benefits

In contrast to some social welfare programs where the goals are not always clear, much less their monetary value, the benefits in number of deaths and injuries of various types prevented in relation to injury-control programs can be estimated with some precision by those who understand the physical forces, technologies, and economics involved. For purposes of balancing these benefits against costs in cost-benefit analysis, however, it is necessary to express the value of life and limb in dollars. The monetary value of a life lost (or a less serious injury) is a subject of enormous disagreement. Those who enjoy their sophistry laced with differential and integral equations can consult some recent economic literature referenced in this section. Here, several of the issues will be mentioned in English.

Various economists and other analysts have entertained several notions of the value of life, such as discounted future earnings. Some have prefered discounted value of losses that occur to others if a person dies at a certain age. Others have rejected both of these concepts on several grounds. Some do not agree with the assumption that maximization of the gross national product is always a socially worthy goal.[20] Carried to its logical extreme, that assumption means no government aid to members of society who will not contribute economically to the gross national product or those about them because of age or infirmity. No cost-benefit theorist who uses the future earnings approach has carried the concept so far as to advocate complete withdrawal of aid to children with multiple congenital anomalies or to the unproductive aged; but the inconsistencies in the approach have led many to abandon it.

Most cost-benefit analysts prefer the notion that the economic value of life and limb should be based on the amount that people are willing to pay to preserve them. The concept is limited somewhat by the absence of the life and limb store where one can go and purchase a bunch of years of life or an arm, leg, and two eyes to go, as it were. There is no easily established market price. Also, in the face of certain death, many people would expend all their assets and whatever they could borrow, beg, or steal from others to remain alive. It would not be appropriate, the cost-benefit theorist argues, to consider willingness to pay when the event is relatively certain as an indication of willingness to pay to reduce less probable risks.

Some economists, among others, have attempted to calculate the value of life by various indications of "revealed preference" in expenditures for activities that reduce risk compared to other uses of resources. If one is willing to accept the premise that people have a ranked set of goals in their heads that guide their behaviors and that they make considered choices among these goals in most of their day-to-day behaviors, then one cannot help but be impressed by the resulting, sometimes ingenious derivation of theories of expected behaviors. An adequate theory of behavior must incorporate a much more complicated mix of intelligence, impulses, habits, a variety of psychophysiologic and sometimes psychopathic states of emotion, and social environments that do not provide an opportunity to understand the options.

This is not to say that the literature on revealed preferences is worthless. If nothing else, it may reveal the extent of inconsistency in human behavior and resultant variation in assumed value of life. In fact, economic value of a life, so calculated, ranges from less than $50,000 to more than $1 million.

The research has been ongoing for decades,[21] but here we need only concern ourselves with recent estimates and some of the accompanying assumptions. One of the most common methods of estimation is calculation of the relative amounts of money accepted in wages for occupations with different death rates. Using relatively hazardous occupations such as mining and flight testing of airplanes during development, one study found the value of life to a male worker aged thirty ranged from $34,000 for some miners to $161,000 for test pilots.[22] The researcher settled on $150,000 as a justifiable population average, although the occupations studied hardly represented the population.

Using a wider range of occupations and controlling for factors such as age, education, marital status, and race of workers as well as some indication of status rank of the jobs and regions of the country, other researchers estimated that workers were accepting risk premiums in wages equivalent to $176,000 per life around 1960, based on wages and death rates in their jobs.[23] One critic, in comments that accompanied the published paper, expressed surprise that the death rates revealed that "it is more risky to be an elevator operator than a marshal, constable, sheriff or bailiff, or that risk is twice as high for waiters as it is for police and detectives!" and wondered whether workers were aware of these differences when they chose their jobs.[24] Another commenter thought perhaps those who find risk stimulating may prefer certain jobs for that reason and questioned whether the controls for personal characteristics adequately accounted for the alleged preferences.[25]

A more ambitious effort to control for a variety of factors that might affect job selection as well as worker's perception of hazard led to a startlingly higher valuation of life. Using data from a survey of workers' views of their jobs and injury rates in those jobs, the researcher controlled for twenty-two variables including commonly measured demographic characteristics but also such factors as speed of work, whether the worker could make decisions on the job, overtime, job security, and availability of training programs. Death and injury rates for a job were modified by whether or not the worker perceived the job as hazardous. The relationship among variables in this analysis suggested that workers value their lives at $1 million to $1.5 million and an average injury at $13,000 to $14,000 in 1970 dollars.[26] If the analysis adequately controls for job characteristics and worker preferences, as it appears to do better than previously mentioned studies, then people trade actually perceived risk for income at a far more dear price than most cost-benefit analysts use as the value of life and limb when balancing them against costs.

Attempts at valuing lives by revealed preferences do not consider the possibility that human beings handle risk in other than a rational fashion based on perfect information. The irony of the assumptions of omniscience and rational decision making by the average worker, driver, or consumer is that those who make the assumptions themselves have difficulty in assembling reliable and valid information. Yet their analyses infer that the general public has such knowledge.

One study used seat belt-wearing rates, the time that is required to use belts, and estimates of belt effectiveness along with wage and other data to infer the value that people place on their lives as indicated by their belt-use behavior. The effect of belt use on fatality reduction was assumed to be 50 percent based on studies showing effects ranging from 40 to 60 percent.[27] Had the researcher looked further, he would have found estimates ranging from 7 percent to 85 percent.[28] The estimate of 50 percent effectiveness is not unreasonable for a scientist who understands the factors that bias such estimates upward and downward (see chapter 1). It stretches the imagination, however, to believe that the public has arrived at a consensus on the effectiveness of seat belts that is precise enough to infer the economic value that they place on their lives based on their belt-wearing rates. Another anomaly in the logic of the research is that no account is taken of the fact that people cannot be assumed to be consistently either belt wearers or nonwearers. A few people consistently use belts on each trip but others use them periodically. Does this mean that they value their lives more on one trip than another? Nevertheless, the researcher claimed that the belt-use data suggested a value of life of $370,000.

The Economics of Injury Control

In addition to simple lack of information about risks, people do not necessarily behave rationally when risks are known. Scientists who actually observe behavior rather than infer it from aggregated statistics have described one of the reactions to perception of increased risk as denial. Numerous studies have documented the phenomenon as a factor in delay in seeking medical care when people have symptoms that suggest cancer.[29] Where the cancers are curable when detected early, the denial and delay contribute to the risk of death. It is conceivable that such a phenomenon contributes to other behaviors that increase risk, such as nonuse of seat belts. The very act of using the belt may be an admission of risk with which many individuals cannot cope.

Evidence that individuals deny their vulnerability in driving was found in a national random-sample survey of new car buyers that attempted to determine whether willingness to pay for reduced risk is related to perception of risk. In the telephone survey, only those people who expressed the expectation that they would buy a new car within the next three years were interviewed. These persons were asked whether their risk of being killed or injured in the next year was "greater than people like youself, the same as people like yourself, or less than people like yourself." Only 6 percent considered their risk greater than others, compared to 40 percent who answered less than others.

The interviewer went on to ask how much the respondent would be willing to add to new car payments per month to reduce crash deaths by 6,000, 12,000, and 18,000 deaths per year. The answers averaged $12 for 6,000 lives, $17 for 12,000 lives, and $20 for 18,000 lives. And, interestingly enough, the average dollar amounts were not significantly correlated to perceived personal risk. Those who claimed that they were less vulnerable than others were willing to pay just as much, on average, as those who considered themselves more vulnerable than others.[30]

We do not know if those who claim to be less vulnerable are more or less likely to use seat belts. If there is a correlation because of denial rather than a realistic valuation of life versus the inconvenience of belt use, the actual value that they place on their lives or, more importantly, the amount they would be willing to pay to reduce risk in general would be inaccurately inferred from their belt use.

Whether the amounts gleaned by asking people what they are willing to pay yield accurate estimates of what they would actually pay is not known. The respondents could inflate the amount to appear charitable or reduce it to influence future car prices. People faced with an unexpected question of that sort, though, probably would not be quick enough to give such strategic answers. The average amounts per monthly car payment noted in the survey, summed over thirty-six payments, come to $432 per car to save 6,000 lives, $612 to save 12,000 lives, and $720 to save 18,000 lives. Since these amounts are far greater than the cost of accomplishing these goals with available technology, it is doubtful that they are so inflated as to significantly reduce car sales were the technology adopted.

That technology has been demonstrated in research safety vehicles that would probably save 18,000 or more lives per year and cost no more than currently priced compacts in mass production.[31] Manufacturers could have put that technology in production at least by 1980 but none chose to do so, despite the fact that major design and retooling was being done during that period in the industry.

Cost-Benefit Analysis and Public Policy

The substantial range in cost estimates and the enormous range in estimated benefits of reducing injury and death suggest that cost-benefit analysis is of dubious value in public-policy decisions regarding injuries. Faced with two- or threefold differences in estimated costs and twenty- to thirty-fold differences in estimated benefits, those making decisions can choose whatever values they like to make costs exceed benefits or vice versa. Only where the costs are trivial or nonexistent do the lowest estimates of benefits exceed the costs, and the highest estimates of benefits would justify almost any program or regulation that promised to reduce injuries. One apparent exception to the latter statement is the ejection seats in fighter airplanes that were purported to cost $4.5 million in 1970 dollars per life saved.[32] Nevertheless, military procurement officers have not seen fit to exclude such protection from fighter aircraft.

In recent years administrators of injury-control programs and regulations have not been oblivious of the pressure for cost-benefit analysis or some other more systematic means of setting priorities. It is difficult, however, to find a case in which a decision to proceed with or drop a particular effort was based primarily on the weighing of costs and benefits. The usual use of cost-benefit analysis in government is to delay decisions or juggle the monetary values on each side of the equation to justify decisions already made on the basis of nonquantifiable values or pork barrel and other political considerations.

The Consumer Product Safety Commission has a bureau of economic analysis that does cost-benefit analysis of ways to decrease the kinds of hazards that show up in their hospital emergency-room surveillance system. The commission has been scolded for ranking products for development of regulatory standards in an order that is substantially different from the ranking of the bureau's benefit-cost ratios.[33] Television receivers and extension cords, for example, have higher priority rank than chain saws but have a lower benefit-cost ratio. Without defending all of the inconsistencies, two points are rather obvious. First, the commission has adopted a policy of giving priority to hazards to children. Second, a lot more people are exposed to television sets and extension cords than are exposed to chain saws.

A benefit-cost ratio does not indicate the magnitude of the benefits and, for that reason, many who advocate use of cost-benefit analysis for decision making prefer the magnitude of benefits minus costs as more relevant than the ratio of benefits to costs. Also, some advocate greater emphasis on hazards to portions of the population for whom exposure is totally involuntary, such as children. In the case of ejection seats for fighter pilots, who not only volunteer but compete for scarce positions, the cost of protection is perhaps justified by the unique value of the people involved or, more likely, the anticipation of political uproar if the protection were not provided.

Closely related to cost-benefit analysis is risk-benefit analysis by which some analysts have attempted to answer the question "How safe is safe enough?" By comparison of risks among various activities and products, the acceptability of the risk is inferred. This approach suffers from the same problems with knowledge of risks on the part of product users as noted previously, as well as of the extent to which acceptance of risk can be assumed to be voluntary where it is known. A risk that is acceptable to knowledgeable members of society at one time may not be so when conditions change, and besides, differences among societies and groups within societies are common.[34]

One study assumed that in the context of the United States, people must of necessity drive motor vehicles but fly in private planes as a matter of choice. (Corporation executives who are ordered to accompany the boss to a meeting in the corporate jet could quibble on that point.) The study contained statements like "automobile and airplane safety have been continuously weighed by society against economic costs and operating performance."[35] How did "society" perform this balancing act? As noted in chapter 7, the airplane was regulated almost from the start, but the automobile was not subject to regulation until three years before that statement was published. These societal approaches were largely idiosyncratic to the history of the vehicles involved. While the formalized attempt to understand the relative merits of various forms of transportation for economic development has a substantial history,[36] its actual effects on transportation policy are doubtful. Health and safety have often been ignored. A recent attempt at analysis of various forms of urban transportation modes,[37] for example, did not give any data on the enormously different fatality rates for passenger cars, buses, or rapid-rail transit (chapter 2). It also neglected other health issues such as the effect of auto emissions on accumulation of lead in children's tissues that is correlated with deterioration of intellectual performance[38] and the correlation of concentrations of motor vehicles in cities and cancer mortality rates, controlling for other environmental sources of carcinogens.[39,40]

The attempt to establish an acceptable level of risk, based on prevalent levels in areas such as transportation, is directed toward defining the limit of expensive, redundant, and "failsafe" systems necessary in the development of newer technologies such as nuclear power generation. The previously mentioned risk-benefit analysis attempted to show that there is a level of risk, consistent across technologies, that is acceptable relative to the economic benefits realized from the technologies. The choice of dollar benefits of a given technology, however, were arbitrary and inconsistent. The time saved in auto travel was valued at $5 per hour but the time saved in air travel was valued at $10 per hour. The major distinction in the risks was whether they were experienced voluntarily or involuntarily, the former resulting in supposedly higher levels of acceptability.[41]

But the issue of the probability of a nuclear power plant catastrophe is far more complicated than either the extent to which the risk is involuntary or the economic benefit to society of the plant. The concentration of fatalities in space and time is one obvious factor in society's tolerance of injuries. Even if there were no potential for genetic damage, a nuclear plant catastrophe that kills several hundreds or thousands of people in a single incident would almost certainly result in a prolonged shutdown of all similarly constructed plants and conceivably all nuclear plants, perhaps permanently. Society, as represented by its government, may tolerate hundreds of motor vehicle deaths per day spread out in time and space or a hundred or so deaths very occasionally in an air crash, but all indications suggest that a nuclear catastrophe is not acceptable.[42]

Some automobile industry executives have implied that motor vehicle deaths are acceptable with the slogan "safety doesn't sell." Since there has never been a sustained attempt to market crash protection in a manner anywhere comparable to the selling of jackrabbit starts and high speeds that increase crash incidence and severity, the notion has not had a reasonable test. Mostly in response to criticism by physicians, the automakers as far back as the 1930s removed some protruding knobs and other energy-concentrating points and edges in vehicle interiors and increased crash padding for a short time. The advertising of these features, however, was not systematic or long-lived. A couple of companies with small shares of the market emphasized safety but did not survive in competition with the style and horsepower emphasis that dominated in the industry.[43]

In 1956, Ford Motor Company's cars were not doing well in competition with General Motors, so the advertising of the 1956 Fords was reoriented to emphasize safety. Among the items mentioned were lap seat belts and crash padding, which then were not standard equipment but could be ordered as options. As demand outstripped supply, Ford sold 160,000 cars with factory-installed belts and 200,000 as added equipment.[44] About 43 percent of the cars were ordered with crash padding as a result of the

The Economics of Injury Control

advertising,[45] no doubt at a profit; but the advertising effort was not continued in subsequent years.

The private marketing studies of auto manufacturers or producers of other hazardous products over the years have not been made public, so we do not know to what extent they have attempted to find out the salability of features that would reduce risk. One exception was a 1971 General Motors study of consumer reaction to seat belts that automatically wrap around the outboard front-seat occupants when they close the doors and air bags that inflate in frontal crashes above a certain severity. A California Congressman obtained a copy of the study in 1979 and demanded that GM release other marketing studies of automatic crash protection in the 1970s; several were forthcoming.[46] All revealed substantial consumer demand for automatic crash protection, particularly the air bag, and willingness to pay the extra cost.

In the 1971 study, new car buyers were shown automatic belts and air bags in cars and films of belts and air bags in crash tests. During the course of the presentations, favorable and adverse publicity about air bags was also presented. The executive summary of the study includes the following statements: *"Consumers are overwhelmingly in favor of some kind of occupant restraint system* . . . , [are] not scared of the Air Cushion concept and that *the Air Cushion Restraint concept is a viable one* to the consumers. . . . After seeing prices quoted, which were higher than those which respondents expected, and had a slight dampening effect—the Air Cushion still maintained half of all preference votes."[47] (Emphasis is in original.)

Spokespersons for General Motors downplayed the study to the press with the comment that people do not always do what they say they would do in a survey. That statement ignores the obvious fact that even if the demand for air bags were half what the survey indicated, GM alone could have sold millions annually and reduced deaths by thousands and injuries by tens of thousands at a profit to the company and at low cost to the consumer because of economies of scale.

The president of GM in the early 1970s promised air bags on all GM cars by 1975. Apparently, he believed the marketing research. Some 750 air bags were sold to corporate fleets in 1972 Mercurys from Ford and 1,000 air bag-equipped 1973 Chevrolets were sold by GM. General Motors offered air bags as an option to the public on the most expensive Cadillacs, Buicks, and Oldsmobiles in 1974 with little advertising or other marketing effort. A *Wall Street Journal* reporter who attempted to buy one of the air bag-equipped cars reported that he and other consumers suffered discouragement from dealers and delays in delivery.[48] About 10,000 cars with air bags were sold despite the lack of marketing by the company.

The fact is that the auto companies know that safety will sell but for reasons or irrationalities that have not been revealed publicly, they seldom attempt to sell it. Indeed, the argument that safety does not sell is an argument of market failure that is the major reason economists give as justification for regulation. Auto executives occasionally have acknowledged that regulation is necessary to prevent competitive disadvantages in prices for those who would introduce safety features with some risk that there would be no consumer demand. Yet the auto companies opposed the Motor Vehicle Safety Act of 1966 and opposed virtually every proposed regulation in the fifteen years after the initial standards.

It should also be noted that the claim that marketing research does not reveal what the public will buy is inconsistent both with the continued conduct of such research and the claim by the companies that they are selling to consumers what consumers want. While such studies are certainly not perfect predictors of the market, their repeated use suggests that they have been found useful for predicting demand.

It is known that some items are marketed whether or not there is demand. One such strategy is the so-called mandatory option in which most, if not all, of the cars of an otherwise popular model sent to dealers will be loaded with an extra such as a vinyl roof, which has an additional cost similar to that of an air bag. Unfortunately for the health of the consumers and the profits of shareholders, the concept does not seem to have been extended to safety features.

In 1982 General Motors placed full-page advertising in newspapers indicating that several of its cars ranked high in relative crashworthiness as shown by insurance company data compiled by the Highway Loss Data Institute. With respect to the "safety doesn't sell" cliche, a company vice president was quoted in a press release, "I doubt the statement was ever true, but it's surely not true today."[49]

One explanation sometimes given for past recalcitrance in designing safer products is that manufacturers fear greater numbers of lawsuits and liability awards if the public's expectations of reduced hazards are aroused. In many cases this argument is demonstrably false because the reductions in deaths and injury that now generate such liability suits would be greatly reduced. In the case of the air bag, insurers knowledgeable in its effectiveness offered a 30 percent reduction in first-party injury coverage to consumers with air bag-equipped cars, and liability coverage to manufacturers at no greater cost than prior coverage. Depending on the price charged for the air bags, the cost to the consumer would be substantially or totally offset over the life of the car by savings in insurance costs.[50]

An interesting issue of liability in relation to cost-benefit analysis was raised in the cases of Ford Pinto gas tanks easily penetrated in rear-end collisions, thus causing fuel leakage and fires. The Pinto was not the only vehicle with fuel leakage in rear-end collisions. In crash tests, the Pinto was but one of six 1973 models from different manufacturers in which the fuel tank ruptured when the car was parked and struck in the rear by another car at less than forty miles per hour. Fuel spilled in all six cars tested and in one a spontaneous fire engulfed the passenger compartment.[51,52]

The notorious reputation of the Pinto was magnified by the revelation that Ford Motor Company knew of the Pinto's propensity to fires, had an $11 device to reduce the problem, but had not adopted it because of an internal cost-benefit analysis that indicated that the costs would exceed the benefits. Specifically, the benefits of prevention of a projected 180 burn deaths, 180 serious burn injuries, and 2,100 burned vehicles were assessed at $49.5 million, while the cost of a $11 modification to 12.5 million vehicles was $137 million. Ford used $200,000 as the value of life in this analysis.[53]

While Ford did withdraw ads that said the Pinto "leaves you with that warm feeling" as the reports of burned people and the awards in lawsuits mounted, the company delayed recall of the vehicle for seven years. In one case, a person burned in a Pinto fire was awarded more than $128 million by the jury, an amount that was later reduced to $6 million.[54]

In addition to the civil liability costs that Ford had not factored into its cost-benefit analysis, the company was indicted by a grand jury in Indiana on three counts of reckless homicide following the fiery deaths of three teenage girls in a Pinto that burst into flames after being struck in the rear. Indeed, "a calculation of the costs of reducing the number of injuries and deaths became evidence of the willfulness and intentionality of the corporate action"[55] in the grand jury indictment. The company was acquitted of the criminal charges after a costly trial. Whether this case has had an effect on the use of cost-benefit analysis in making decisions regarding protection of the public or workers from health hazards would be an interesting topic for research.

The highest court in the land has also addressed the use of cost-benefit analysis. The Supreme Court has ruled that "cost-benefit analysis by OSHA is not required by the statute because feasibility is."[56] In the case in question proprietors of cotton mills had resisted a standard by OSHA limiting the amount of cotton dust in the plants on the basis that the costs would exceed the benefits. Whether that estimation is actually valid would depend on many of the assumptions about value of life that were discussed previously. The Court ruled that protection of the worker's health and safety "to the extent feasible," the wording of the OSH act, was not to be construed as inapplicable because someone's estimate of benefits exceeded their estimate of costs.

Conclusion

Few persons would argue that in the consideration of injury-control options no attention should be given costs. The choice between two strategies that would cost approximately the same but would have substantially different impacts is easy, as is the choice between efforts that have widely different costs but a similar result. The world is usually not quite that simple. To the extent that costs per life saved or injury severity reduced can be calculated and compared across a variety of strategies, usually called cost-effectiveness rather than cost-benefit analysis, few people would theoretically object to allocation of available resources to the efforts that would have the most impact. In practice, however, the range of options suggested by the analysis in chapter 4 is seldom, if ever, considered. Choices based on cost-effectiveness can also result in money being taken away from an established program for a new or different effort. When that occurs, the principle of the allocation of resources on efficiency grounds often slips on the banana peel of politics, a subject to be approached with appropriate trepidation in the final chapter.

References

1. C.F. Adams, *Notes on Railroad Accidents* (New York: G.P. Putnam's Sons, 1879).
2. M.V. Nadel, *The Politics of Consumer Protection* (Indianapolis, IN: Bobbs-Merrill, 1971).
3. L.G. Anderson and R.F. Settle, *Benefit-Cost Analysis: A Practical Guide* (Lexington, MA: Lexington Books, 1977).
4. E.J. Mishan, *Introduction to Normative Economics* (New York: Oxford University Press, 1981).
5. P. Self, *Econocrats and the Policy Process: The Politics and Philosophy of Cost-Benefit Analysis* (Boulder, CO: Westview Press, 1975).
6. E.M. Trisko and E.W. Shomo, "A Study in Fire Department Cost Allocation," *Governmental Finance* 3(1974):24-28, 33-36.
7. Self, *Econocrats and the Policy Process*, pp. 69-70.
8. "Auto Safety Costs $3 Billion a Year, Manufacturers Report to Safety Agency," *Product Safety and Liability Reporter*, October 8(1982):674.
9. B. O'Neill and A.B. Kelley, "Costs, Benefits, Effectiveness and Safety: Setting the Record Straight," *Professional Safety* 20(1975):28.
10. B. O'Neill, et al., "Automobile Head Restraints: Frequency of Neck Injury Claims in Relation to the Presence of Head Restraints," *American Journal of Public Health* 62(1972):399.
11. C.J. Kahane, *An Evaluation of Head Restraints: Federal Motor Vehicle Safety Standard 202* (Washington, DC: National Highway Traffic Safety Administration, 1982).
12. L.B. Lave, "Conflicting Objectives in Regulating the Automobile," *Science* 202(1981):893.

13. Lave, "Conflicting Objectives in Regulating the Automobile," p.894.

14. Z. Griliches, "Hedonic Price Indexes for Automobiles: An Econometric Analysis of Quality Change," In: Z. Griliches, ed., *Price Index and Quality Change: Studies in New Methods of Measurement* (Cambridge, MA: Harvard University Press, 1971).

15. *The Contributions of Automobile Regulation* (Washington, DC: National Highway Traffic Safety Administration, 1978).

16. *The Value Line Investment Survey* (New York: Arnold Bernhard and Co., 1981).

17. D.L. Bodde, "Riding the Experience Curve," *Technology Review* 78(1976):53.

18. "AOPA Discloses Air Bag Cost Figures," *The Highway Loss Reduction Status Report* 16(June 10, 1981):2.

19. *The Secretary's Decision Concerning Motor Vehicle Occupant Protection* (Washington, DC: U.S. Department of Transportation, 1976).

20. E.J. Mishan, *Cost-Benefit Analysis* (New York: Praeger, 1976).

21. M.W. Jones-Lee, *The Value of Life: An Economic Analysis* (Chicago: University of Chicago Press, 1976).

22. D. Usher, "An Imputation to the Measure of Economic Growth for Changes in Life Expectancy." In: M. Moss, ed., *The Measurement of Economic and Social Performance* (New York: National Bureau of Economic Research, 1973).

23. R. Thaler and S. Rosen, "The Value of Saving a Life: Evidence from the Labor Market." In: N. Terleckyz, ed., *Household Production and Consumption* (New York: Columbia University Press, 1976).

24. M. Kosters, "Comments on 'The Value of Saving a Life: Evidence from the Labor Market.'" In: N. Terleckyz, ed., *Household Production and Consumption*. (New York: Columbia University Press, 1976).

25. R.E. Lipsey, "Comments on 'The Value of Saving a Life: Evidence from the Labor Market.'" In: N. Terleckyz, ed., *Household Production and Consumption*. (New York: Columbia University Press, 1976).

26. W.K. Viscusi, "Labor Market Valuations of Life and Limb: Empirical Evidence and Policy Implications." *Public Policy* 26(1978):359.

27. G. Blomquist, "Value of Life Saving: Implications of Consumption Activity." *Journal of Political Economy* 87(1979):540.

28. L.S. Robertson, "Estimates of Motor Vehicle Seat Belt Effectiveness and Use: Implications for Occupant Crash Protection." *American Journal of Public Health* 66(1976):859.

29. Summarized in L.S. Robertson and M.C. Heagarty, *Medical Sociology: A General Systems Approach* (Chicago: Nelson-Hall, 1975).

30. L.S. Robertson, "Car Crashes: Perceived Vulnerability and Willingness to Pay for Crash Protection," *Journal of Community Health* 3(1977):136.

31. N. DiNapoli, et al., *Research Safety Vehicle Phase II, Volume II; Comprehensive Technical Results* (Springfield, VA: National Technical Information Service, 1977).

32. Usher, "An Imputation to the Measure of Economic Growth for Changes in Life Expectancy."

33. H.G. Grabowski and J.H. Vernon, "Consumer Product Safety Regulation," *American Economic Review* 68(1978):284.

34. B. Fischhoff, et al., *Acceptable Risk* (Cambridge: Cambridge University Press, 1982).

35. C. Starr, "Social Benefit Versus Technological Risk: What Is Our Society Willing to Pay for Safety," *Science* 165(1969):1232.

36. H.A. Levine, *National Transportation Policy: A Study of Studies* (Lexington, MA: Lexington Books, 1978).

37. J.R. Meyer and J.A. Gomez-Ibanez, *Autos, Transit and Cities* (Cambridge, MA: Harvard University Press, 1981).

38. H.L. Needleman, et al., "Deficits in Psychologic and Classroom Performance of Children With Elevated Dentine Lead Levels," *New England Journal of Medicine* 300(1979):689.

39. J.A. Campbell, "The Effects of Road Dust 'Freed' from Tar Products Upon the Incidence of Primary Lung-Tumours of Mice," *British Journal of Experimental Pathology* 18(1937):215.

40. L.S. Robertson, "Environmental Correlates of Intercity Variation in Age-Adjusted Cancer Mortality Rates," *Environmental Health Perspectives* 30(1980):197.

41. Starr, "Social Benefits Versus Technological Risk," p. 1238.

42. D. Ford, *The Cult of the Atom: The Secret Papers of the Atomic Energy Commission* (New York: Simon and Schuster, 1982).

43. J.W. Eastman, " 'Doctors' Orders,' The American Medical Profession and the Origins of Automobile Design for Crash Protection, 1930-1955," *Bulletin of the History of Medicine* 55(1981):407.

44. Statement of Alex L. Haynes of Ford Motor Company. In: *Automobile Seat Belts, Hearings Before a Subcommittee of the Committee on Interstate and Foreign Commerce, U.S. House of Representatives* (Washington: U.S. Government Printing Office, 1957).

45. "IIHS Research Chief Tells NAII: Safety Will Sell," *Insurance Institute for Highway Safety Status Report* 17(May 24, 1982):4.

46. "Congressman Charges Air Bag Data 'Suppressed,' " *Insurance Institute for Highway Safety Status Report* 14(December 21, 1979):1.

47. Advertising and Marketing Section, *Consumer Opinions Relative to Automotive Restraint Systems Report* #71-27P (Detroit: General Motors Corporation, 1971).

48. A.R. Karr, "Saga of the Air Bag, or the Slow Deflation of a Car-Safety Idea," *Wall Street Journal*, November 11, 1976, p. 1.

49. Press release from General Motors Corporation, June 7, 1982.

50. K.E. Warner, *Mandatory Passive Restraint Systems in Automobiles: Issues and Evidence* (Washington, DC: Congress of the United States, Office of Technology Assessment, 1982).

51. A.B. Kelley, *Cars That Crash and Burn* (film) (Washington, DC: Insurance Institute for Highway Safety, 1973).

52. Statement of W. Haddon, Jr., before the Committee on Interstate and Foreign Commerce Subcommittee on Commerce and Finance, *Amendments to the National Traffic and Motor Vehicle Safety Act of 1966*, (Washington, DC: U.S. House of Representatives Committee Print, May 29, 1973).

53. M. Dowie, "Pinto Madness," *Mother Jones* (September/October, 1977).

54. J. Perlman, "Pinto Trial: Complex Plan Spelled Success," *Los Angeles Times* (September 17, 1978):Section X, p. 1.

55. V.L. Swigart and R.A. Farrell, "Corporate Homicide: Definitional Processes in the Creation of Deviance," *Law and Society Review* 15(1980-81):161.

56. "Excerpt from Court Decision on Health Standards," *New York Times* (June 18, 1981):B8.

9 Values, Politics, and the Future of Injury Control

If the merit of recent economic analysis for increasing efficiency and efficacy in policy choices regarding injuries is questionable, its importance in setting the agenda for public decisions is even more so. The social forces that contribute to the initiation of injury-control policies in private organizations and government action or inaction are based on an uncertain mix of people's value systems, beliefs, and organizational cultures; the traditional roles of government that evolved in the society's history; and the ability of interested parties at any given juncture to direct the attention of government leadership and the courts toward or away from a specific problem.[1]

Blatant inconsistencies within value systems, if systems is the proper word, are evident in retrospect. Democracy in ancient Greece flourished among people who owned slaves. As a nation of supposedly free people, the United States has been free of slavery for only little more than half of its existence; and women did not gain the right to vote until the twentieth century. The relatively free exchange of goods and services in market economies lagged behind the development of political freedoms in the form of representative democracies by centuries.[2] Despite the apparent high value placed on health, with 10 percent of the economy devoted to medical care and the proportion growing, the proper role of government in protecting health is not a settled issue.

The most extreme libertarians argue that the appropriate role of government is to do little more than control the money supply, enforce criminal laws and contractual agreements among individuals and corporations, and conduct international affairs, which includes maintenance of a defense force. The most extreme socialists argue that the earth's resources should be shared on a more or less equal basis and that this goal can only be accomplished by government ownership and allocation. The mixture of private and public responsibilities in the economies of the United States and other Western-style democracies represent rejections of these extremes based at least in part on the inhumanity and dreariness that has prevailed historically in societies that have approached either of them. The country has moved only slightly back and forth between these philosophies, the small vacillation being dependent on the general state of the economy, the attractiveness of political candidates who advocate particular viewpoints, and the beliefs about successes or failures of a given philosophy in attempts at application to problems of recent memory. U.S. government tends to be moderate and pragmatic, looking for solutions to problems within constitutional limits as they are brought to the public agenda.

Some political analysts have suggested that public-policy decisions be considered a market.[3] In analysis of a legislature with the "horse-trading" of votes among issues of varying importance to specific legislators, the tools of market analysis may be useful; but as an indicator of voter choice, the concept is questionable. The voter must vote a candidate up or down and cannot give him points on issues A, B, and C equivalent to relative numbers of dollars spent on commodities.[4] Decision by referendum is an alternative pursued to some extent in certain state governments; but the rules for placing an issue on the ballot, the wording of the proposition, and the lack of general expertise among the electorate on technical issues make the use of referendum on technical issues problematic and on national issues presently impossible.

Because many injury-control programs and policies require expertise, governmental efforts have been assigned to agencies with more or less specific guidance from the legislature as to the direction and limits of the efforts. Oversight hearings involving the agency officials as well as other knowledgeable and/or interested parties, budgetary allocations and limitations, and additional legislation to promote or limit a given agency's actions are the legislative means of influencing agency behavior. Appeal to the courts by interested groups not satisfied with particular private or regulatory decisions is not uncommon. Enormous inconsistencies in public policy nevertheless persist.

Values and Beliefs

In the state of Connecticut, drivers obtaining or renewing licenses are given the opportunity to designate on the license that they wish to be an organ donor in the event of death. Those licensees younger than eighteen years old, however, are denied the privilege of making this ultimate contribution to fellow human beings. It does not seem to have occurred to the state legislators that anyone who is not old enough to make a judgment regarding the disposition of his or her body is not old enough to make judgments about the operation of a vehicle that is by far the most common source of death in that age group. In fact, states commonly license drivers younger than eighteen but deny them trivial privileges, such as the use of pinball machines in Tennessee.

Another law in Connecticut requires that children riding in cars be secured in a restraint that meets federal standards if they are less than one year old. One to four year olds must be in such a restraint except when riding in the back seat with a seat belt fastened.[5] The legislature seems to

Values, Politics, and the Future

have decided that a two year old is more valuable than a six year old. Actually, the law is a slightly modified copy of a law enacted in almost half the states by 1982, following the lead of the first such legislation in Tennessee, which also placed a four-year-old upper limit on the requirement.[6] Those who place high value on children's lives can only admire the pediatricians, among other interested groups, who lobbied successfully for the legislation in the face of legislative inertia. But the willy-nilly adoption of legislation based on precedent rather than a careful consideration of the value implications is less admirable. It appears that our elected representatives charged with molding public policy through deliberative bodies are often no more consistent in their values, or "utilities" if one is a utilitarian theorist, than individuals in their day-to-day behaviors.

In other cases, treasured beliefs about questions that can be factually determined are not easily modified, even if the facts do not support the beliefs. The belief that education is inherently good leads to the maintenance of demonstrably harmful programs such as drug and driver education in the public schools (chapter 5). When the public schools are given the task of solving too many of society's problems, they solve few of them well and compound the ones we have by graduating students who have not mastered even the fundamental tasks of reading, writing, and arithmetic, not to mention biology, chemistry, and physics.

Drug education may have actually fed on itself. Use of drugs among isolated groups resulted in drug-education programs that apparently have spread the problem, creating the perceived need for more drug-education programs. The increase in homicides, suicides, and motor vehicle fatalities per capita among the young in the 1960s and 1970s is perhaps partly attributable to alcohol and other drug use inadvertently promoted by education programs intended to reduce use. Other factors undoubtedly contributed to the problem and more evidence on the role of education is needed, but the spread of drug-education programs on the basis of the evidence available cannot be justified.

High-school driver education greatly increases early licensure of teenage drivers. When the self-selection bias is removed, the high-school youngsters drive no better than teenagers who learn by other means; and the number of prople killed by teenage drivers, two other road users for every teenage driver who dies,[7] is augmented by the increased licensure. This evidence has been available to legislatures and school boards for years, but no states and only a few school boards have taken action to reduce the harm that their predecessors unintentionally caused.

Lobbyists use statements from seemingly neutral organizations to support the program. However, at least some of these organizations fund their activities through—and in some cases profit from the sale of materials for—driver education courses; they are thus less than neutral observers. Education is so sacrosanct in the public's beliefs and teachers' organizations, protecting their jobs, are so successful in lobbying that these harmful programs remain firmly ingrained in the political woodwork. Consideration of the combination of high costs and harm rather than of benefits, much less a sense of the immorality of taking the taxpayers' money for programs that increase the taxpayers' risk, has hardly penetrated the political system. Whether someone harmed by these programs will appeal to the courts, as is common when executive or legislative bodies fail to confront problems, and will do so successfully is a matter of speculation at this point. In many jurisdictions, so-called sovereign immunity statutes protect public officials from lawsuits, but higher courts have occasionally found such statutes a violation of individual rights.

Both the law and widely held beliefs about injuries are bound up in the Gordian knots of the concepts of fault and intent. If a drunk teenager shoots a neighbor, is his drug-education teacher to blame? If he runs over his neighbor in the street with a car, is his driver-education teacher at fault? On the basis of intent, certainly not. But at what point in the accumulation of evidence that the drug- or driver-education programs increase the number of such incidents do we expect the teachers, school board members, and legislators to accept the facts—and with them the responsibility and perhaps a penalty for continued harm if they take no action?

Freedom

Among the value issues that are frequently explicit or implicit in debates regarding public policies for injury control is the question of the extent to which a given policy affects freedom of choice. While few would question the prohibition of the freedom to injure with intent, in cases where injury results from various types of negligence, the issues become muddy. If an infant is strangled to death when its throat is caught by crib slats that are wide enough apart for the child to place its body but not its head between them, is the parent or the manufacturer negligent? The parent who left the infant alone for an hour to go to a bar for a few drinks would probably be accused, but the attentive parent whose back was turned preparing dinner surely would not. The more difficult question is whether the parent should have thought of the possibility when purchasing the crib and found one with narrow slats. Since the hazard of widely spaced crib slats is not common knowledge, most observers would not blame a parent on such grounds.

The manufacturer of the crib might be judged guilty of negligence in a lawsuit. In states with strict liability laws, manufacturers who do not employ state-of-the-art design for safety of their products are liable for the harm that would have been prevented by such design.

The issue of freedom of choice arises when a government body proclaims that children are strangled by cribs when slats are spaced beyond a certain limit and that manufacturers will no longer be allowed to sell cribs with widely spaced slats. The manufacturer's freedom of choice to design the crib in certain ways has been curtailed and its price is conceivably increased by the use of extra materials. Furthermore, the variety of cribs available to parents has been narrowed both in terms of design and price. Loss of freedom to pay less is the only issue in the case of the parents because the removal of an option that the vast majority would not have chosen if they had sufficient knowledge is not usually considered loss of freedom.[8] Vast amounts of guilt and recrimination as well as the loss of children can be avoided by prohibiting the offending cribs.

Extreme libertarians would argue that, at most, the proper role of government is to inform the parents of the risk and therefore preserve the maximum freedom of choice. More practical people understand that no such information program could reach all prospective parents and that an effort to do so on a continuous basis as new families are formed would cost more than the increased price to modify the cribs. The loss of freedom by manufacturers and parents is trivial when balanced against the freedom that will be enjoyed by the children who escape death or brain damage from insufficient oxygen.

Only a few radicals would quarrel with the latter argument when adults are making choices that affect the lives of children. The number of dissenters increases as the person making the choice is the person who suffers any adverse consequences. Some of these outcries are based on false assumptions about who is making choices for whom. Much of the debate regarding motor-vehicle safety standards, for example, reads as though the only person who will ever use the vehicle is the original purchaser. This is not true: vehicle occupants who die in crashes include not only children but many adults who were not party to the choice of original equipment, such as persons who drive company-owned vehicles as part of their jobs.

A study of the age of occupants injured, ownership of vehicles, and relation of the injured persons to the owners of the vehicles in which injuries occurred estimated that 75 to 80 percent of the persons injured did not have a say in the purchase of the vehicle and its equipment.[9] The manufacturers and the original purchasers are making choices, whether informed or uniformed, that will determine the degree of risk to all future users including many who have no choice in the vehicle's use or protective characteristics. Certainly pedestrians and other individuals struck by motor vehicles have no choice in the designs of the vehicles' front ends and their energy-absorbing capability.

The clearest cases of freedom to choose risk being abridged by public policy are the laws in numerous countries, including relatively libertarian democracies, that require adult use of seat belts in cars and trucks, the use of motorcycle helmets, and the use of various types of protective equipment by workers in industry. The seat belt case is not one of pure self-protection because the movement and weight of unbelted occupants can increase the severity of injuries to other occupants in crashes, belted or not. The author recalls one crash investigation that reported that the weight of the unbelted rear-seat occupant, multiplied by the crash forces in the frontal crash, crushed the belted front-seat occupant between the impacted seat back and the dashboard after his belt was severed by the extra force.

The U.S. has no belt use laws but the issue has been debated and adjudicated with respect to mandatory helmet use by motorcyclists. Although the motorcycle organizations that have successfully lobbied to repeal such laws represent only a minority of motorcyclists, a majority of whom favor helmet laws according to public-opinion polls, the appeal to freedom for the minority has been the principal argument. In the cases in which the issue was fought in the courts after failure in the legislatures, the courts have almost uniformly ruled that freedom to ride a motorcycle bareheaded is not included among those constitutionally guaranteed. One such court opinion stated:

> While we agree with plaintiff that the act's only realistic purpose is the prevention of head injuries incurred in motorcycle mishaps, we cannot agree that the consequences of such injuries are limited to the individual who sustains the injury. . . . The public has an interest in minimizing the resources directly involved. From the moment of the injury, society picks the person up off the highway; delivers him to a municipal hospital and municipal doctors; provides him with unemployment compensation if, after recovery, he cannot replace his lost job, and, if the injury causes permanent disability, may assume the responsibility for his and his family's substinence. We do not understand a state of mind that permits plaintiff to think that only he himself is concerned.[10]

Even if society through government were so inhumane as to offer none of these services, persons other than the motorcyclist and immediate family would not remain immune from bearing the cost of the severe head trauma. Testifying before a state legislative committee considering helmet legislation, one lawyer noted four cases in which motorcyclists with brain damage successfully sued motor vehicle operators involved in the collisions for a total of $11 million. He said, "When a motorcyclist chooses to ride without his helmet, he is not only placing his own head at risk; he is also placing at risk for the other drivers on the road their bank books, their homes, and their children's college education."[11]

We have no way of breaking freedom down into countable units so that we can say x number of units associated with bareheaded motorcycle riding is worth y number of units of freedom of those who have to care for and pay the costs of a brain-damaged individual, not to mention the lost freedom of the injured person. Clearly, the issue is more complicated than the simpleminded slogan of the motorcyclists' lobby: "Let those who ride, decide."

The Politics of Injury Control

A politician has written that "[s]cience is a process that seeks truth—politics is a process which seeks survival."[12] Politicians must deal with not just the variations of the truth as scientists understand them but also with the values and beliefs of their constituents, the pressures of their colleagues and lobbying groups, and the realization that to fail to have sufficient numbers of their constitutents agree with them precludes fighting, sometimes for the truth, another day. And, as the nonscientist reader may have gathered from previous criticism in this book, some would-be scientists are more politicians than seekers of truth.

Using the principles of science, we know how to build vehicles that would seldom kill occupants in a crash and would reduce pedestrian injury. Cigarettes and matches can be made to self-extinguish when dropped, reducing their potential as an ignition source. Many materials can be made nonflamable or fire-resistant. Indeed, most of the options for injury control discussed in chapter 4 are technically feasible and few can be rejected on economic grounds. Persuading the producers and users to adopt the technology or forcing the recalcitrant to do so in the political arena has been a far more difficult task than developing the technology.

The origins of the agencies charged with protecting the public from hazards are varied and somewhat idiosyncratic. Major new laws or modifications of old ones that give the agencies general policy direction have more often originated in the terms of activist presidents such as Theodore Roosevelt, Franklin D. Roosevelt, and Lyndon B. Johnson. Scandals regarding deaths from such sources as contaminated foods and drugs, aircraft disasters, and malfeasance in government and private organizations have increased public awareness and given impetus to new and changed policies. Muckraking exposes by journalists and citizens' groups have enhanced the perception of wrongdoing. Scientific evidence that amelioration is available is also an important element.

An interesting example is the Motor Vehicle Safety Act of 1966. In 1965, hearings by the Senate Subcommittee on Executive Reorganization were held on federal government efforts to reduce motor vehicle injuries. The subcommittee was chaired by a former state governor, Abraham Ribicoff, who, while governor, had gained publicity from a crackdown on speeding. He saw a *New York Times* article in late 1964 on Haddon, Suchman and

Klein's book, *Accident Research*, and was intrigued by the point that injuries could be reduced by increasing crashworthiness of vehicles in addition to efforts at crash prevention. He decided to call upon auto executives to testify about their activities on the issue.

During the hearings, the committee staff learned that a lawyer advising them was under surveillance by a private detective hired by General Motors Corporation in an apparent attempt to find information to discredit him. When this maneuver was made public by the committee, the resulting uproar led the chairman of the board of GM to apologize to the committee and the lawyer. After that, the passage of legislation was only a matter of working out the details among the appropriate congressional committees (the Subcommittee on Executive Reorganization did not have jurisdiction) and the administration. All of the ingredients for action were in place: the scientific evidence, an activist government, and a juicy scandal to bring the issue to the public's attention.[13]

The young lawyer that GM had investigated was Ralph Nader, who used his new-found celebrity status and money from a lawsuit against GM to form organizations active in the passage of other consumer product, safety, and health legislation in the late 1960s and early 1970s, some of which was mentioned in chapter 7. Nader and his raiders, as they were called, were highly critical of the newly formed or upgraded agencies that emerged during the period, as well as of the older regulatory agencies.[14] While scientists sometimes are appalled at the quality of evidence used by so-called citizens' lobbies, whether the pro-regulation types or more recently formed anti-regulation types, these lobbyists have become a part of the political spectrum that must be considered in attempts to modify public-injury control policy.

The reputation of the federal government as a protector of the public's interest was seared by the Vietnam War, the Watergate scandal, and an economy whipsawed by the vicissitudes of dealing with the foreign governments controlling major portions of energy supplies. Antigovernment rhetoric was successful in political campaigns in the ensuing decade. A regulatory agency in this political environment could be headed in one administration by a former Nader raider and in the next by an administrator with no expertise in injury control and whose apparent assigned mission was to rescind as many regulations as possible.

Regulatory Agencies

Federal regulations do not spring from the head of an agency's administrator full blown but, unless exempted specifically in enabling legislation, must go through a process specified in the Administrative Procedure Act.[15] This act requires, among other things, that proposed regulations along with justification of need must be published in the *Federal Register* and adequate time allowed for public comment and revision before issuance of a final rule. In many cases comment is received in publicized open hearings as well as in written form.

The reader who does not subscribe to the *Federal Register* may be surprised to learn that he or she can actually propose a regulation for the Consumer Product Safety Commission. If the rule is within the commission's jurisdiction and relevant in terms of the commission's priority products, the citizen or group with sufficient technical expertise and the time and interest to do so can submit a rule by way of the Commission's offeror system. The commission has adopted rules offered by citizens' groups as well as by industry and independent standard-development organizations.[16] In other cases of equal or greater merit, however, citizen efforts have been rebuffed.[17]

The more usual process involves development of a proposed rule by the agency's technical staff, one or more periods of public comment and revision based on that comment, followed by final adoption or dropping of the revised proposal. During this process the rule may be debated by opponents and proponents in hearings or letters, or it may become the center of a political donnybrook.

Researchers interested in identifying organized groups with interests in a given issue usually need go no further than the regulatory agency's dockets on the issue or transcripts of agency and legislative hearings. The latter can be found in libraries that routinely access government documents in state capitols as well as in some university and other libraries. If public hearings are to be held on an issue, one or another of the groups in favor and opposed will usually contact as many others of their persuasion as they can think of to present the appearance of a large backing for their point of view. For example, in hearings on recreational boating safety and facilities in 1979, there were presentations by federal government departments, state recreation departments, various yacht clubs, engine and boat manufacturers, marine trade groups, and associations of dock facility owners. Several letters from interested members of the public were also entered in the record.[18]

When there is major conflict between the affected industry and the agency, between the agency and a citizens' group, or between the agency and the Congress or White House, the press is likely to be informed and the public will receive a more or less accurate description of the issue and of interested parties from that source. The accuracy of depiction depends on who has the reporter's ear and his or her diligence and competence in understanding the issue. Some reporters give only one side of an issue, often in line with the ideological bent of the media's management, others quote conflicting statements without sufficient information for the reader or listener to decide on the truth, and still others will transmit a more complete story. On occasion, a competent story will be inaccurately altered by a rushed or less than competent editor, embarrassing the reporter if it carries a byline and distorting the issue in the public's mind.

Perhaps the most controversial of health and safety regulations in recent years is the so-called air bag proposal. The issue is of interest not only because it has been controversial but because the technology would have a greater impact on reducing motor vehicle deaths than all of the standards adopted to date.

The first patent for an automatically inflatable bag that would absorb crash forces in severe frontal crashes and spread the forces over larger body surfaces than padding or seat belts was obtained in 1952. In the succeeding years, several companies worked on developing the concept into a workable system. Major motor vehicle manufacturers and suppliers kept the newly formed National Highway Safety Bureau informed of some of the developments.[19] When scientists in the agency were convinced that the system was sufficiently developed, a new standard was proposed. The agency issued an advanced notice of proposed rule making in 1969 to become effective January 1, 1972.[20] This original proposal set performance requirements for an "inflatable occupant restraint system" that, after various comments were received, was changed to a more general performance standard specifying automatic provision for minimum crash forces on the head, chest, and knees of a test dummy in a 30-mph front and front-angle crash into a rigid test barrier. The standard could then be met by automatic wrap-around seat belts as well as air bags.[21]

The auto industry argued during the comment period that the technology was not sufficiently developed, was too costly, and that it did not allow sufficient lead time. These were not new arguments, having been used in opposition to several of the initial standards for 1968 models.[22] Failing to budge the agency beyond a one-year delay, Henry Ford II and Lee Iacocca, then of Ford Motor Company, met with President Richard M. Nixon and John Ehrlichman in the White House and attempted to convince the president to delay the rule making. Like other of the transcripts of the White House tapes, there are many unintelligible passages, but Mr. Ehrlichman was directed by the president to look into the matter.[23] Subsequently, the agency was ordered, over its strong opposition, to accept the buzzer and interlock devices developed by Ford; the agency's compliance, as noted in chapter 5, met with adverse public reaction. The unpopularity of these devices was subsequently used by Mr. Iacocca[24] and economists opposed to regulation—one of whom had the dates and other facts wrong[25]— as an example of the follies of pernicious regulators. In fact, it was one of Ford's worse ideas and the company apparently knew it. Ford ran television ads in 1970 describing the interlock that said, "You probably won't even like it."[26]

After the interlock was banned by Congress, the administrator of the agency and later the secretary of transportation held hearings on the passive restraint rule in 1975 and 1976, respectively. The secretary found that the benefits of either air bags or automatic belts would greatly exceed the costs but dropped the rule—despite his finding that something more than 12,000 lives per year would be saved—in favor of a "demonstration project" in collaboration with the auto industry. He said his choice was based on concern over public acceptance,[27] ignoring the public-opinion surveys favoring increased automatic crash protection presented in the hearing. The original estimate of the secretary that the demonstration project would involve approximately one-half million automobiles was reduced to less than 70,000 in the actual, nonbinding statements of intent from the auto companies a few months later.

Following the election of Jimmy Carter, a new secretary of transportation announced hearings on the issue. The auto companies then backed out of the previous agreement for a demonstration project. The 1977 hearings produced no new evidence but a different decision was rendered. The new rule required passive restraints in large 1981 models, compact to mid-sized 1982 models, and all 1983 models. Groups both for and against went to court, the former to step up the timetable for the standard and the latter to kill it. The court let it stand.

After the 1980 election, President Reagan appointed a new administrator of the National Highway Traffic Safety Administration (NHTSA), who soon announced a one-year delay in implementation in 1981 and, after additional hearings he rescinded the standard. The automakers testified that they would use only automatic belts that could be easily detached, and the administrator said that he doubted that the public would use such belts, ignoring any change in the rule that would reduce the likelihood of nonuse or an alternative approach.[28]

Various insurance companies and citizens' action groups again appealed to the courts. In a sharply stated opinion, the United States Court of Appeals for the District of Columbia Circuit agreed with the petitioners that the dumping of the standard was "arbitrary, capricious, an abuse of discretion, a violation of law as defined by Section 10 of the Administrative Procedure Act."[29] The standard was ordered reinstated by the court. The government, as well as domestic and foreign automobile manufacturers, appealed the decision; and in November 1982, the Supreme Court agreed to hear the case. If the Supreme Court ruling is consistent with its ruling on the cotton dust standard (chapter 8), one can expect the standard to be upheld, as required in principle by the Motor Vehicle Safety Act of 1966. The outcome is nevertheless problematic at this time.

Even if the Supreme Court affirms the lower court's decision, the timing of the rule's application and the question of whether the industry will respond with the most efficacious technology at the least cost is very much in doubt—given the failure to do so with respect to other standards noted in chapter 8. Following the appeals court ruling, the industry claimed that it could not possibly meet the standard in 1983 models and the NHTSA administrator projected 1986 as the earliest possible date. An internal study at NHTSA, however, found that the standard could be met in 80 percent of the 1984 models.[30] With a regulatory agency at war with itself and congressional attention focused on the immediacy of a recession, an increase in automatic occupant crash protection could be far longer in coming than the technology or economics alone would determine.

Theories of Regulatory Life Cycles

Economists and political scientists have attempted to construct theories to explain the behavior of regulatory agencies. Central to these theories is the notion of developmental and declining stages. The analogy to the life cycle of a person is used: gestation, youth, maturity, old age. In contrast to human development, some theorists include the possibility of revitalization by scandal or some other crisis.[31]

Some of the factors involved in gestation of an agency were noted previously. The youth of an agency is supposedly characterized by enthusiastic aggressiveness coupled with inexperience leading to mistakes, which gives organized opposition a chance to gain strength. In maturity, the agency is said to become apathetic and captured by the regulated industry. It is characterized by service to the industry rather than acting as a watchdog, a backlog of cases, increased amounts of litigation, and losses in budgetary and other forms of support from the executive and legislative branches of government. Old age brings further declines in funding, resulting in poor staff quality and failure to adapt to new conditions.

Reasoning by analogy is often a dangerous path to the truth. One tends to look for instances that fit the analogy and ignore contrary evidence. Much of the empirical evidence on behavior of regulatory agencies over the long run is based on agencies charged solely with economic regulation: market entry, fair pricing, and fraudulent claims or practices. One recent study of some of the hypothesized correlates of the age of an agency[32] included the Federal Aviation Administration (FAA), the National Transportation Safety Board (NTSB), and the Occupational Safety and Health Administration (OSHA) along with five agencies that regulate strictly economic issues. NTSB was not discussed in chapter 7 because it investigates transportation injuries, mainly those that occur in catastrophes such as plane crashes, and recommends ameliorative steps; it has no authority to impose regulations or to make any other changes in conditions that lead to damage to people, property, or systems. Its inclusion in the study is thus dubious while OSHA was so young at the time of the study that the application of a life cycle theory is questionable.

Nevertheless, the study found little support for the life cycle theory, at least as a monotonic function of the age of the agencies studied. When the effect of initial start-up budgets was removed, no evidence of declining support of the agencies in terms of budget allocations was found. The notion of capture of the agencies by means of personnel moving back and forth between the agency and the regulated industry was not supported. The percentage of the top jobs in the agencies that were filled by persons with prior jobs in the regulated industry fluctuated over time, but a general upward trend was not detected. In the FAA, the percentage declined from 60 percent in 1957 through 1960 to none in 1973 through 1975. Apparently the agency was, in time, able to develop its own experts so that it no longer needed to depend on expertise from the industry. The percentage of top people in the agencies who took jobs in the regulated industries tended to decline rather than increase in time—also contrary to the capture theory that describes jobs in the regulated industry as rewards for those who served the industry during their government tenure.

Although backlogs of cases were unrelated to agency age, the research did find an increase in legal staff correlated with the age of the agency. While those who dislike lawyers might interpret this trend as evidence of senility, it probably reflects the tendency of regulated industries' increased attempts to tie up the agency in lawsuits in order to prevent or modify regulations. That involvement may result in a decline in effectiveness of an agency, but it cannot be taken as evidence of lack of agency effort to do its job.

One writer has suggested that we add to the notions of market failure and regulatory failure the concept of theory failure.[33] It is doubtful that some grand theory of regulation deduced with mathematical precision will be forthcoming to explain and predict the motivations and actions of persons in regulatory agencies and regulated industries or of the politicians and citizens' organizations looking over their shoulders, much less the near infinite numbers of combinations of interactions among the people involved. Regulatory agencies have made and will make mistakes, but the scrutiny these agencies receive in a society that is not fond of regulation is likely to keep in check serious failures by acts of commission and bring about rapid correction when they occur. The continued rates of injury associated with motor vehicles, guns, cigarette-generated fires, light aircraft, industrial work, and certain consumer products suggest that failure in the form of omission remains the primary problem.

Persons opposed to all regulation are fond of bringing up cases such as the interlock seat belt system, the public acceptance of which the regulatory agency misjudged based on poor research (chapter 5) but the use of which was opposed by the senior staff of the agency and allowed only at the insistence of the regulated industry to the White House. The use of a potential carcinogen as a flame retardant for children's sleepwear in response to a requirement for reduced flammability is also a favored example. In each of these cases, however, the industry made the choice of the technology to be used to meet the standards; and, while the agencies involved could have provided better research or guidance regarding the standard's potential effects, the industries involved are not without resources to research those matters. Indeed, General Motors knew from its marketing studies that the public greatly preferred air bags to automatic seat belts,[34] and yet it used the interlock in an attempt to force seat belt use in most of its cars rather than offer air bags in any but the most expensive models (chapter 8).

It will remain the responsibility of scientists with expertise and concern for public health, citizens' organizations, and insurers or other businesses that understand the issues and the effects of lack of action to keep the omissions and excesses of the regulatory agencies on the public agenda. The regulated industries could avoid the politicking and court costs, much liability, and all regulation if they stayed ahead of potential regulation by use of their expertise to reduce the involvement of their products in injury. Too few have acted in that responsible a fashion.

Decisions in Organizations

The story of organizations whose leaders make socially responsible decisions is not told often enough. *The Wall Street Journal* recently reported that McCulloch Corporation, a division of Black and Decker Manufacturing Company, "advocates application of all state-of-the-art safety devices as standard equipment."[35] Since 1975, the company has installed brakes on its chain saws to halt movement of the chain if the saw jerks upward in use. It withdrew from the Chain Saw Manufacturers Association in 1978 because of resistance of other members to improve industry safety standards.

We do not know whether the distinction between organizations that act responsibly and those that do not is idiosyncratic to the leadership of a given organization or is characteristic of organizations by some sort of typology. Some organizational analysts believe that each organization has a culture, an "amalgam of beliefs, mythology, values and rituals that, even more than its products, differentiates it."[36] To some extent this is undoubtedly true, whether it is a manufacturing, government, or other kind of organization. A simple description of these attributes, though, does not explain how they develop or why they lead to decisions favorable to the public interest in some cases and adverse in others.

Some obvious factors that could be investigated by social scientists in this regard include the educational and social backgrounds of the sequential leadership of organizations. Do those trained in professions with stronger codes of ethics foster a more socially responsible organizational culture? Does the age and sex mix of the leadership make a difference? Does new leadership adapt to the old culture or are certain types of leaders able to reorient the culture? Are certain types of individuals attracted to organizations of a particular type, thus reinforcing and perpetuating an organizational viewpoint? To the social scientist, the emphasis in several organizations on power or violence, sometimes interspersed with sexual overtones, seems more than coincidental.

The cover of the November 1982 issue of the speed buff magazine *Car and Driver* included a headline, "Radar Detectors Tip the Balance of Justice in Your Favor." The magazine's primary emphasis in its descriptions of cars is speed and power, but occasionally things get a little more kinky. One article begins, "Everybody here knows the deal about future cars, right? They look like atomic carpet sweepers. They're made out of balsa wood and spun sugar. And you can only see them at auto shows in the company of strange women in whip me, whip me, Ming-the-Merciless costumes."[37] While that is hardly an accurate description of most car promotional campaigns, it is clear from the designs of cars on the road, their names, and the way they are advertised that there is more than a little suggestion of sex and violence.

One can only speculate as to why manufacturers build vehicles capable of speeds more than twice the maximum legal speed limit and give them names that emphasize a mixture of power and virility: Mustang, Firebird, Charger. The shapes of the vehicles and the points and edges on their fronts that are a hazard to pedestrians, even at low speeds, are suggestive of phallic symbols. Advertisements of sexy women lounging on or in them emphasize the image. It is not clear whether the designs and advertising result from assumptions about the psychology of the potential buyers or represent macho psychosexual power fantasies of those who design the vehicles and their advertising. Whatever the explanation, the nation's roads are not the appropriate place for the resolution of psychiatric problems at the cost of physical damage to hundreds of thousands of people annually.

The editors of speed buff magazines such as *Car and Driver* become apoplectic every time there is a suggestion that the top speed of vehicles be limited or that crash protection be increased. They helped to foment a pro-speed lobby that blocked a proposed rule to limit designed-in top vehicle speed capability in the early 1970s; but more recently they have not been able to get the 55-mph speed limit overturned. Public-opinion polls have made it clear that the public is terrorized by the speed buffs and wants the limit to remain as is.[38]

Television and movie producers of entertainment shows have used the theme of sex with violence in cars as a partial replacement for guns as the preferred form of violence. In contrast to scenes of shootings, people are seldom portrayed as injured in wild car chases, though several vehicles always get destroyed. On June 12, 1982, the 9:00 P.M. CBS movie, "Georgia Peaches," began with scenes in which a young man in a car was being chased by police. He did two 180-degree turns, ran a motorcycle policeman off the road, spread gasoline on the road through a pipe controlled from inside the car, and ignited it by a friction device, setting off a wall of flame in front of following police vehicles. The participants in such scenes are often stereotyped "good ole boys" from the South, just having a little fun showing off to their girlfriends by frustrating the bumbling police. The credits include homage to governors and police departments that cooperated in the production. President Jimmy Carter, then governor of Georgia, was honored thus by the producers of "Smokie and the Bandit," another film in the genre.

While hard scientific data on the effects of such displays is difficult if not impossible to obtain, the potential of vehicle violence to influence the behavior of drivers cannot be ignored. Young people in the past have admitted acting out scenes from television programs and movies. Several cases were reported in support of a legal defense based on exposure to violence on television. In one, a fourteen-year-old boy killed his eleven-year-old brother unintentionally with a gun while acting out a scene from a television movie they had seen the night before.[39] Among other reported incidents, the rape of a nine-year-old girl with a bottle by a fifteen-year-old boy, watched by three onlookers, was copied from a similar incident in a television movie.[40] The behavior that included the shooting of President Ronald Reagan was said by the defendant's psychiatrists to be patterned after a movie with an assassination theme: the president's assailant claimed to have seen the movie eighteen times.[41] It would be naive to believe that vehicle violence in television and movies has no effect on the trauma daily inflicted by motor vehicles, especially those driven by immature young people.

The issue of censorship is a constitutional issue, and we may have to depend on the conscience of writers, producers and network executives to exercise self-restraint in the use of violent themes. State and local governments are not compelled by issues of censorship, however, to allow film makers to use public roads for the portrayal of vehicles traveling at illegal speeds and performing other illegal maneuvers. Nor are the states compelled to register vehicles whose designed top-speed capabilities are twice the legal speed limit on the states' roads.[42]

Gun lobbyists have argued that the right to bear arms is a constitutional issue; but the constitutional provision for state militias is not usually interpreted in court cases as a right to walk around the streets with a gun in violation of the law.[43] The National Rifle Association (NRA), the flagship organization of the lobby, likes to portray itself as an association of ordinary citizens concerned only with personal liberty, fighting off the tyranny of big government. The NRA has long-standing ties with the gun manufacturers and the expenses of its target shooting programs have been decreased through loans of guns from the Department of Defense, which makes it something more than the voice of its dues-paying membership. For years the military sold surplus guns to NRA members at a discount, a practice that contributed to the rise in membership.[44] Thus, the taxpayer strongly in favor of gun control was being taxed to support the principal organization opposing that view.

Although the NRA claims to be a force against tyranny, its ordinary dues-paying members are not given a vote on the organization's policies. Only lifetime members who have paid $150 for that designation have the right to vote on policy. The gun manufacturers exert their influence by way of large advertising budgets devoted to the NRA's magazine and more recently to political action committees that oppose politicians or referenda favoring gun control. In a 1982 California ballot proposition on gun control, the gun lobby spent $6 million to defeat the proposed restrictions.[45]

In some circles it is not considered proper to question the motives of others. But the assumption of motive is inherent in proposals that regulation be replaced by incentive systems. Popular theories of organizations characterize government executives as primarily motivated by power and business executives as primarily motivated by money. In one study of business executives' views of economic regulation, based on interviews with them, individual income and corporate profits were not the primary reasons given for opposition to regulation. The most important factor was resentment at not being in complete control of the business.[46] Some businessmen are certainly capable of a primary concern for power, just as some government executives have used their positions to increase personal wealth. Simple theories of singular motivations are inadequate to explain organizational decisions.

A plausible theory of organizational decisions adverse to injury control that is worthy of consideration is based on pluralistic ignorance. Few government or business executives would ever consider deliberately killing an individual with a gun or knife, but some of them have been party to collective decisions that they know will mean death or disability to large numbers of people. Indeed, in the group context of the organizational decision, each person, as an individual, may be in his (or rarely her) own mind completely opposed to the action being taken. Not knowing the feelings of the others, wanting to be considered a tough decision maker, or afraid to advance a position contrary to the prevalent organizational culture, an individual may acquiesce to a policy that leads to injury and death—or even propose it—to go along with the assumed view of the crowd.

Whether evidence of such pluralistic ignorance can be gained by interview or other form of data gathering when, by definition, the individuals have reason not to reveal their true feelings is not apparent. Incidents abound in which individuals in government and private organizations expressed sympathy with the injury-control efforts that their organizations opposed but swore their confidants to secrecy regarding their views. Others have resigned but remained silent. A few have participated in court cases against their old employers. Occasionally, an important document revealing a government or private organization's culpability will be leaked to trusted members of the press, a citizen advocate, a competitor, or even a scientist working on an issue. Such documents can arrive over the transom or in the mail, source unknown but appreciated.

Another rather obvious problem in some organizations is general ignorance. Manufacturers of products that are less frequently or severely involved in injuries than motor vehicles and guns are probably often surprised to find their products in a list of hazards such as that compiled from the emergency room surveillance system of the Consumer Product Safety Commission. Designers and manufacturers of hazardous toys, clothes, furniture, and dwellings probably never consider the potential for harm if their products are swallowed, burned, or are fallen against or from, respectively. An architect invited to an injury-control conference that the author attended in 1981 admitted to the group that he and most of his colleagues, after meeting building codes, gave little thought to the potential effects of their designs on a range of injuries.

Policies for Injury Control

What for a while was a push for regulatory reform, that is, the tinkering with regulatory agency structures to make them more effective, has recently been under vigorous attack from those who would like to dump all regulations. This latter view has the appearance of throwing out the baby of health and safety, which has been more than a little effective, with the bathwater of some economic regulations that have been of more benefit to the economic interests they were supposed to regulate than to the public. It is too early to tell whether deregulation is a trend or a post-Vietnam War, post-Watergate aberration.

In the more than likely event that it is the latter, some thoughts and evidence regarding regulatory reform with respect to injury control are offered to close out this discussion. So-called market solutions, such as changes in the tax code as an economic incentive, have been proposed as an alternative to "command and control" regulation. The argument that incentive systems would be more efficient or effective than an agency's application of specific design or performance requirements is not supported by sufficient evidence.

Values, Politics, and the Future

Although not intended primarily as such, the system of worker's compensation for injuries in work places should have acted as a strong incentive to modify machinery and work practices for the reduction of injuries. The amounts expended for worker's compensation in some states increased much more rapidly in the 1970s than the inflation rate. In three plants of one company, each located in a separate state, however, there was no reduction of objectively verifiable injuries and changes in the worker's compensation rates above inflation. The self-insured company, with less than 2,000 employees in the three plants, was paying $100,000 per month for worker's compensation by 1980 but had not taken any increased actions to reduce injuries except when OSHA inspectors issued citations for violations of its standards. While it would be inappropriate to generalize to all industry on the basis of three plants of one company, the interstate differences in days lost from injury in correlation with worker's compensation show increases rather than decreases.[47] Apparently, the workers reacted to economic incentives, demanding more time off for injury when it became affordable, but the industries did not.

Legislation giving tax incentives to manufacturers who install air bags in their vehicles has been introduced in Congress but has not been voted out of committee. It would be an interesting social experiment to see if companies would respond to financial incentives in this way, having previously rejected use of air bags despite evidence in their marketing studies that they were profitable.

The development of incentive systems or piecemeal standards for use of this and that vehicle component results in enormous gaps between the technological possibilities and actual realization. The involved parties are debating and litigating the merits and feasibility of regulations and incentive systems for belt use, automatic seat belts, and air bags while the other technologies of the research safety vehicles lie on the shelf.

Despite the gains realized from extant standards (chapter 7), enormous differences in death and injury rates are found among vehicles in use. Examining death rates by make and model from the fatal accident reporting system computer tapes, which include virtually every fatal motor vehicle crash in the country, the author found that, from 1975 through 1980, there was one death in the 1975 models of the Honda Civic for every 727 sold in the U.S. in that model year, compared to one death in the 1975 model Volvos for every 2,106 sold in that model year during the same six-year period. The Civic in its own way was as misnamed as the muscle cars. By 1982 even Volvo had succumbed to the temptation of advertising power: its commercials portrayed the Turbo model as reminiscent of a muscle car, thus completing the circle of irresponsible advertising by auto manufacturers.

A twofold difference in injury insurance claim rates and death rates among cars is not unusual based on size differences alone, but most of the cars made in Japan have had worse rates than those made elsewhere.[48,49] These cars became popular in the United States because of lower prices and better ratings on mechanical reliability and gas mileage than their U.S. counterparts. The Japanese manufacturers reportedly can produce a car for about $2,000 less than U.S. manufacturers[50] but in most cases have not used that price advantage to improve the crashworthiness of their cars.

A comprehensive approach to regulating for motor vehicle injury reduction could be stated in a simple standard. A new vehicle sold in the United States should not be capable of exceeding a speed on a level road at any point in a five-mile test run that would injure with life-threatening severity in a frontal or front-angle crash, according to crash forces measured on a test dummy in crash tests into a solid barrier at the vehicle's maximum speed. The manufacturers would be free to modify the crashworthiness or the maximum speed capability or both in any way they saw fit to meet the standard. The consumer would be assured of relatively uniform crashworthiness among vehicles and the regulatory agency would be able to determine the maximum speed capability and crash test the vehicle at that speed to assure compliance. Other regulations would still be needed for side and rear impacts, rollovers and pedestrian protection, each improved in the research-safety vehicles; but the majority of fatalities to occupants—those that now occur in frontal impacts—would decline rapidly and become a rarity after the ten years or so that would be required to replace the existent fleet.

A comprehensive regulation to cover even a small segment of the widely varied products under the aegis of the Consumer Product Safety Commission (CPSC) is more difficult than that for transportation vehicles. A number of manufacturers and importers have readily admitted that they do no testing of hazard potential in use of their products.[51] CPSC has neither the budget nor the staff expertise to pretest even a fraction of these potentially hazardous products, and it has experienced delays in issuing hazard notifications and recalls after receiving reports of death or severe injury associated with a specific product.[52]

In both regulation and recall, CPSC and other agencies must regulate with one eye on the public's health and the other on the courthouse. A mistake can lead to lengthy and costly litigation. The relatively small business with only one or a few products can be wiped out if it must meet the cost of a major recall campaign. While no simple solution to such problems seems evident, it is doubtful that some clever manipulation of an already incomprehensible tax code could persuade producers to increase expertise in product hazards and the means to reduce them.

Many large businesses that produce a variety of products have or are capable of maintaining in-house research by hazard-control experts. One possibility to decrease the number of untested hazardous products is to require that the products of small firms be tested by independent testing firms, or that an expansion of facilities at the Bureau of Standards provide such a service before they are marketed. A certification from such sources would not entirely eliminate hazards, but it would reduce them. Some producers would no doubt resist such a policy, but reminder of the losses to other businesses from recalls and liability suits might bring them around. Guns and ammunition, industrial machines, light aircraft,[53] and farm equipment[54] should come under greater scrutiny.

Manufacturers of all products and commercial users that expose workers and customers to hazards should take heed of the new issues of liability based on old precedents that are being suggested by legal scholars or being litigated. Aside from increasingly large awards in liability suits for defects and worker compensation costs that could often have been reduced by increased protection at less expense, legal precedence holds commercial users and manufacturers liable for failure to use available technology to protect life, limb, and property. In 1932, the owner of a tugboat, the *T.J. Hooper*, was judged liable when his boat lost a barge because it did not have a radio receiver on board, despite the fact that government regulations at the time did not require such a receiver.[55] One filing for bankruptcy in 1982 was made not to protect the company from immediate creditors but in anticipation of losses in lawsuits brought by workers for failure to provide protection from the asbestos inhalation that evidence indicated the company knew would result in lung damage. Continued failure to modify the hazardous characteristics of products, or failure to include technology that would reduce the risk of use, may be a far greater threat to the economic viability of a company and the accompanying power of its management than the costs of changes in the products.

References

1. C.E. Lindblom, "The Science of 'Muddling Through,' " *Public Administration Review* 19(1959):79.

2. R. Heilbroner and L. Thurow, *Economics Explained* (Englewood Cliffs, NJ: Prentice-Hall, 1982).

3. J.Q. Wilson, *The Politics of Regulation* (New York: Basic Books, 1980).

4. P. Self, *Econocrats and the Policy Process: The Politics and Philosophy of Cost-Benefit Analysis* (Boulder, CO: Westview Press, 1975).

5. S. Muenchow and M.E. Lang, "Falling Through the Loopholes," *The New York Times* (October 31, 1982), Section 11, p. 26.

6. R.S. Sanders, "Legislative Approach to Auto Safety: The Tennessee Experience." In: A.B. Bergman, ed., *Preventing Childhood Injuries* (Columbus, OH: Ross Laboratories, 1982).

7. R.S. Karpf and A.F. Williams, "Teenage Drivers and Motor Vehicle Deaths," *Accident Analysis and Prevention*, in press.

8. B.M. Mitnick, *The Political Economy of Regulation: Creating, Designing and Removing Regulatory Forms* (New York: Columbia University Press, 1980).

9. S.P. Baker, "Who Bought the Cars in Which People Are Injured? An Exploratory Study," *American Journal of Public Health* 69(1979):76.

10. Simon v. Sargent, 346 F. Supp. 277 (D. Mass. 1972), affirmed without opinion, 409 U.S. 1020 (1972).

11. Testimony of S. Teret quoted in S.P. Baker, "On Lobbies, Liberty and the Public Good," *American Journal of Public Health* 70(1980):573-74.

12. R.D. Lamm, "The Environment and Public Policy." In: K.R. Hammond, ed., *Judgment and Decision in Public Policy Formation* (Boulder, CO: Westview Press, 1978).

13. C. McCarry, *Citizen Nader* (New York: Saturday Review Press, 1972).

14. S.P. Sethi, "Corporations and the Citizens at Large." In: S.P. Sethi, ed., *Up Against the Corporate Wall: Modern Corporations and Social Issues of the Seventies* (Englewood Cliffs, NJ: Prentice-Hall, 1977).

15. 5 U.S. Code 551-553, 1976.

16. J.A. Hermanson, "Regulatory Reform By Statute: The Implications of the Consumer Product Safety Commissions 'Offeror System,' " *Public Administration Review* 38(1978):151.

17. L. Berger and F.P. Rivara, "Minibikes: A Case Study in Under-Regulation," *Business and Society Review* (Summer, 1980):41.

18. *Recreation Boating Safety and Facilities, Hearings Before the Subcommittee on Coast Guard and Navigation of the Committee on Merchant Marine and Fisheries, U.S. House of Representatives, 96-14* (Washington, DC: U.S. Government Printing Office, 1979).

19. E.g., transcript of a meeting of representatives from American Motors Corporation, Chrysler Corporation, Ford Motor Company, General Motors Corporation, Eaton Yale and Towne Inc. and William Haddon, Jr., and senior staff and a consultant of the National Highway Safety Bureau, U.S. Department of Transportation, July 19, 1968.

20. Communications Department, *Background Manual on the Passive Restraint Issue* (Washington, DC: Insurance Institute for Highway Safety, 1977).

21. K.W. Warner, *Mandatory Passive Restraint Systems in Automobiles: Issues and Evidence* (Washington, DC: U.S. Congress Office of Technology Assessment, 1982).

22. "Safety and Other Problems." In: L.A. Sobel, ed., *Consumer Protection* (New York: Facts On File, Inc., 1976), p. 30.

23. "Part of a Conversation Among President Nixon, Lide Anthony Iacocca, Henry Ford II and John D. Ehrlichman in the Oval Office on April 27, 1971, between 11:08 and 11:43 A.M.," *Automotive Litigation Reporter* (November 18, 1982):1784-98.

24. L.S. Robertson, "Gimcrack From Ford?", *Wall Street Journal* (October 15, 1979):25.

25. M.L. Weidenbaum, *Government-Mandated Price Increases* (Washington, DC: American Enterprise Institute, 1975).

26. Communications Department, *Background Manual on the Passive Restraint Issue* (Washington, DC: Insurance Institute for Highway Safety, 1977).

27. *The Secretary's Decision Concerning Motor Vehicle Occupant Protection* (Washington, DC: U.S. Department of Transportation, 1976).

28. K.W. Warner, *Mandatory Passive Restraint Systems in Automobiles*, pp. 32-34.

29. *State Farm Mutual Insurance Co., et al. v. Department of Transportation, No. 81-2220* and *National Association of Independent Insurers, Automobile Owners Action Council, et al. v. National Highway Traffic Safety Administration, No. 81-2221* (Washington, DC: United States Court of Appeal for the District of Columbia, 1982).

30. "Auto Safety Agency Report Says Industry Can Comply with 1984 Restraint Deadline," *Product Safety and Liability Reporter* (October 22, 1982):710.

31. M.H. Bernstein, *Regulating Business by Independent Commission* (Princeton, NJ: Princeton University Press, 1955).

32. K.J. Meier and J.P. Plumlee, "Regulatory Administration and Organizational Rigidity," *Western Political Quarterly* 31(1978):80.

33. C.S. Diver, "A Theory of Regulatory Enforcement," *Public Policy* 28(1980):257.

34. Advertising and Marketing Section, *Consumer Opinions Relative to Automotive Restraint Marketing Systems Report #71-27* (Detroit, MI: General Motors Corporation, 1971).

35. R. Vicker, "Rise in Chain-Saw Injuries Spurs Demand for Safety Standards, But Industry Resists," *Wall Street Journal* (August 23, 1982):1.

36. S. Salmans, "New Vogue: Company Culture," *The New York Times* (January 7, 1983):D1.

37. M. Jordan, "Volkswagen and Audi Future Cars: If These Are Really Dream-Mobiles, Where Are the Girls with the Whips and Chains?" *Car and Driver* 28 (November, 1982):105. Reprinted from *Car and Driver* magazine with permission. Copyright 1982 Ziff-Davis Publishing Co.

38. National Highway Traffic Safety Administration, *55 MPH Fact Book* (Washington, DC: U.S. Department of Transportation, 1978), p. 19.

39. Merwin Sigale, "TV 'Intoxication' Murder Trial to Open," *Washington Post* (September 26, 1977):A4.

40. M. Mintz, "Judge is Selected for Violence Suit Against TV Network," *Washington Post* (August 1, 1978):A4.

41. L.A. Kiernan, "Hinkley, Jury Watch 'Taxi Driver' Film," *Washington Post* (May 29, 1982):A1.

42. W. Haddon, Jr., "Why Be Able to Do 140 If 55 Is the Limit," *The New York Times* (October 4, 1982):A18.

43. United States v. Miller, 307 U.S. 174, 178 (1939).

44. S.P. Sethi, *Up Against the Corporate Wall: Modern Corporations and Social Issues of the Seventies* (Englewood Cliffs, NJ: Prentice-Hall, 1977).

45. R. Lindsey, "Bradley Loses Close Contest On Coast," *The New York Times* (November 4, 1982):A22.

46. R. Lane, *The Regulation of Businessmen* (New Haven, CT: Yale University Press, 1954).

47. L.S. Robertson and J.P. Keeve, "Worker Injuries: The Effects of Worker's Compensation and OSHA Citations," *Journal of Health Politics, Policy and Law*, in press.

48. *Insurance Losses, Personal Injury Protection Coverages: Passenger Cars, Vans, Pickups, and Utility Vehicles: 1979-1981 Models* (Washington, DC: Highway Loss Data Institute, 1982.

49. National Highway Traffic Safety Administration, *The Car Book* (Washington, DC: U.S. Department of Transportation, 1981).

50. J. Holusha, "General Motors: A Giant in Transition," *The New York Times Sunday Magazine* (November 14, 1982):76.

51. R.D. Pittle, "The Consumer Product Safety Commission: Its Clout, Its Candor, and Its Challenge." In: R.N. Katz, *Protecting the Consumer Interest: Private Interest and Public Response* (Cambridge, MA: Ballinger, 1976).

52. S.P. Sethi, *Promises of the Good Life: Social Consequences of Private Marketing Decisions* (Homewood, IL: Richard D. Irwin, 1979).

53. R.G. Snyder, "Crashworthiness Investigation of General Aviation Accidents," Society of Automotive Engineers Business Aircraft Meeting, April 8-11, 1975, and R.G. Snyder, "Civil Aircraft Restraint Systems: State-of-the-Art Evaluation of Standards, Experimental Data, and Accident Experience," Society of Automotive Engineers Paper No. 770154, 1977.

54. E.g., T. Karlson and J. Noren, "Farm Tractor Fatalities: The Failure of Voluntary Safety Standards," *American Journal of Public Health* 69(1979):146.

55. A.R. Hricko, "T.J. Hooper and the Air Bag," *Federation of Insurance Council Quarterly* 27 (1977):233.

Index

Aaronson, S., 161
Abbreviated Injury Scale (AIS), 3, 5
Acceleration, 24-26
Accident Research, 192
Accidents, 2-3, 12, 59
Accounting, 169
Active strategies, 85
Adams, C.F., 159, 180
Adams, J.R., 112
Administrative Procedure Act, 192, 195
Administrative rules, 86-87, 133
Advertising safety, 176-177
Age, 5-6, 9-10, 13, 18-19, 45, 54-57, 59-60, 123-124, 128
Agents of injury, 23-24, 71, 83, 85, 139
Aggression, 52, 59, 64
Air bags, 76, 86, 169, 177-178, 194-195, 198, 203
Air Commerce Act of 1926, 147
Aircraft, 24, 132, 146-147, 155, 175, 191, 197, 205
Akinyemi, J., 159
Alcohol, 12, 15-16, 37-38, 50-51, 53-54, 58-60, 72, 82-83, 86, 91, 96-97, 118-124, 131, 134
Alcohol education, 95-97, 187-188
Alcoholism, 124
Alcohol Safety Action Projects, 123
Allgaier, E., 111
Aluminum wiring, 153
American Motors, 169
American Safety Belt Council, 101
Amnesia, 7
Amperage, 39
Andenaes, J., 135
Anderson, L.G., 180
Andressand, D.C., 137
Andrews, W.H., 160
Annegers, J.F., 20
Antihistamines, 53
Ariens, J., 43
Ashton, S.J., 43

Asphyxiation, 23, 33-36, 79-80
Assault, 5, 15, 32, 45, 51, 64, 127
Association of Home Appliance Manufacturers, 155
Atomic explosion, 40
Auto manufacturers, 166-169, 194, 199
Automatic couplers (trains), 146
Automatic seat belts (cars), 169, 177, 194-195, 198, 203
Azar, N., 115

Bailey, J.S., 112
Baker, S.P., 20, 42-43, 67-68, 87-89, 160, 206
Balloons, 34
Balls, 34
Baltimore Gas and Electric Co., 155
Bankruptcy, 205
Banks, W.W., 69
Baptiste, M.S., 88
Barancik, J.I., 20
Barmack, J.E., 112, 136
Barry, P.Z., 21, 66, 114
Baumann, D.D., 69
Beds, 78
Bed disability, 3-4
Behavior-change program evaluation, 111
Behavioral science, 17, 65, 91
Behavior modification, 91, 103-108
Beitel, G.A., 135
Beliefs, 64-65, 185-187, 198
Berg Electronics, 114
Berger, L.R., 68, 206
Bergner, L., 43, 161-162
Bernstein, M.H., 207
Bicycles, 7, 55, 75-76, 139, 153
Biggs, J.P., 136
Biomechanics, 17, 25, 28
Birmingham, England, 85
Black and Decker Manufacturing Co., 198
Blanchet, M., 20
Blomquist, G., 181

Blumenthal, M., 135
Boats, 16, 33-34, 80, 148, 193
Boat Safety Act of 1971, 148
Bodde, D.L., 181
Borkenstein, R.F., 21, 67
Boston, 64
Bowers, W.J., 136
Bowman, B.M., 41
Box, P.C., 115
Brain damage, 80, 189-191
Brakes, 30-31, 46, 52, 64, 72, 141, 146
Bridge abutments, 73
Brisbane, 157
British Board of Trade, 145
British Road Safety Act of 1967, 120-121
Brocklehurst, J.C., 69
Bruun, K., 69
Bueche, F., 41
Bukenmaier, C.C., Jr., 115
Bull, J.P., 20
Bullets, 24-25, 27, 31-32, 77-78
Bumpers, 31
Bureau of Labor Statistics, 16, 22
Bureau of Labor Statistics Producer Price Index, 167-168
Bureau of Mines, 151
Burg, A., 68-69
Burns, 35-36, 55, 102-103, 154
Burns, M., 67
Busses, 24, 175
Buzzer-light reminder system, 104, 168, 194
Byington, S.R., 136

Caffey, J., 20
Cairns, H., 137
Campbell, B.J., 159
Campbell, D.T., 22, 136
Campbell, J.A., 182
Cancer, 11, 81, 86, 173, 175
Car and Driver, 199
Carbon monoxide, 37-38, 82
Cars, 23-24, 29, 48, 58, 73, 143-144, 166-170, 175
Car size, 29, 58, 203

Carter, J., 195, 200
Chain saws, 174-175, 198
Chain Saw Manufacturers Association, 198
Chambers, L.W., 135
Chatterjee, B.F., 20
Chein, I., 67
Chelius, J.R., 160
Chemical energy, 36-38, 82-83
Chemists, 16-17
Chen, E., 68
Chicago crackdown on drunk drivers, 122
Child abuse, 86
Children, 8, 26, 31, 33-34, 46, 54-56, 65, 78, 97-98, 152-153, 156-157, 170, 175, 188-189
Child-resistant packaging, 153
Child restraints, 75, 86, 98-99, 129, 132, 186-187
Christenson, C.L., 160
Christopherson, E.R., 113
Chronic ailments, 62
Chrysler Corporation, 169
Cigarettes, 36, 59, 80-81, 101, 139, 191, 197
Clothing, 139, 202
Clinical counseling, 97-99
Clotfelter, C.T., 136
Cochrane, R.C., 161
Cohen, A., 115
Colvez, A., 20
Committee on Medical Aspects of Automotive Safety, 19
Compliance with laws, 133-134
Compression, 27
Conybeare, J.A.C., 137
Conger, J.J., 111
Connecticut crackdown on speeding, 126-127
Conrad, J., 137
Consumer products, 16, 197
Consumer Product Safety Act of 1973, 152
Consumer Product Safety Commission, 16, 33, 55, 152, 174, 193, 202, 204
Consumers, 139

Index

Convenience, 101
Cooking, 36, 80
Cost-benefit analysis, 163-164, 170-171, 174-175, 178-179
Cost-effectiveness analysis, 180
Costs, 10-11, 86, 142, 158, 163-170, 179-180, 188
Council, F.M., 112
Crash protection, 75
Cribs, 34, 153-154, 188-189
Criminal Code of Canada, 121
Culture, 63, 91

Dalgaard, J.B., 137
Dalton, K., 67
Dardis, R., 161
Data sources, 14-16
Davis, J.H., 44
Day of week, 56, 58
Death at the wheel, 62-63
Death penalty, 128
Deceleration, 24-25, 28-30
Defensive Driving Course, 94-95
DeHaven, H., 27-28, 42
DeMuth, W.E., Jr., 43
Denton, G.G., 115
Denial of risk, 65, 173
Dershewitz, R.A., 113
Deterrence theory, 118, 120-121, 127, 129
Detroit, 143
Deutsch, D., 159
Developmental stages, 34-35, 54-58
Dietz, P.E., 43, 67, 87-88
DiMaio, V.J.M., 43
DiNapoli, N., 182
Dinitz, S., 137
Disability, 5, 7, 72
Disease, 2, 9, 12, 27, 41, 65, 86
Disulfirum, 83
Divided attention, 51-52
Diving, 7
Done, A.K., 161
Dose-response, 37
Dowie, M., 183
Driver education, 17, 92-96, 187-188
Driver license suspension, 95, 126

Drivers, 46-49, 51-52, 56, 58, 60, 63-64, 75, 92-96, 118-127, 141-142
Drivers licensure, 62, 93-95, 126, 186-187
Drowning, 23, 33-34, 79-80, 86, 157
Drug education, 96-97, 187-188
Drugs, 15-16, 37, 53, 59, 82-83, 96-97

Earplugs, 106
Eastman, J.W., 182
Economics, 163
Economic value of life, 170-174, 179
Economists, 12-13, 130-131, 139, 141, 145, 150, 152, 157-158, 170-171, 194
Economy of scale, 169-170
Education, 86-87, 91-100, 128, 187
Educators, 65, 91-92
Edwards, D.S., 66
Edwards, M.L., 112
Ehrlichman, J., 194, 207
Elasticity, 25, 27
Electrical energy, 36, 38-39
Electrical outlet covers, 97, 99
Elgrishi, A., 69
Ellingboe, J., 67
Ellis, N.C., 112
Elman, D., 114
Embry, D.D., 113
Employment, 7
Energy, 1-2, 17, 23-29, 50, 66, 74
Energy-absorbing steering assemblies, 140-141, 166
Engineers, 16-17
Environment, 23, 29, 85
Epidemiology, 1-2, 12-13, 23, 34, 84
Erikson, K.T., 67
Evans, L., 66, 159
Experience, 56
Experiments, 17, 84
Explosion, 34-35, 76
Exposure, 33-34, 37, 55-57

Factors and phases of injury process, 71-73
Fairlie, H., 69
Falls, 10, 23, 25-26, 32-33, 63, 78-79, 86, 99, 156-157

Farm equipment, 205
Farrell, R.A., 183
Fatal crash reduction program, 126
Fatalism, 63
Fault, 2, 48, 60, 62
Fear, 8
Feck, G., 88
Federal Aviation Administration, 146-147, 196-197
Federal Bureau of Investigation, 32
Federal Highway Administration, 68
Federal Railroad Administration, 146
Federal Register, 193
Feldman, K.W., 43
Feshbach, S., 69
Field studies, 17, 84
Fife, D., 138
Finland, 121-122
Fire, 34-36, 64, 76, 80-81, 86, 141, 154, 178-179, 191
Firearms, 7, 16, 31-32, 64, 77-78, 97, 128-129, 139, 149, 152, 197, 200-201, 204
Fischer, R.P., 44
Fischhoff, B., 182
Fisher, R.S., 43
Fitch, H.G., 115
Flammability, 17, 23, 81, 153-155, 198
Fleischer, G.A., 113
Floods, 34
Foldvary, L.A., 137
Following distances, 143
Food starches, 36
Football, 7
Forbes, T.W., 68
Force, 26-28
Ford, D.R., 88, 182
Ford, H., III, 194, 207
Ford Motor Co., 104, 169, 177-179, 194
Ford Pinto gas tanks, 178-179
Foust, D.R., 41
Fowler, R., 112
France, 40
Franti, C.E., 111
Freedman, K., 138
Freedom, 117, 185, 188-191

Frost, H.M., 42
Fuchs, C., 112
Fuel economy, 75, 166-167
Furniture, 55, 139, 202
Fuses, 86

Gallagher, S.S., 113
Gas tanks, 36, 72, 178-179
Geiger, H.J., 44
Geisel, M.S., 136
Geller, E.S., 114
Genetics, 60
General Motors Corporation, 163, 169, 177, 192, 198
General Services Administration, 104, 140
Germaine, S., 88
Gertner, H.R., 21
Gibson, J.J., 41
Ginsburg, M., 42
Glass, 55
Glauz, W.D., 135
Gochman, D.S., 69
Gomez-Ibanez, J.A., 182
Gordon, D.I., 66
Grabowski, H.G., 182
Gravity, 23-26, 28
Grease, 36
Grief, 8
Griffin, L.I., III, 66
Griffin, W.O., 43
Griliches, Z., 181
Grossman, R.G., 20
Guilford, J.P., 68
Guilt, 8, 189
Gumbel, E.J., 136
Guns. *See* firearms.
Gun laws, 128-129

Haddon, W., Jr., 11, 19, 21, 41-42, 67, 71-73, 87-88, 114, 159, 183, 191, 206, 208
Hahn, C.P., 66
Handgun Control, Inc., 8
Harris, D., 43, 161
Hartunian, N.S., 21
Haskins, J.B., 113

Index

Hassall, C., 88
Hassler, C.R., 42
Hatch, E., 113
Hawkins, G., 135
Haynes, A.L., 182
Headaches, 7
Head restraints, 165-166
Head trauma, 5, 7
Health departments, 100
Hearing, 7
Heat energy, 24, 35-36, 41, 80-81
Heilbroner, R., 205
Heinzmann, A.T., 115
Helmets, 76, 130-131, 134, 190-191
Hemophilia, 27, 76
Hemorrhage, 72, 76
Henderson, J.V., 21
Henriques, C.F., Jr., 43
Hermann, J., 115
Hermanson, J.A., 206
Heumann, M., 137
Highway Loss Data Institute, 178
Highway Safety Act of 1966, 140
Hill, P.S., 112
Hiroshima, 40
Hirst, L.F., 19, 88
Hoffman, E.R., 68
Holburn, H., 137
Holusha, J., 208
Home injuries, 3, 50, 55, 97-98, 100
Homicide, 1, 9-11, 51, 86, 128, 187
Honda Civic, 203
Honolulu, 157
Hopkins, B.L., 115
Hormones, 52, 54
Hospitals, 15-16
Hosts of injury, 23, 83
Hot dogs, 34
Howes, D.R., 161
Hricko, A.R., 280
Human abilities, 66, 71
Human error, 65
Human limitations, 45-49, 71-72
Human tolerance, 16, 26-28, 72
Hunt, M.S., 161
Hunter, P., 113
Hydrogen bomb, 40

Iacocca, L., 194, 207
Ignition interlock system, 104-105, 194-195, 197
Impulsiveness, 19
Incentives, 17, 86, 105-107, 202-203
Income, 73, 86, 142
Injury: causes, 1, 12, 23, 34, 36, 83; fatal, 8-10, 33, 36, 39, 48-49, 51, 56-58, 60, 63, 120-121, 125-126, 130-132, 142-149, 152-154, 203; incidence, 1-6, 11, 55, 150-151; severity, 2-10, 11, 13-14, 118
Injury control, 2, 60, 71, 84, 163, 174, 179, 185-186, 188, 191, 202
Injury Severity Score (ISS), 3, 5
Insurance, 15, 195
Insurance Institute for Highway Safety, 42, 138
Interstate Commerce Commission, 146

Jail for alcohol offenses, 121-122
Jamieson, B.D., 112
Janeway, R.N., 42
Japanese auto manufacturers, 204
Jeep CJ5, 28
Johansson, G., 66
Johnson, C.A., 69
Johnson, L.B., 140, 191
Joksch, H., 42
Jonah, B.A., 138
Jones, M.H., 112
Jones-Lee, M.W., 181
Jordon, M., 207

Kahane, C.J., 180
Kansas City patrol experiment, 127
Karate-chop dashboard, 29
Karlson, T., 20, 208
Karpf, R.S., 68, 206
Karr, A.R., 182
Katz, A., 69
Keeve, J.P., 22, 160, 208
Kelley, A.B., 43, 115, 180, 183
Kelling, G.L., 136
Keltner, J.I., 69
Kemper, W.J., 136
Kennedy, R.F., 163

Kiernan, L.A., 208
Killebrew, T.J., 114
Kinetic energy, 26, 33-34, 46, 75
Klein, D., 21, 69, 192
Kleinbaum, D.G., 22
Knife, 27
Komaki, J., 115
Kosters, M., 181
Kraus, A.S., 68
Kraus, J.F., 20, 111
Kravitz, H., 113
Kupper, L.L., 22
Kurke, D.S., 115

Lamm, R.D., 206
Lane, J.C., 137
Lane, R., 208
Laner, S., 114
Lang, M.E., 205
Lave, L.B., 180-181
Law-enforcement crackdowns, 122, 126, 132-134
Laws, 18, 86-87, 117-134
Laws requiring protective equipment, 129-133
Lawson, L., 115
Lead, 54
Lester, D., 113
Levin, H.S., 20
Levine, D.N., 159
Levine, H.A., 182
Liability, 15, 178-179, 188, 198, 205
Libertarians, 185, 189
Life lost in years, 9
Lifton, R.J., 21
Lin, Y., 161
Lindaman, F.C., 162
Lindblom, C.E., 205
Lindgren, B., 159
Lindsey, R., 208
Linneman, P., 161
Lipsey, R.E., 181
Liskey, N.E., 67
Load, 27, 29
Lobbyists, 190-192, 200-201
Loftin, C., 137
Luce, E.A., 43

Luke, J.L., 67
Lukin, J., 138

McCarroll, J.R., 67
McCarry, C., 206
McCulloch Corporation, 198
McDermott, F., 135
McKeon, P.J., 161
McKeown, T., 21
McKibben, W., 138
McKinnon, G.P., 43
McLoughlin, E., 114
Malfetti, J.L., 113
Malecki, J.A., 115
Management, 17
Mandatory options, 178
Mandatory sentences, 129
Manufacturers, 65
Marihuana, 53
Marketing research 177-178
Market solutions, 202
Markkanen, T., 69
Mass, 24-28, 75-76, 78
Mass media, 100, 193-194
Mast, T.M., 66
Matches, 80-81, 139, 191
Mattresses, 34, 36, 153-154
Maximum Abbreviated Injury Scale (MAIS), 3, 5-6
Mayer, S., 43, 161
Mechanical energy, 24-28, 41
Medical care, 10
Medical examiners, 16
Memory, 7
Mendeloff, J., 160
Mendelson, J.H., 67
Menstrual cycle, 52
Mental retardation, 8
Meyer, J.R., 182
Mileage, 56-57, 62, 92-93
Miller, R.E., 113
Miller, W.C., 111
Mine Safety and Health Administration, 151, 160
Minibikes, 55, 64, 75
Minimum age for purchasing alcohol, 123-124, 134

Index

Mining injuries, 151-152
Mintz, M., 208
Mishan, E.J., 180-181
Mitnick, B.M., 206
Moffatt, G.H., 136
Morganstern, H., 22
Moritz, A.R., 43
Moskowitz, H., 67
Motives, 201
Motorcycles, 7, 28, 48-49, 75, 92, 141-144
Motor vehicles, 3, 5-7, 9-11, 13, 16, 23, 28-31, 36, 51, 72-77, 86, 139-145, 149, 152, 155, 175, 191, 197
Motor vehicle safety standards, 13, 139-145, 165-167, 189, 204
Motor vehicle sales, 168
Motor vehicle size, 29-30, 75, 167
Muenchow, S., 205
Mulhern, T., 112
Munger, B.L., 43

Nadel, M.V., 180
Nader, R., 192
Nagasaki, 40
Nagin, D., 136
National Bureau of Standards, 154, 205
National Center for Health Statistics, 19, 21, 41, 154
National Fire Protection Association, 156
National Health Survey, 2
National Highway Traffic Safety Administration, 10, 21-22, 42, 66, 87, 104, 123, 126, 135-136, 149, 165, 195-196, 207-208
National Institute for Burn Medicine, 154
National Institute for Occupational Safety and Health, 148
National Institute of Mental Health, 69
National Rifle Association, 201
National Safety Council, 94, 101
National Traffic and Motor Vehicle Safety Act of 1966, 140, 178, 191, 195

National Transportation Safety Board, 196
Neck injury, 166
Needleman, H.L, 68, 182
Negligence, 2, 188-189
Newspapers, 36
Newton, G.D., 136
Newton, Sir Isaac, 24-26
New York Board of Health, 157
New York City Health Department, 156
New York Times, 191
Nicholas, G.G., 43
Nixon, R., 194, 207
Noise, 106
Nonconformity, 59
Nonverifiable injuries, 150-151
Noren, J., 208
Northeastern Ohio Trauma Study, 5
Nuclear industry, 85, 176
Nuclear reactions, 40

Occupational Safety and Health Act of 1970, 148
Occupational Safety and Health Administration, 148-151, 179, 196-197, 203
OECD, 115
O'Neill, B., 42, 68, 111-112, 114, 138, 180
Ontario Department of Transportation, 102
Olson, N.R., 42
Ontario belt use law, 131
Optical illusions, 108-109
Options analysis, 71
Organizational cultures, 185, 198
Organizations, 17, 185, 193, 197-202
Osteoporosis, 27, 76

Pacifiers, 34
Pain, 8, 10
Palomba, C.A., 161
Palomba, N.A., 161
Panic, 66
Partenen, J., 69
Paterson, L., 114

Passing maneuver, 48
Passive strategies, 85-87
Payne, A., 68
Payne, D.E., 112, 136
Pearn, J.H., 162
Pease, K., 113
Pedestrians, 28-29, 31, 48, 51, 54, 63-64, 75-76, 97, 141-144, 189
Peltzman, S., 21, 159
Perception of hazard, 54-55, 108-111
Perel, M., 114
Perlman, J., 183
Persuasion, 86-87, 91-108
Phillips, B.M., 114
Phobias, 8
Physicians, 15, 97-99
Physics, 16-17, 24-28
Pierce, J.A., 68
Pittle, R.D., 208
Planek, T., 112
Plastic surgery, 77, 82
Plea bargaining, 129
Plumlee, J.P., 207
Pluralistic ignorance, 201-202
Poisoning, 37, 83
Poison Prevention Packaging Act of 1970, 152
Police, 5, 12, 15, 32, 65, 119, 126-127, 134, 200
Political science, 157-158
Politics, 180, 185, 191
Posters, 103
Potential energy, 33
Power, 199, 201, 205
Prescott, S., 68
Preston, B., 113
Preusser, D.F., 112, 138
Price of cars, 167-169
Pritz, H.B., 42
Private professional and industrial standards, 155-156
Probability of arrest, 120, 128
Productivity, 11
Prosthetic devices, 77
Psychologists, 13, 103, 145
Psychophysical states, 49-54
Psychophysical traits, 49-54

Public health principles, 1-2, 83-87
Public policy, 163, 174-180, 202-205

Quartantelli, E.L., 69

Race, 128
Rafaelson, O.J., 67
Rail transport, 145-146
Rainey, R.V., 111
Random breath tests, 119
Rape, 5, 127
Ray, H.W., 112
Raymond, S., 111
Reaction time, 46
Reagan, R., 195, 200
Rear brake lights, 110
Recreation, 7
Reflectorized pavement markers, 110
Refrigerator Safety Act of 1956, 152
Regulation of agents and vehicles, 139, 143-145, 147-149, 151, 153, 155-157, 163, 178, 202-205
Regulatory agencies, 139, 192, 196-198, 204
Rehabilitation, 92, 95
Reilly, R.E., 115
Reisinger, K.S., 113
Renwick, J.H., 88
Research 11-19
Research safety vehicles, 174, 204
Revenge, 8
Rhode Island child restraint use law, 132
Ribicoff, A., 191
Rich, F.R., 135
Riddick, L., 67
Riggins, R.S., 111
Rimel, R.W., 20
Rick, 1, 59, 64-65, 86, 91, 93, 141-142, 171, 173, 175-176, 189-190
Risk-adjustment theory, 142-143, 145, 150
Risk-benefit, 86, 175-176
Rivara, F.P., 68, 206
Road curvature, 109-110
Road illumination, 111
Road marking, 108-109

Index

Road signs, 110-111
Roberts, B.J., 20
Roberts, R.S., 135
Robertson, L.S., 21-22, 42, 66-69, 87-88, 112-115, 135-137, 159-160, 181-182, 207-208
Rockwell, T.H., 115
Roll, R., 136
Rollover crashes, 28
Roosevelt, F.D., 191
Roosevelt, T., 191
Roper, R.B., 112
Ropes, 34, 80
Rosen, S., 181
Rosenberg, C.E., 88
Rosner, B., 138
Ross, H.L., 22, 69, 135-136
Rowe, A.R., 135-136
Rubinsky, S., 115
Rumar, K., 66, 159
Running through red lights, 142
Rural driving, 58
Rutowski, W., 43
Ryther, P.I., 160

Sadof, M.G., 112
Safety Appliance Act of 1893, 146
Salmans, S., 207
Salpukas, A., 68
Sameth, S., 159
Sandels, S., 68
Sanders, C.R., 20
Sanders, R.S., 205
Scandel, 191-192
Schmidt, F., 66
Schulz, R., 20
Schupack, S., 112
Schuster, D.H., 68
Screening traits, 58-63
Scurvey, 27
Seat belts, 13-15, 26-28, 75, 85, 91, 100-102, 104-105, 129-131, 134, 141-143, 172, 190, 194
Secretary of Transportation, 195
Seizures, 7
Selection bias, 92-93
Self, P., 180, 205

Sell, R.G., 114
Sethi, S.P., 206, 208
Settle, R.F., 180
Severity of punishment, 134
Sex, 5-7, 13, 18, 45, 52, 56-57, 59, 199-200
Shaoul, J., 112
Sharp, M.C., 135
Shaw, D.J., 114
Shaw, R.B., 159-160
Shear, 27
Shinar, D., 115
Shomo, E.W., 180
Sigale, M., 208
Sight, 7
Sims, J.H., 69
Simulators, 106-107
Singer, R.D., 69
Skull fracture, 7
Smart, C.N., 20, 21
Smith, N., 115
Smith, R.S., 160
Smoke, 34, 81
Smoke detectors, 81, 99, 103
Snow, J., 83
Snyder, R.G., 41, 208
Socialists, 185
Social Security, 9, 73
Society of Automotive Engineers, 156
Sociocultural environment, 63-65, 71, 73
Sociologists, 13
Solem, L., 44
Soviet Union, 40
Space heating, 36
Speed, 24-28, 30-31, 46, 47, 64, 72, 75, 78, 108-110, 118, 141-143, 165, 199, 204
Speed adaptation, 47, 49
Speeding laws, 125-127, 199
Speed perception, 47-48
Spiegel, C.N., 162
Spinal cord trauma, 5, 7, 76
Spitz, W.U., 43, 67, 69
Sports, 45, 83
Sports Car Club of America, 92
Spouse abuse, 86

Sprinkler systems, 86
Stanley, J.C., 22
Stapp, J., 27-28, 42
Stairs, 55, 100
Starr, C., 182
Stephenson, R.J., 42
Stockholm International Peace Research Institute, 44
Stopping distance, 29-31, 46
Strain, 27
Strang, P., 135
Strate, R.G., 44
Stress, 27
Stuart, C., 159
Stuart, R.B., 113
Suburbanization, 13
Suchman, E.A., 21, 41, 191
Suffering, 8, 10
Suicide, 1, 9-11, 16, 53, 85-86, 99, 117, 128, 187
Sweden, 131, 144
Swigart, V.L., 183

Tabachnick, N., 67
Talbott, E., 114
Tate, C.L., Jr., 88
Tatum, S., 111
Technology, 139, 147, 174, 176, 191, 194, 198, 203, 205
Teenagers, 53, 56, 93-94, 187-188
Television, 17, 64, 101-103, 174-175, 200
Ten strategies for injury control, 71, 73-74
Tension, 27
Thaler, R., 181
Three Mile Island, 85
Thurow, L., 205
Tiffin, J., 66
Time of day, 56, 58
Tingvall, C., 137
Tires, 31, 72, 141, 143, 155
Tittle, C.R., 135-136
Tornados, 63
Toxicology, 37-38, 53-54
Toys, 202
Training, 91-92

Trains, 24, 145-146, 155, 175
Tranquilizers, 53
Trees, 73, 76
Trethowan, W.H., 88
Trisko, E.M., 180
Trucks, 24, 29, 49, 143-144
Tryon, G.H., 43

Ulmer, R.G., 112
United Kingdom, 40
United States, 40, 74, 117, 185
Urbanization, 13
U.S. Coast Guard, 22, 33, 148, 160
U.S. Congress, 105, 140, 146, 152, 193, 195, 203
U.S. Constitution, 117
U.S. Court of Appeals for the District of Columbia Circuit, 195
U.S. Department of Commerce, 147, 154
U.S. Department of Health and Human Services, 148
U.S. Department of Labor, 149, 151
U.S. Department of the Interior, 151
U.S. Department of Transportation, 101, 140, 146, 158
U.S. Fire Administration, 43
U.S. Senate, 163
U.S. Supreme Court, 179, 195
Usher, D., 181-182
Utility poles, 73, 76
Utility theory, 142, 187

Value Line Investment Survey, 181
Values, 91, 185-187, 198
VanDine, S., 137
Vectors of injury agents, 23, 45
Vehicle design, 76, 170, 189
Vehicle emissions, 167, 175
Vehicles of injury agents, 23, 28, 45, 50, 71, 74, 83, 85, 139
Velocity, 24-27, 30-33
Verifiable injuries, 150-151
Vernon, J.H., 182
Vicker, R., 207
Victoria, Australia, 119-120, 130-131
Violators, 60-62, 95-96, 125

Index

Violence, 199-200
Viscusi, W.K., 181
Visual acuity, 62-63
Voelker, C.A., 135
Voltage, 39
Volvo, 203
Von Buseck, C.R., 159
Vulcan, P., 137

Walker, H.M., 136
Wall Street Journal, 177, 198
Waller, P.F., 21, 114
War, 8
Warner, K.E., 183, 206-207
Washington, D.C., 64
Wasielewski, P., 159
Watson, G.F., 137
Wechsler, H., 67
Weidenbaum, M.L., 207
Weight, 24-26, 29, 166-167
Weiss, E.B., 42
Weiss, N.H., 88
Wells, J.A.K., 138
Westinghouse automatic brakes, 145
Wettick, R.S., Jr., 136
White House, 193, 198

Wichita State University, 147
Wigglesworth, E.C., 158
Wilks, A., 137
Wilson, J.Q., 205
Williams, A.F., 68, 89, 111, 113, 135-136, 138, 206
Williams, R.L., 136
Williamson, J.W., 113
Windshields, 140-141
Windsor, Ontario, 143
Witt, T.S., 161
Wixom, C.W., 114
Work injuries, 3, 18-19, 45-50, 107-108, 148-152, 171-172, 203
Worker's Compensation, 150-151, 203, 205
Wright, P.H., 115
Wright, R.K., 44

Yeaton, W.H., 113

Zador, P.L., 112, 135, 137
Ziegler, P.M., 114
Zimring, F., 135-136
Zohar, D., 115

About the Author

After receiving the Ph.D. in sociology at the University of Tennessee, **Leon S. Robertson** taught at Wake Forest University, did postdoctoral work at The Johns Hopkins University, and served on the faculty of Harvard University Medical School. He now teaches and conducts research in the Department of Epidemiology and Public Health at Yale University. Dr. Robertson was previously a senior behavioral scientist in the Insurance Institute for Highway Safety. He is coauthor of *Biology and Social Behavior, Changing the Medical Care System*, and *Medical Sociology*, as well as of numerous research articles on injuries and other health issues.